"That journalism in the United States and worldwide is in a deep and seemingly worsening crisis is becoming increasingly clear. The business model of commercial journalism is in its death throes, yet societies desperately need this grand public good if any semblance of democracy or freedom is to survive. *Reimagining Journalism in a Post-Truth World* is a hearty attempt to take stock of the swirling changes, make the best of a very bad situation, and rethink journalism by reconfiguring the existing cast of characters, institutions, and options. It is a necessary contribution to a larger conversation our entire society, not just the journalism community, needs to have. The sooner, the better."

—*Robert W. McChesney, Gutgsell Endowed Professor, Department of Communication, University of Illinois at Urbana-Champaign, and co-author,* The Death and Life of American Journalism

"This refreshing look at journalism's current quandaries is a concise chronicle of the anti-media, anti-fact world journalism must now navigate. More than bemoan how fake news and political propaganda are impersonating journalism, the authors offer solutions that need to be more seriously embraced than past journalism reform efforts."

—*Jan Schaffer, J-Lab Executive Director, American University*

"Fake news, declining trust in institutions, eroding business models—journalism faces challenges from every quarter, but the need for accurate news and information to cut through the noise and enlighten the public is essential for our democracy. The deep research of *Reimagining Journalism in a Post-Truth World* provides illuminating context for understanding the obstacles confronting the industry and assembles a foundation of useful ideas that may help lift journalism, and our society, into a better future."

—*Michael D. Bolden, Managing Director, Editorial and Operations, JSK Journalism Fellowships, Stanford University*

"Amid the change that has become media's only constant, Ed Madison and Ben DeJarnette offer journalism's champions a chance to consider what's been won and lost in the Internet revolution—and what lessons mean most. Their take offers critical context on trends that blossomed and died, theories that dominated and receded, and—beyond the flash—innovation with real promise. In considering fundamental purpose as well as financial reality, the authors amplify the central and urgent question of how journalism can succeed and thrive best: by connecting directly with the public it aims to serve."

—*Melanie Sill, News Strategist and Former Content Chief at the* Sacramento Bee, *the* News & Observer *and KPCC-Southern California Public Radio*

Reimagining Journalism in a Post-Truth World

Reimagining Journalism in a Post-Truth World

How Late-Night Comedians, Internet Trolls, and Savvy Reporters Are Transforming News

Ed Madison and Ben DeJarnette

Foreword by Frank Sesno

PRAEGER™

An Imprint of ABC-CLIO, LLC

Santa Barbara, California • Denver, Colorado

Library of Congress Cataloging-in-Publication Data

Names: Madison, Ed 1958– author. | DeJarnette, Ben author.
Title: Reimagining journalism in a post-truth world : how late-night comedians, Internet trolls, and savvy reporters are transforming news / Ed Madison and Ben DeJarnette ; foreword by Frank Sesno.
Description: Santa Barbara, California : Praeger, 2018. | Includes bibliographical references and index.
Identifiers: LCCN 2017041449 (print) | LCCN 2017057492 (ebook) | ISBN 9781440854767 (ebook) | ISBN 9781440854750 (hard copy : alk. paper)
Subjects: LCSH: Journalism—United States—History—21st century. | Journalism—Objectivity—History—21st century. | Online journalism—United States—History—21st century. | Television broadcasting of news—United States—History—21st century. | Television talk shows—Political aspects—United States—History—21st century. | Television comedies—United States—Influence.
Classification: LCC PN4867.2 (ebook) | LCC PN4867.2 .M33 2018 (print) | DDC 071.309/05—dc23
LC record available at https://lccn.loc.gov/2017041449

ISBN: 978-1-4408-5475-0 (print)
         978-1-4408-5476-7 (ebook)

22 21 20 19 18   1 2 3 4 5

This book is also available as an eBook.

Praeger
An Imprint of ABC-CLIO, LLC

ABC-CLIO, LLC
130 Cremona Drive, P.O. Box 1911
Santa Barbara, California 93116-1911
www.abc-clio.com

This book is printed on acid-free paper ∞

Manufactured in the United States of America

For my father, who blazed many trails.
—Ed Madison

*To the pioneers—inside and outside of the profession—who help us
imagine a brighter future for journalism.*
—Ben DeJarnette

Contents

Foreword

The crisis in American journalism goes far beyond the practitioners who pursue it and the politicians who complain about it. At a time of anxiety and complexity, competing narratives and deep political polarization, the inability to agree even on basic facts threatens to submerge us in confusion and conflict. Journalism's convulsions over the past two decades have taken a terrible toll. Legacy news organizations hemorrhaged revenue and staff. Business models collapsed. Politically driven media exploded and won massive audiences. Public trust evaporated. An unlikely presidential candidate attacked journalists as dishonest enemies of the people. And won.

This crisis was not born overnight, and it is not attributable to any single source. Rather, it is the result of a combination of factors that have been building for years and that are as striking as the ironies they have produced. The Internet connected us, but also helped tear us apart by amplifying our discontent. Social media democratized expression, but invited everyone to the playing field, no matter how qualified or knowledgeable. The elitist hold on information was broken, but peddlers of extremism and conspiracy gained access to a global audience.

In *Reimagining Journalism in a Post-Truth World*, Ed Madison and Ben DeJarnette put journalism's journey in stark perspective and bring a clarifying, deeply researched urgency to the conversation about what's gone wrong and what can be done about it. They chart the indelible changes in journalism that have created what they rightly refer to as an "anti-media, anti-fact culture shift." They look at the problem generationally—today's "Tiffany Network" just may be Comedy Central—and they break the challenges into component parts. Then they pose the most important question of all: What can be done to reimagine journalism so that it contributes to genuine public understanding and productive civic discourse?

The authors approach their work from distinct and yet complementary perspectives. As a broadcast media veteran who began his career in the thick of Watergate, Ed Madison brings keen insights to his work as a journalism professor and researcher. Ben DeJarnette is an early-stage journalist with millennial sensibilities and fresh ideas. Collectively, they bring a voice to this topic that is neither cynical nor naïve. They offer a thoughtful approach and a constructive tone at a critical time in the trajectory of journalism.

The authors show clearly that at a time when *BuzzFeed* and *Breitbart,* Reddit and *The Intercept, Vox* and *VICE* News have carved up the audience, not only is there no single repository of information—no single narrative—but we appear to have lost the ability to coalesce around a basic version of events. Whether it is the size of an inauguration crowd or the shortcomings of our health care system, we argue over observable facts, disagree on the evidence, and dismiss news that upsets us as biased or fake.

As *Reimagining Journalism* points out, many of the changes in the way news is reported and consumed started with CNN. When the network went on the air in 1980, citizens could, for the first time in human history, see and hear events as they happened around the world, 24 hours a day. I joined the network in those early years—when CNN was still referred to as Chicken Noodle News. We didn't have many viewers, and we experienced more glitches and gaffes than we cared to admit, but we had a mission and we proudly tilted at the windmills of the mighty broadcast networks. CNN was a rough-around-the-edges startup, but we were committed to news, and we reveled in the knowledge that we were scaling the walls of tradition and bringing our viewers the news as it happened. We held an idealized sense that solid reporting and pictures that spoke for themselves would lead to a more informed public. CNN founder Ted Turner believed his upstart network could unmask dictators, expose wrongdoing, nurture democracy, and promote nuclear disarmament. Maybe more news to more people really could transform the world.

When I was hired, I got the line that is now a part of CNN lore. "Just remember, we don't have stars. The news is the star," I was told. We didn't talk about ratings. I once made the mistake of asking the famously gruff Ed Turner, who was in charge of news gathering (and no relation to Ted) about the ratings of one of our programs. He exploded. "Don't EVER ask me about ratings! I don't give a DAMN about ratings and neither should YOU!" That was then. Today, the cable news universe is dominated by opinion and "analysis." Newscasts are virtually nonexistent. Beyond cable, every news platform—legacy and newcomer alike—is driven by ratings, metrics, and analytics. Executives at major news organizations pursue computer scientists and data analysts as if *they* are the stars.

Madison and DeJarnette take in this broad landscape as they look over the horizon. They address the questions that anyone involved in producing, studying, or consuming the news—and that's just about everybody—should be asking: How are new technologies and the media companies they shape altering not just the media but the way people get and process information? What are the implications for journalism? In this hyperpolarized culture, can journalism play a role to bridge divides rather than widen them? What can the news media learn from John Oliver and media satirists about how to convey complexity, nuance, irony, and truth? How should Facebook's breathtaking profits and vast human network shape its sense of responsibility to the public? What can be done to restore public trust in journalism?

In addressing those and other questions, the authors apply data, perspective, and a keen understanding to this crucial and complex topic. They examine the impact of "fake news." They consider "news deserts." They look at what satire teaches us about objectivity, facts, and truth-telling. They explore how consolidation and the collapse of ad revenues have ravaged local and regional news organizations that no longer have the resources to send human beings—reporters—to see and hear and question city councils and school boards in cities and towns across America. They consider the attitudes and behaviors of millennials, who came of age amid social media, to understand how they are reshaping the media world through their appetite for shorter stories, more video, and more irreverent discourse.

Reimagining Journalism is an essential read for anyone who has weighed in with an opinion about the media, studied journalism, or wondered about what's gone wrong with the news. Ed Madison and Ben DeJarnette make clear that we are experiencing a news crisis as journalism, savaged by politicians, economics, and the public alike, seeks a future. But the authors give us hope, too. The public still wants credible news and can be a resource in its own right, millennials also consume in-depth reporting, and the long-form narrative *can* draw an audience. Despite the repeated, overwrought, and dangerous attacks on the news media and dismal levels of public trust, many news organizations experienced a significant jump in readers, viewers, and listeners in 2016.

It won't be easy to reimagine journalism because the problems are, in many cases, already deeply engrained in the new journalism ecosystem. But there are important explanations and promising ideas in this book, and anyone who reads it will have a deeper appreciation for journalism's extraordinary journey in recent years and where it may be going. What will it take to "reimagine" journalism? Courage and creativity. What price will we pay if we do not rise to the challenge? The disruption and polarization we've experienced so far could be just the beginning.

Frank Sesno
Director, School of Media and Public Affairs,
The George Washington University;
former Washington Bureau Chief—CNN

Preface

Journalism has always had its critics, particularly people in power who resist public scrutiny. However, presently the profession is meeting some of its greatest challenges as questions persist about its credibility and relevance.

This book tackles this daunting topic at an equally daunting time as we find ourselves engaged in debate about the merits of journalism and its role in society. Although many people have objected to specific examples of news coverage, few until now have questioned the entire enterprise. I count myself as an advocate for journalism and a believer in its resiliency, with good reason.

During my junior year of high school, I walked into a guidance counselor's office and was struck by an inconspicuous poster that would fundamentally affect my future. Growing up in Washington, DC, during the turbulent 1960s and 1970s with a dad who was a journalism pioneer and a mom who taught elementary school, I was exposed to the importance of media, specifically the news media. I knew quite early that I wanted to follow in my dad's footsteps—and that poster offered a potential pathway. It announced a six-week internship at WTOP-TV—Channel 9, which at the time was owned by the *Washington Post*. The station was also conveniently located across the street from my high school. The prerequisite for consideration was writing an essay on the significance of media and an in-person interview, if you made the cut. I made the cut—but was not chosen.

The devastating news was communicated in a phone call: "This is for kids who don't have a parent who can give them a leg up," I was told, affirming their knowledge of my father's career history. However, a few days later there was a reprieve. "We've talked about it as a committee . . . one of the other three students selected dropped out . . . and we unanimously agree that you deserve the spot." That phone call opened the door to my own pathway as a media professional.

The Watergate scandal unfolded over the next few months, and, at age 16, I was not only an eyewitness but an active participant in reporting stories about unfolding history. There was talk of our government facing a constitutional crisis and concern about the future of our democracy. Similar sentiments are expressed today. I share this story to provide a contextual foundation for this work and to foreshadow our belief in the power of journalism to consistently light a pathway forward. Also, to acknowledge my parents who instilled in my siblings and me the importance of public service and gratitude. These are values I've sought to emulate and pass along as a journalism professor to my students, and as a father to my children.

—Ed Madison

I still remember the first book I ever read about journalism. It was Bernie Goldberg's bestseller *Bias: A CBS Insider Exposes How the Media Distort the News*, which my parents gave me for Christmas shortly after I joined my high school newspaper staff. The central premise of Goldberg's book—that the essence of good journalism is "objectivity"—stuck with me throughout my formative years in journalism, when above all else, I aspired to be a "neutral" journalist, impartially conveying the facts in service of the Truth.

I don't remember what finally shattered my Goldbergian view of the journalistic universe, but I can tell you it's now long gone. These days I watch more Samantha Bee than David Muir, read more op-eds and explainers than hard news, and believe more in Santa Claus than the idea of "objective truth." It's why the title of this book, *Reimagining Journalism in a Post-Truth World*, doesn't strike me as entirely foreboding. In fact, what it partly suggests is a more honest form of journalism, stripped of the illusion that truth is singular, finite, and objective. I think Reagan Jackson says it best (see Chapter 1): "I have no interest in objectivity—in fact I distrust anyone who thinks that they are somehow able to be a neutral outside observer. What are you outside of exactly? Certainly not the constructs of race, power, or privilege."

Objectivity was a worthy goal, but ultimately a false promise. Now it's time to come clean and move forward—to shift our sights from neutrality to *fairness*, from balance to *inclusion*, from objectivity to *honesty*.

That's the future I hope to see for journalism. Consider this my contribution to the cause.

—Ben DeJarnette

Acknowledgments

First and foremost, I want to acknowledge my co-author Ben DeJarnette, who tirelessly worked to make this project possible. I could not have mustered the courage to take this topic on alone. Ben is a brilliant writer and thinker, and it has been a privilege to collaborate with him. I also want to thank our editor, Hilary Claggett; our agent, Stan Wakefield; and our editorial assistant, Iam Pace. I am grateful for having numerous great mentors throughout my professional career, including Bob Shanks, Woody Fraser, Bob Loudin, Jane Caper, Reese Schonfeld, Hilary Schacter, John Goldhammer, Dick Colbert, Carol Randolph, Peter Zabriskie, and Malcolm Boyes. Later, in my academic career, I must acknowledge Juan-Carlos Molleda, Tim Gleason, Julie Newton, Randy Kamphaus, Leslie Steeves, Kim Sheehan, Janet Wasko, Patricia Curtin, Deb and Dan Morrison, Mark Blaine, Andrew DeVigal, Lisa Heyamoto, Todd Milbourn, Rebecca Force, John Russial, Scott Maier, Tom Wheeler, Carl Bybee, Peter Laufer, Tom Bivins, Ron Beghetto, Jerry Rosiek, Joanna Goode, Edward Olivos, Jill Baxter, Hank Fien, Michelle Swanson, Lori Shontz, Matt Coleman, Ross Anderson, Art Pearl, Eric Newton, and Jenefer Husman. Finally, I must thank Esther Wojcicki, Tara Guber, Robert Gould, Maya Lazaro, Nic Walcott, Erik Bender, Jordan Tichenor, Riley Stevenson, Bethany Grace Howe, Sumi Lewis, Emma Oravecz, and our Journalistic Learning Initiative team.

—Ed Madison

Writing a book takes a village, and I don't trust myself to offer a full accounting of the villagers who contributed inspiration, ideas, quotes, and ice cream in support of the cause. Instead, let me say it this way: Thank you to my colleagues, classmates, and professors at the University of

Oregon for their endless supply of wisdom and insight; to my interviewees for their big ideas and enviable ability to articulate them; to my editors, past and present, for their lessons in the grind of writing; to my family and friends for their unflinching support, now as ever; to my girlfriend, Grace, for all the things words can't describe (and the ice cream, too); and to my brilliant co-author, Ed, for his vision, smarts, and good humor, and for his unwavering belief in me.

—Ben DeJarnette

How Journalism Became a Dirty Word

"The FAKE NEWS media . . . is not my enemy, it is the enemy of the American People!"[1]

—@realDonaldTrump

In October 2015, before the news cycle became entirely consumed by scandal and poll numbers, by 24-hour chatter over Donald Trump's undersized hands and Hillary Clinton's private e-mail servers, the presidential election race served up its first troubling sign of the crisis in American journalism.

It happened during the third Republican presidential debate in Boulder, Colorado, as the line of questioning veered between vacuous and combative. Within 15 minutes, the moderators had asked the candidates to explain their "biggest weakness," quizzed Donald Trump on his "comic-book version of a presidential campaign," and prodded Jeb Bush about his falling "stock" in the race. By the time CNBC's Carl Quintanilla turned to Ted Cruz with a question about his problem-solving ability, the Texas senator was ready to unload.

"Let me say something at the outset," Cruz fired back. "The questions that have been asked so far in this debate illustrate why the American people don't trust the media. This is not a cage match . . . The questions that are being asked shouldn't be trying to get people to tear into each other. It should be, 'What are your substantive solutions to people who are hurting?'"[2]

As Cruz delivered his punch line, a focus group of prospective voters turned their reaction dials in unison—a very good sign for Cruz. A dial-test score of 100 is considered perfect. Cruz's zinger landed a 98. "That's the highest score we've ever measured," tweeted Republican pollster Frank Luntz. "EVER."[3]

In an election season when political pundits rarely agreed—not even on the facts—Cruz's attack against the media inspired a rare moment of unity. *Washington Post* media columnist Erik Wemple piggy-backed on Cruz's barb to criticize the news media for its obsession with "electability issues and optics questions" instead of substantive policy concerns; conservative radio personality Rush Limbaugh praised Cruz's courage in taking on the "assassins" in the mainstream media; and even left-wing comedian and political commentator Bill Maher admitted that Cruz, his political antithesis, had made a good point. "Oh my god," Maher tweeted, "did I just hear Ted Cruz say something awesome that I agree with? Yes. The media is even stupider than the [politicians]."[4]

Criticism of the news media has a long history in American politics, stretching back to George Washington's complaint that news editors were "stuffing their papers with scurrility and nonsensical declamation."[5] But it's hard to remember a time when such rhetoric played better with the public than during the 2016 campaign, including the debate in Colorado, where Marco Rubio received the night's biggest applause for equating the mainstream media to a Democratic super PAC, and Cruz scored a major victory on social media for his jab at the moderators.

"#Cruz isn't my top candidate (yet), but he had me cheering during that moment," tweeted @BamaStephen. "He had a great night."[6]

"I was driving, listening on the radio—my face lit up and I shouted 'oh yeah!!'" wrote @coachanthony79. "That was awesome!"[7]

Added @SandyLannis: "Yes! @tedcruz is most articulate, principled, brilliant, gutsy person running from either party; glad he attacked unfair [mainstream media]."[8]

As much as journalists might like to dismiss this polemic as an election-year anomaly, the public's disdain for the media is, in fact, a trend decades in the making. In 1976, not long after journalism's Watergate triumph, a Gallup survey found that 72 percent of Americans had a "great deal" or "fair amount" of confidence in the news media. During the 1990s, a decade in which 24-hour networks like Fox News and MSNBC burst onto the scene, that number dropped below 55 percent. And by the time voters headed to the polls in 2016, an all-time low 32 percent of Americans expressed confidence in the news media—including just 14 percent of self-identified Republicans and 26 percent of people under 50 years old.[9]

The trend line is no less foreboding when specifically examining newspapers or television news, which a 2016 Gallup survey identified as two of the four least-trusted U.S. institutions, ahead of only Congress and big business.[10] Meanwhile, even individual journalists haven't been immune from the public's mistrust. In 2007 when the Pew Research Center asked respondents to name the news figure they most admired, more Americans picked *The Daily Show* host Jon Stewart than esteemed news anchors such as Jim Lehrer of *PBS NewsHour*, Tim Russert of NBC's *Meet the Press*, Diane Sawyer of ABC, and Wolf Blitzer of CNN. (Among respondents under 30, Stewart tied for the highest share of votes, alongside then Fox News commentator Bill O'Reilly.)[11] These results are partly an endorsement of Stewart's acerbic wit and journalistic chops, but as Stewart himself points out, they also speak to the failures of the mainstream media. "The embarrassment," Stewart told Fox News anchor Chris Wallace in 2011, "is that I'm given credibility in this world because of the disappointment that the public has in what the news media does."[12]

Once revered as a pillar of democracy, journalism today feels more like a dirty word and a tarnished brand. Maybe this explains why Stewart and his satirical colleagues regularly shirk the "journalist" label, why many ex-newspaper and television reporters, as if afflicted with a disease, sheepishly call themselves "recovering journalists," or why even those who fall squarely within journalism's ranks often do their best to distance themselves from the rest of the profession. "There really is no such thing as 'the media,'" *Washington Post* columnist Paul Farhi wrote in a defensive open letter to readers. "It's an invention, a tool, an all-purpose smear by people who can't be bothered to make distinctions."[13] ABC *Nightline* anchor Ted Koppel drew a similar distinction in an interview on Fox News, blaming partisan commentators like O'Reilly for making *real* journalism irrelevant. "You have changed the television landscape over the past 20 years," he told O'Reilly. "You took it from being objective and dull to subjective and entertaining. And in this current climate, it doesn't matter what the interviewer asks [Donald Trump]—Mr. Trump is gonna say whatever he wants to say, as outrageous as it may be."[14]

Journalism's current crisis of trust has seen plenty of finger pointing, but it has also inspired, in Jeff Jarvis' words, a long overdue "journalistic truth and reconciliation conversation."[15] To date, this conversation has largely played out in a torrent of think pieces and essays about Donald Trump, "fake news," and the 2016 election—and we certainly have plenty to say about all three. But we also recognize that the crisis of journalism is bigger than one president or one election. In this introduction, we will outline six fundamental trends that contributed to the erosion of public trust in journalism, beginning with the most fundamental of them all: the disruptive power of the Internet.

Journalism's Gatekeepers Lost Control of Their Gates

Every night for 19 years, *CBS Evening News* anchor Walter Cronkite ended his newscast with the same assurance to his viewers: "And that's the way it is."

And that's the way it is. Only in a world without cable news, without *Breitbart*, without Twitter trolls, and without late-night satirists, would a journalist dare make so bold and sweeping a claim. But to paraphrase Cronkite, that's the way it *was* in broadcast television. No "alternative facts." No alternative realities. And barely any alternative voices. Before cable television and the Internet, the news was the news, composed of the same top stories and delivered in the same gravel-voiced tenors regardless of the outlet. Anchors might add occasional touches of flair (like a signature sign-off), but there was nothing truly novel in the news media. If ABC was Coke, then CBS was Pepsi. Each had its own flavor, but the ingredients were pretty much the same.

The homogeneity of broadcast television first showed signs of cracking in the 1980s, when CNN, the country's original 24-hour news channel, debuted. The big three networks, perhaps too comfortable in their dominance, were quick to dismiss CNN as a fringe player, privately calling it Chicken Noodle News. But when CNN was the only network to broadcast live from inside Iraq during the Persian Gulf War, big audiences tuned in, foreshadowing the growth of cable news and the rise of MSNBC and Fox News Channel.

These newcomers challenged the primacy of network television in the 1990s, but it was the *Internet* that caused the real disruption to legacy media's distribution monopoly. As the gates to mass publishing fell, new flavors of journalism began to emerge—from the Drudge Report's politicized journalism to *VICE*'s gritty immersive reporting—and the democratized Web became home to a wider spectrum of voices and perspectives, including those critical of the mainstream media. Suddenly, anyone with an Internet connection and a Twitter account could help turn #NBCFail into a trending hashtag, allowing media criticism to go viral and giving readers' isolated misgivings an opportunity to evolve into collective mistrust. And unlike the pre-Internet era, dissatisfied audiences now had somewhere else to go.

Arguably, no trend has reshaped the media landscape more dramatically than this one—the proliferation of news options on an ungated Web. And in early 2017, perhaps nowhere were the impacts of this new reality more apparent than in the White House briefing room.

Professional Journalism Lost the Power to Enforce Its Own Rules

On January 17, three days before Donald Trump's presidential inauguration, the press corps sent an open letter to Trump offering him a glimpse of what he could expect over the next four years. "While you have every right to decide your ground rules for engaging with the press, we have some, too," the letter read. "It is, after all, our airtime and column inches that you are seeking to influence. We, not you, decide how best to serve our readers, listeners, and viewers."[16]

The letter came only six days after Trump famously shouted down CNN reporter Jim Acosta in his first press conference as president-elect, calling Acosta's network "fake news" following its coverage of an investigation into Trump's relationship with Russia. That incident sparked outrage in the media and inspired the combative letter, which promised that "we," the press corps, would decide how much airtime to offer to Trump spokespeople, that "we" would set the ground rules about "off the record" interviews, and that "we" would even work together to hold Trump's administration to account.

"You have tried to divide us and use reporters' deep competitive streaks to cause family fights," the letter explained. "Those days are ending. We now recognize that the challenge of covering you requires that we cooperate and help one another whenever possible. So, when you shout down or ignore a reporter at a press conference who has said something you don't like, you're going to face a unified front."[17]

If the promise for collaboration and a "unified front" among dozens of competitive news organizations seems almost beyond belief, that's because it was. In reality, the letter was penned by Kyle Pope, editor and publisher of the *Columbia Journalism Review*, who was expressing the unity he *wished* existed in Washington's press corps. Pope's use of the collective "we" was misleading, but it was also anachronistic, a throwback to an era when journalism's rules and standards—the ones taught in journalism schools, enshrined in codes of ethics, and reinforced by press clubs and award programs—were universally accepted across the news business.

That journalism—Cronkite's journalism—came with a sense of collective identity, a sense of "we" that no longer exists in the age of cable news and the Internet. Consider the fact that shortly after shutting down Jim Acosta, Trump took a question from Matthew Boyle, a reporter from the alt-right news site Breitbart. Regardless of the well-intentioned screeds by journalism critics like Pope, a *Breitbart* employee is about as likely to repeat CNN's question as Trump is to duplicate Obama's climate policies.

Pope's open letter reflects a broader failure by mainstream journalists to recognize the limitations of their influence on the Internet. In 1997, for example, at the dawn of the digital age, the American Society of Magazine Editors (ASME) released a set of "Guidelines for New Media" that instructed publishers to clearly identify advertising on their websites. According to John Motavalli, ASME's leadership believed "the traditional magazine world would still dominate cyberspace," as it had in print publishing. Instead, the organization's guidelines were "widely mocked and ignored," offering an early glimpse at what would happen to professional norms on the Internet, where journalism's core values, including "balance" and "neutrality," could no longer be taken for granted.[18]

News Publishers (and Audiences) Gravitated toward the Political Poles

In August 2016, 24-year-old Tomi Lahren became the latest fiery ideologue to "break the Internet" when she delivered a three-minute rant about biracial quarterback Colin Kaepernick's decision to protest racial discrimination by kneeling during the national anthem. Lahren, then only two years removed from college, referred to Kaepernick as a "whiny, indulgent, attention-seeking crybaby" and proceeded to blast him for choosing to "sit on a bench and bitch and moan about [his] perceived oppression."[19]

That kind of rhetoric would be a fireable offense at any legacy broadcast network, but Lahren's segment didn't appear on ABC or CBS. It appeared on TheBlaze, a right-wing digital network founded by former Fox News personality Glenn Beck. And her audience loved it. Within weeks, the clip had been viewed more than 65 million times on Facebook, helping make Lahren one of the most talked-about political commentators of 2016. "I do not bullshit, I am genuine and authentic," she said in an interview with *The Guardian*. "I don't say these things to go viral or to be controversial, but I say things that a lot of people wish they could say but are fearful of saying."[20]

Lahren is only the latest partisan news commentator to find fame on the Internet, where anyone with a smartphone and Internet access can now engage in the kind of content creation, curation, and distribution work once reserved for card-carrying journalists. Digital media celebrants argue that such democratization has been a net positive for society, pointing to social media's role in the Arab Spring revolutions, the triumphs of crowd-sourced reporting, and the growth of community media as evidence that digital media really *can* be a force for democratic good. But even the Web's most ardent defenders acknowledge that the digital revolution also came with a dark side. Comment sections and digital aggregators like Reddit and

Digg found themselves overrun by racist, sexist, and xenophobic Internet trolls. Social media platforms wrote algorithms that bifurcated the Web into insular filter bubbles. And opportunistic upstarts dressed up propaganda to look like real news and then fed it to partisan news consumers who couldn't get enough. "We built the structures for hate to flow along the same pathways as knowledge, but we kept hoping that this wasn't really what was happening," social media scholar danah boyd wrote for *Points.* "We aided and abetted the media's suicide. The red pill is here. And it ain't pretty."[21]

But the red pill also isn't new. Within months of President Reagan's 1987 decision to roll back the Fairness Doctrine, a Federal Communications Commission policy that required broadcasters to commit airtime for exploration of diverse and opposing viewpoints on controversial themes, a young talk show host named Rush Limbaugh was being syndicated on 56 stations across the United States. Within four years, Limbaugh was on more than 600 stations, reaching huge audiences with his then-novel brand of no-holds-barred conservative commentary.[22] Subsequent efforts to reinstate the Fairness Doctrine in the 1990s were unsuccessful (in no small part because of the political mobilization of Limbaugh's supporters), and talk show hosts like Sean Hannity and Laura Ingraham on the right and, to a lesser degree, Alan Colmes and Stephanie Miller on the left, followed Limbaugh's game plan—and shared his success—by catering to the political extremes.

The trend toward polarization that started on talk radio only accelerated on the Internet, where left-wing progressives turned to MoveOn and *ThinkProgress,* disaffected conservatives embraced *Drudge Report* and *Breitbart,* and the mainstream outlets found themselves stuck in the middle, espousing a "view from nowhere" that's subject to criticism from both left and right.[23] The result, according to the Pew Research Center, is a news and information ecosystem that's becoming increasingly fractured: "When it comes to getting news about politics and government, liberals and conservatives inhabit different worlds," a 2014 Pew study found. "There is little overlap in the news sources they turn to and trust."[24]

Most recently, this polarized media ecosystem has been weaponized by blatant propaganda, which uses fabrication and misinformation to appeal to partisan audiences. During the 2016 presidential campaign, these sensational "fake news" stories sprinted around the Internet, driving millions of clicks that in turn generated thousands of dollars for their unscrupulous publishers. One of those publishers, a recent college graduate named Cameron Harris, estimates he made about $1,000 an hour from advertising revenue on his bogus news site ChristianTimesNewspaper.com, which posted headlines like "Protesters Beat Homeless Veteran to Death in Philadelphia" and "NYPD Looking to Press Charges Against Bill Clinton for Underage Sex Ring."[25]

Interestingly, Harris is not a political ideologue himself, nor are the Macedonian twentysomethings who created more than 100 bogus news sites in 2016 focused on the U.S. election. For these profiteers, fake news is just business, and clicks are the currency. "The info in the blogs is bad, false, and misleading," one Macedonian student acknowledged. "But the rationale is that 'if it gets the people to click on it and engage, then use it.'"[26]

The brazenness of the propaganda (and the extent to which news consumers shared it, uncritically, on social media) took many people by surprise in 2016, but as Bill Kovach and Tom Rosenstiel warned as early as 2001, the economic conditions that fueled this movement have been building for years. "For the first time in our history," they wrote, "the news increasingly is produced by companies outside journalism, and this new economic organization is important. We are facing the possibility that independent news will be replaced by self-interested commercialism posing as news."[27]

Rolling Stone's Matt Taibbi similarly interpreted the rise of propaganda as a symptom of market forces. "I think for a long time now, Americans have been consuming facts as consumers," he told Trevor Noah on *The Daily Show*. "I think we shop for facts the same way we shop for hats, shoes, or radial tires; we shop for the things we like. And I think people are choosing their own reality now."[28]

This trend toward a post-truth society has alarmed political leaders across the world, including President Obama, who spent much of his lame-duck period speaking out about the perils of fake news. In November 2016 Obama told HBO's Bill Maher that "it's very hard to figure out how we move democracy forward" without "some common baseline of facts," and during a press conference in Germany, he warned that "if we are not serious about facts and what's true and what's not . . . [and] if we can't discriminate between serious arguments and propaganda, then we have problems."[29]

The president even devoted a section of his farewell speech to the issue of truth in the media, urging Americans not to retreat into their own bubbles, "surrounded by people who . . . share the same political outlook and never challenge [their] assumptions." He continued:

> The rise of naked partisanship, and increasing economic and regional stratification, the splintering of our media into a "channel for every

taste"—all this makes this great sorting seem natural, even inevitable. And increasingly, we become so secure in our bubbles that we start accepting only information, whether it's true or not, that fits our opinions, instead of basing our opinions on the evidence that is out there. And this trend represents a third threat to our democracy . . . Without some common baseline of facts, without a willingness to admit new information and concede that your opponent might be making a fair point, and that science and reason matter, then we're going to keep talking past each other. And we'll make common ground and compromise impossible.[30]

Because news publishers no longer control society's media and information gates, they are largely powerless to stop the virality of fake news and the fracturing of news audiences on the Internet. However, there *is* at least one digital-era gatekeeper that could help reverse the tide if it wanted to: Facebook. In 2016 a Pew Research Center study found that 67 percent of American adults were registered Facebook users, and 44 percent accessed news on the site—up from 30 percent only three years earlier.[31]

As a result of the platform's growing reach, Facebook's algorithms now increasingly shape the news diets of millions of Americans. And in 2016 those algorithms served up lots of garbage. According to an analysis by *BuzzFeed*, the 20 most viral fake election stories generated a total of 8.7 million shares, reactions, and comments on Facebook, compared to only 7.4 million shares, reactions, and comments for 20 of the top-performing legitimate election stories.[32]

It's true, of course, that human users—not algorithms—were the ones choosing to share these stories with their friends. But by allowing investigative reports from the *New York Times* to appear alongside half-baked propaganda from the Conservative Tribune—and by providing few visual cues to distinguish the two—Facebook enabled a problem that critics argue it might have easily fixed. As techno-sociologist Zeynep Tufekci wrote for the *Times*, "When the company decided it wanted to reduce spam, it established a policy that limited its spread. If Facebook had the same kind of zeal about fake news, it could minimize its spread, too."[33] Another Facebook engineer agreed, telling *BuzzFeed* that the company could slow fake news if CEO Mark Zuckerberg simply gave the order. "There is a lot more we could be doing," the unnamed employee said, "using tools already built and in use across Facebook to stop other offensive or harmful content."[34]

So will Zuckerberg answer the call? Many critics say he has a moral obligation to do so, citing the role that Facebook plays as a modern news and information filter and invoking the company's "responsibility" to the public. Their hope is that Facebook, along with fellow digital media giants

Twitter and Google, might yet embrace their role as gatekeepers of the modern Web and choose to filter out fake and hyperpartisan news, doing for journalism what journalism can no longer do for itself. However, this white-knight logic neglects an important point: the Internet's new gatekeepers aren't journalists—and they have plenty of reasons to keep it that way.

The Internet's New Gatekeepers Don't Share Journalism's Values

During an August 2016 event in Italy, an inquisitive university student asked Zuckerberg whether his company intended to become a news editor. The question came at a moment of soul searching for the social media giant: three months earlier, Gizmodo had broken the news that Facebook's "news curators" were deliberately stifling conservative news sources on the platform's Trending Topics feed, sparking an uproar of criticism from Republicans and leading to Facebook's eventual decision to replace its human curators with supposedly "neutral" algorithms.[35]

The snafu underscored Facebook's increasingly influential role as a gatekeeper of the modern Web, and for a fleeting moment in May 2016, when Zuckerberg used the word "newsworthy" to describe his vision for Trending Topics, it seemed that Facebook might start approaching this gatekeeping role with a greater sense of journalistic responsibility.[36] In Italy, however, Zuckerberg doused those hopes with a splash of reality. "No, we're a technology company," he told the student, "not a media company."[37]

Zuckerberg has appeared to give some ground since the election, announcing a range of efforts to make fake news less viral on the platform; launching the Facebook Journalism Project, an initiative intended to "establish stronger ties" with the news industry; and publishing a 3,600-word manifesto affirming Facebook's commitment to "reduce sensationalism and help build a more informed community," among other lofty goals.[38] But none of these modest steps even remotely suggest that Facebook plans to assert "news judgment" in the way that professional journalists have for more than a century. In fact, Zuckerberg's vision for the company (he has called Facebook a "platform for all ideas" and repeatedly expressed a desire "to make the world more open and connected") is fundamentally at odds with this gatekeeping approach, and so is his business model.[39] In 2016 Facebook generated $26.9 *billion* dollars from digital advertising, a 57 percent increase from 2015 that helped the company turn a record profit of $10.2 billion, up 177 percent.[40] Surely, it's no coincidence that this spike overlapped with the explosion of fake and sensational news on the platform. In reality, these vices are not bugs in Facebook's platform so much as features of the machine—a machine that works best when audiences become glued to their screens, no matter what brings them there. As John Hermann wrote for the *New York Times*:

> Unlike traditional media organizations, which have spent years trying to figure out how to lure readers out of the Facebook ecosystem and onto their sites, these new publishers are happy to live inside the world that Facebook has created. Their pages are accommodated but not actively courted by the company and are not a major part of its public messaging about media. But they are, perhaps, the purest expression of Facebook's design and of the incentives coded into its algorithm—a system that has already reshaped the web and has now inherited, for better or for worse, a great deal of America's political discourse.[41]

So, sure, Zuckerberg might be earnest about combatting blatant propaganda on Facebook, if only to ward off government regulation and prevent a revolt by advertisers. But the idea that Facebook will assume responsibility for curating and filtering news in the "public interest" is wishful thinking. As long as Facebook's bottom line remains beholden to clicks, likes, and shares, the public should expect its infrastructure and algorithms to reward the types of content that deliver on these metrics. That's good news if you run a hyperpartisan news blog or specialize in "trendy" social videos, but it's bad news for the rest of the news media, including a pillar of American journalism that's already in crisis: the watchdog press.

Journalism's Watchdogs Lost Their Teeth

On January 29, 2002, less than 15 minutes into George W. Bush's first State of the Union address, the president fired the opening salvo of a yearlong campaign to take the United States to war. "Iraq continues to flaunt its hostility toward America and to support terror," Bush told the country. "The Iraqi regime has plotted to develop anthrax, and nerve gas, and nuclear weapons for over a decade. This is a regime that has already used poison gas to murder thousands of its own citizens. . . . This is a regime that agreed to international inspections—then kicked out the inspectors. This is a regime that has something to hide from the civilized world."[42]

A Senate Intelligence Report would later reveal that U.S. intelligence agencies were deeply divided over the justifications for war in Iraq. But the narrative spun by the Bush administration—and reported uncritically by the news media—featured no such uncertainty.

Instead, Secretary of Defense Donald Rumsfeld spoke matter of factly about Iraq's "weapons of mass terror" and linked Iraq, without credible evidence, to the attacks on 9/11; National Security Advisor Condoleeza Rice gravely warned that "we don't want the smoking gun to be a mushroom cloud," repeating a line drafted by the ad hoc White House Iraq Group and first published, without attribution, in the *New York Times*; and President Bush assured the public there was "no doubt" that Saddam Hussein's regime continued "to possess and conceal some of the most lethal weapons ever devised."[43] The country's only remaining choice, these officials told a credulous press, was to invade Iraq.

The White House's fervor for war should have planted suspicion in the minds of famously skeptical journalists. It should have raised questions about the administration's ulterior motives in Iraq, about the defense contractors that stood to gain from an extended war, about the United States' entanglement in foreign oil markets, about the credibility of intelligence on weapons of mass destruction, and about the unintended consequences of war and the human toll of sending yet more troops into the Middle East. Indeed, had there been a sufficiently adversarial relationship between the press and the political establishment, these questions would have led every newscast and topped every front-page news feature on the subject.

But that didn't happen. Instead, journalists succumbed to what *New York Times* columnist Paul Krugman called "a definite culture of fear," one in which "criticizing the push for war looked very much like a career killer."[44] Despite the stakes, this culture pervaded even the country's most fiercely independent news outlets, including the *Times*, where Judith Miller and Michael Gordon published unverified claims about WMDs that were fed to them by unnamed government sources. Years later, Miller would claim that she and Gordon were simply doing their jobs ("Were we not supposed to report what it was that had the intelligence community so nervous about Saddam? Were we supposed to keep that from the American people?" she asked *The Daily Show* host Jon Stewart in 2015). But her argument was as hollow as it was disingenuous, and Stewart saw right through it. "[The Bush administration] gave that story to you," he said. "A reporter's job is to look at the context of it and find out what it is within that that is true and what is a manipulation."[45]

In fairness to Miller, some researchers have argued that the media did not manufacture the public's support for war so much as reinforce it, citing evidence that a majority of Americans mistrusted Saddam Hussein well before the Bush administration's PR campaign.[46] But even if Americans *were* predisposed to support an invasion, that doesn't let the news media off the hook. As watchdogs of government, journalists are meant to serve as a check on power, to question an administration's claims and motives, to hold their public statements to scrutiny, and to dig beneath the rhetoric to separate fact from fiction. But in the run-up to the Iraq War, many reporters instead settled for a role as stenographers, idly transmitting sensational fodder that flowed from the White House Iraq Group to senior administration officials to unscrupulous journalists. The press failed the public by becoming the "passive recipients of news," Brett Cunningham wrote in 2003, "rather than aggressive analyzers and explainers of it."[47]

Unfortunately, this plague of journalistic impotence has only become more severe since the Iraq War. Consider that during the 2012 presidential campaign, political journalists routinely allowed the Obama and Romney teams to review and edit their own comments before publication, a policy that caused quotes to "come back redacted, stripped of colorful metaphors, colloquial language and anything even mildly provocative," according to the *Times*.[48] Many journalists justified these agreements as the cost of doing business—a necessary concession to ensure valuable access to campaign staff. But critics rightly saw them as a breach of journalistic ethics and a sign that journalism's fierce watchdogs were being replaced by cozy lapdogs, content to let political journalism be "contrived and distorted by the very people whom these media outlets purport to cover adversarially," Glenn Greenwald wrote for *Salon*. "We would be far better off," he continued, "without anonymous quotes from government officials repeating administration spin or sliming political opponents, and we would also be far better off without doctored quotes based on their veto power over what can be published—even if the price is that we do without their official statements."[49]

The controversy over journalism as stenography erupted anew in 2015, when CNN, Fox News, MSNBC, and other cable news outlets regularly aired Donald Trump's campaign speeches live, without editing or fact checking. During the Republican primaries alone, this wall-to-wall coverage helped Donald Trump earn more than $4 billion in free media, according to MediaQuant, and it allowed the candidate to repeat outlandish claims without journalistic scrutiny.[50]

This unfettered airtime undoubtedly helped Trump's candidacy, but in a sign of the increasingly symbiotic relationship between media and politics, it also helped the news outlets themselves, which saw huge ratings whenever Trump made a controversial promise to build a wall or ban Muslims from entering the country. "It may not be good for America, but it's damn good for CBS," Les Moonves, CBS's chief executive officer, said candidly of the Trump campaign.[51] Executives at other networks may have been more restrained, but their entanglement with Trump's star power was the same. As Brett Edkins wrote for *Forbes*: "Cable news is happy to court higher ratings by covering Trump's latest tweet, and Trump is happy to oblige by stirring controversy."[52]

The coziness of journalism's relationship with Washington's power players became even more apparent after Trump's election, when the president-elect invited a handful of TV executives and anchors to join an off-the-record "reset" meeting at Trump Tower. One by one, CNN president Jeff Zucker (who was a top executive at NBC during Trump's rise to fame on *The Apprentice*); MSNBC president Phil Griffin; and on-air personalities Martha Raddatz, George Stephanopoulos, Lester Holt, and Chuck Todd, among others, dutifully filed into the building's lobby, presumably fearing that failure to attend the meeting would cause them to lose access—and ratings—during the Trump presidency. Their calculation may have been correct, but agreeing to go off the record to appease the most powerful figure in American government was, as Poynter's Benjamin Mullin wrote, "in opposition to the values journalists everywhere are supposed to embody" and a "disservice" to the American public.[53]

Of course, plenty of important investigative journalism *did* take place during the campaign, from the incisive reporting on Trump's charitable giving to the uncovering of archival video and audio tapes that helped inform voters' judgment of the two candidates. This reporting lived up to the Fourth Estate's proud reputation for watchdog journalism, and it helps explain the surge of donations and subscriptions received by investigative powerhouses like *ProPublica* and the *Washington Post* following Trump's election.

The problem, as Dana Milbank explained in the *Post*, is that these "watchdogs of democracy, growling at falsehoods and barking at abuses in the system," were the exception in 2016, not the rule. "In general," Milbank wrote, watchdogs were outnumbered "by those who cover politics as horse race, praising the maneuvers of whichever candidate is ahead in the polls. This avowedly neutral approach—process journalism—is apolitical. But it's also amoral—a he-said-she-said approach that in this case confused tactics for truth and what works for what's right."[54]

If news organizations hope to regain the trust of the American public, they will need to rededicate themselves to public-interest journalism that puts the needs of citizens first. In part, this means rejecting "access journalism" and returning to a more adversarial relationship with power. But in an age of social media, fractured audiences, and democratized publishing, building public trust will also require more fundamental changes to the relationship between journalists and the communities they serve. The good news is that many pioneering newsrooms started making these pivots more than two decades ago.

The bad news: much of the profession didn't follow their lead.

Journalism's Reform Movement Lost Momentum

By today's standards, there was nothing particularly unusual about news coverage of the 1988 presidential race. Dozens of campaign reporters followed the candidates across the country, documenting moments of staged drama like Michael Dukakis's ill-fated appearance atop a military tank; news magazines produced exclusive features detailing the candidates' childhoods, medical histories, and personalities (while giving short shrift to their issue stances); and anchors regularly led their broadcasts with updates on the "race" for the White House, putting "titillation above education," candidate Bob Dole lamented, and obsessing over journalism's latest shiny toy: public opinion polls.[55] "Simply put," Peter D. Hart, a pollster, told the *New York Times* in 1988, "polls have become the crutch of the media."[56]

Although ubiquitous today, sensational tabloid fodder and nonstop "horse race" coverage were still quite new to American politics in 1988. An analysis by Harvard professor Thomas E. Patterson found that only 45 percent of news stories sampled in 1960 focused on campaign strategy and success (the "game schema"), compared to nearly 55 percent that focused on policy and leadership (the "policy schema"). But over time, this commitment to substantive election coverage eroded under the weight of commercial pressures and the convenience of public opinion polling, and by 1992, the balance had been lost: during that year's presidential campaign, the game schema appeared in more than 80 percent of the stories in Patterson's sample, whereas the policy schema appeared in less than 20 percent.[57]

Alarmed by this trend, a group of editors in the 1990s began pushing their newsrooms to adopt a more civic-minded approach to reporting. In Kansas, for example, the *Wichita Eagle* surveyed readers before the 1990 governor's race to determine what issues deserved the most coverage; in Florida, the *Tallahassee Democrat* organized a series of community dialogue meetings at the state capitol building and added a "public agenda page" to the print newspaper; and nationally, PBS hosted the National Issues Convention, a gathering that brought together more than 400 citizens from around the country to discuss national issues.[58]

Seeking to build momentum around this movement, the reform-minded editors spearheading these projects began attaching a name to their work—"public" or "civic" journalism—and soon adopted a more far-reaching mission that reimagined journalism's role not only in political coverage but also in community life at large. "Public journalism is a set of values about the craft that recognizes and acts upon the interdependence between journalism and democracy," Davis Merritt, editor of the *Wichita Star*, explained to NPR. "It values the concerns of citizens over the needs of the media and political actors, and conceives of citizens as stakeholders in the democratic process rather than as merely victims, spectators or inevitable adversaries."[59] Ed Fouhy, founding executive director of the Pew Center for Civic Journalism, described the movement as "a fundamental change in the way we do our business," and media scholar Jay Rosen, an early champion of these reforms, wrote that "public journalism tries to place the journalist within the political community as a responsible member with a full stake in public life."[60] In his book *What Are Journalists For?*, Rosen further explained the movement's rationale:

> Journalism would do well to develop an approach that can (1) address people as citizens, potential participants in public affairs, rather than victims or spectators, (2) help the political community act upon, rather than just learn about, its problems, (3) improve the climate of public discussion, rather than simply watch it deteriorate, and (4) help make public life go well, so that it earns its claim on our attention. If they can find a way to do these things, journalists may in time restore public confidence in the press, reconnect with an audience that has been drifting away, rekindle the idealism that brought many of them into the craft, and contribute, in a more substantial way, to the health and future prospects of American democracy.[61]

Rosen and other advocates believed that this new relationship between journalists and citizens would strengthen democracy and promote participation in civic life. But even as the movement gained traction in the early 1990s, many journalists remained fiercely resistant to the idea that news organizations should set aside traditional journalistic values such as independence and "objectivity" to become more active participants in community life. Some critics warned that "community boosterism" would hurt the credibility of the press ("Too much of what's called public journalism appears to be what our promotion department does, only with a different kind of name and a fancy, evangelistic fervor," said *Washington Post* executive editor Leonard Downie), whereas others argued that giving citizens a more participatory role in journalism would be a dereliction of duty.[62] "What in God's name are we thinking about?" *Philadelphia Daily News* editorial page editor Richard Aregood asked incredulously in 1994. "We are abandoning a piece of our own jobs if what we are doing is asking people what we should do. Are we to draw up panels of our readers and ask them what they want and put them in the newspaper? We may as well go into the mirror business."[63]

Despite the embrace of public journalism at the *Virginian-Pilot*, the *Wichita Eagle*, the *Wisconsin State Journal*, and dozens of other publications, a survey of Associated Press managing editors in 1997 found that only 7 percent of respondents strongly agreed that civic journalism was "an important way for many news organizations to reconnect with their alienated communities."[64] The movement continued to lose steam in the early 2000s as digital-era disruption stole the industry's attention, and by 2003, when the Pew Center for Civic Journalism folded, the momentum for far-reaching reform had fizzled.

However, that was *then*, before the collapse of print advertising revenue, before the growth of social media, before "fake news," and before Donald Trump. Today, as the news business grapples with political and economic upheaval, the principles of public journalism can be seen resurfacing under new names like "solutions journalism" and "engaged journalism," and reform advocates see an opportunity for progress. "Engaged journalism is a much evolved descendant" of public journalism, "born into a radically changed landscape," Geneva Overholser, a senior fellow at the Democracy Fund, wrote in 2016. "Newsrooms that had been averse to change [are now] desperately looking for answers."[65]

The prospects for engaged journalism continued to improve following the election, when journalists at the *New York Times*, the *Washington Post*, *Rolling Stone*, and other major media outlets all acknowledged the need to spend more time *listening* to the public and explicitly addressing the public's concerns. But what remains to be seen is whether this renewed appetite for change can reverse a decades-long trend of growing public mistrust; whether it can pierce the Internet's filter bubbles and bridge a bifurcated media landscape; and whether, in doing so, it can somehow achieve one of the news business's most elusive goals: reaching millennials.

Journalism's Traditional News Products Lost a Generation

For the country's three major broadcast networks, 2005 could have been a landmark year. In the span of only six months, CBS's Dan Rather, NBC's Tom Brokaw, and ABC's Peter Jennings all stepped aside from their evening news anchor desks, opening the door for transformative change at a time when many media critics believed it was desperately needed. Between 1980 and 2005, nightly evening news viewership dropped from 52 million to 27 million—a 48 percent decline—and research suggested that many young viewers were turning away from the broadcast networks altogether.[66] In a 1998 study, for example, Stephen Earl Bennett found that only 45 percent of respondents under 30 said they'd watched a TV news show the day before, compared to 86 percent of people over 30, revealing a generational gap that threatened the long-term viability of broadcast news.[67]

The three broadcast networks might have used this moment of transition to overhaul their formats or to invite young, edgy news anchors into the roles previously filled by Boomers. Instead, the networks played it safe by promoting Elizabeth Vargas, Brian Williams, and Bob Woodruff, three establishment news anchors in their mid-40s, and the evening newscasts continued to lose audience share and relevance, slipping to a record-low 21.4 million nightly viewers by 2010.[68]

The struggle to attract young audiences has not been confined to broadcast news.[69] In 2016 the Pew Research Center found that only 5 percent of 18- to 29-year-olds and 10 percent of 30- to 49-year-olds often get news from print newspapers, compared to 48 percent of the 65-and-over demographic.[70] Some of the discrepancy can be attributed to a shift from print to digital readership—young audiences were more than twice as likely to get news from websites or apps—but the Pew data revealed that regardless of medium, millennials and Gen Xers were consuming significantly less news than their older counterparts. As for the prediction that young Americans would begin to consume more news as they got older, Pew found little evidence to support it: "Today's younger and middle-aged audience seems unlikely to ever match the avid news interest of the generations they will replace," the report concluded, "even as they enthusiastically transition to the Internet as their principal source of news."[71]

One popular explanation for this trend is that young people are simply less interested and engaged in public affairs than older generations. It's hardly an original theory: in a July 1990 cover story, *Time* sounded the warning about a generation of Americans who "crave entertainment" and have attention spans "as short as one zap of a TV dial."[72] That article was lamenting the apathy of Gen Xers (who are now in their 40s and 50s), but it just as easily could have been written two decades later about millennials, the most recent target of Boomer scorn. As retired *Washington Post* columnist Robert G. Kaiser put it: "Today's young people skitter around the Internet like ice skaters, exercising their short attention spans by looking for fun and, occasionally, seeking out serious information," he wrote for The Brookings Essay. "Audience taste seems to be changing, with the result that among young people particularly there is a declining appetite for the sort of information packages the great newspapers provided."[73]

Kaiser's critique mirrors the hand-wringing of many industry insiders, who place the blame for legacy journalism's shrinking reach at the feet of "apathetic" and "disengaged" millennials. However, this argument is increasingly running into conflicting data. For one, although millennials are less likely than older generations to trust the news media *in general*, that trust gap disappears when examining specific news sources, including *The Daily Show* and *Politico*, which millennials trust in greater proportions than both Gen Xers and Baby Boomers.[74] Meanwhile, according to a 2015 survey by the Media Insight Project, 85 percent of millennials say keeping up with the news is at least somewhat important to them, and nearly 70 percent consume news daily. "This newest generation of American adults is anything but 'newsless,' passive, or civically uninterested," the report concluded. "Millennials consume news and information in strikingly different ways than previous generations, and their paths to discovery are more nuanced and varied than some may have imagined."[75]

Rather than disengaging from civic life, it appears millennials may actually be turning off David Muir to start watching John Oliver, Trevor Noah, and Samantha Bee; ditching the Sunday sports section for *The Ringer, The Undefeated*, and *Bleacher Report*; trading in newspaper opinion columns for essays on *Salon* and *Slate*; and replacing 1,500-word business stories from the *Wall Street Journal* with a series of 20-word bursts texted to their phones by *Quartz*. "Today's young people (the 'millennials') are interested in local, national, and international issues," Christopher Sopher, a Truman Scholar and news-consuming millennial, wrote for Nieman Lab. "Most news outlets simply aren't very good at reaching or serving [them]."[76]

In 2015 the American Press Institute outlined a series of "best practices" for reaching millennial news audiences, which included adopting a more approachable writing voice, investing in visual journalism, and embracing new platforms. These strategies are already operational at digital-era startups like *BuzzFeed* and *VICE*, as well as at national outlets like the *New York Times* and *Washington Post*, which, recognizing the need to adapt, were quick to hire social media editors, build mobile news apps, and experiment with podcasts and other new media formats. This all bodes well for the future of national news organizations, many of which, after years of uncertainty, appear to be trending toward sustained profitability.

However, the outlook remains less cheerful for another pillar of journalism, local news, where growth and evolution have been largely overshadowed by a different concern: survival.

Journalism's Local Newsrooms Lost Their Scale

Following Donald Trump's surprise election victory, the Internet buzzed with essays and think pieces about the contributing role of fake news, filter bubbles, polling failures, identity politics, sensational news coverage, and false equivalence. But in an article for *Politico*, media economist Ken Doctor pointed to a less obvious explanation for Trump's success: the shrinking of local newsrooms. "While it seems that everyone reads the *New York Times*, *Wall Street Journal* or *Washington Post*, in reality, they don't, and they never did," Doctor wrote. "They relied on the local paper. It's now shrunken in size, in content, in authority—and in confidence to address its community's issues of the day."[77]

Between 1990 and 2014, the number of full-time journalists working in U.S. newsrooms declined from 56,900 to 32,900—a 42 percent drop—and more than 200 daily newspapers closed their doors for good.[78] The deepest cuts have come at midsize metropolitan dailies, and with the exception of 2016, when political advertising helped stabilize the industry's sagging revenue figures, newsroom consolidation has shown few signs of slowing down. In fact, within months of November's election, the *Detroit Free Press* and the *Detroit News* announced dozens of layoffs and buyouts, Gannett cut more than 250 jobs from its newspaper properties in New Jersey, and the *Issaquah Press* in Washington printed its final issue. (By the time you read this, the list of casualties will almost certainly be longer.)

The exact impact of these declines on public discourse and civic society is hard to measure, because there is no control group (read: a world with fully staffed newsrooms) against which to compare the status quo. But what we do know is that investigative news teams are being scaled back or eliminated en masse, that experienced (and expensive) reporters are receiving a disproportionate share of the pink slips and buyouts, that newspapers in cities like Baltimore and Philadelphia are producing significantly less public-affairs journalism than in decades past, and that across the profession, news organizations are experiencing, in Doctor's words, "an ungodly decline in numbers, knowledge, and know-how."[79]

At the very least, these facts allow some informed guesses about the social cost of shrinking newsrooms. Pulitzer Prize winner Paul Starr, for example, predicted in 2009 that the decline of newspapers would be accompanied by a rise in political corruption, a correlation that's been observed in other countries around the world; Nieman Journalism Lab director Joshua Benton noted that the hollowing out of local newsrooms has accelerated the news media's retreat from rural America, where journalism is less profitable than in affluent, urban centers like New York City;

and a report by the Federal Communication Commission speculated that the decline of investigative reporting capacity in states like West Virginia has already cost human lives. "Several publications brilliantly documented that the Upper Big Branch mine in West Virginia had '1,342 safety violations in the past five years,'" Steven Waldman wrote for the FCC. "But it requires no stretch of the imagination to think that the 29 people who died in the 2010 mine explosion might have been spared had more journalists aggressively reported these safety problems before the accident."[80]

The most common explanation for this decline in local journalism is the collapse of print advertising revenue in the Internet age—and for good reason. Historically, advertising played the largest role in underwriting the work of U.S. newspapers, often accounting for more than 75 percent of their total revenue. The windfall from advertising allowed media companies to pull in double-digit profit margins while still funding a robust reporting operation, including the scores of beat writers who served as public-interest watchdogs at statehouses, school board meetings, and city halls across the country.

This model sustained journalism for the better part of a century, but it came crashing down once the Internet created new avenues for corporate advertisers to connect with consumers. Between 2000 and 2013, newspaper revenue from print advertising plummeted 64 percent—from $63.5 billion to $23 billion—and although newspapers have managed to claw back some of that money through *digital* advertising, which contributed $3.5 billion to industry coffers in 2014, most of the gains have gone instead to five technology and social media companies: Facebook, Google, Yahoo, Verizon, and Twitter.[81] Together, these companies brought in 65 percent of all U.S. digital advertising revenue in 2015 and accounted for nearly 80 percent of the market's year-over-year growth, an ominous sign for news organizations that increasingly find themselves fighting over scraps.[82]

The story often spun from these numbers, of course, is that newspaper companies were powerless victims of technological change, left with no choice but to lay off reporters and rapidly downsize their news operations. But what this economic determinism overlooks is the supporting role played by the media's ownership class, which managed for years to maintain double-digit profit margins even as their newsrooms shriveled. Consider the case of Gannett, a media chain that in 2000 reported its ninth consecutive year of record profits.[83] With the Internet then emerging as a threat to its advertising-based business model, Gannett might have decided to reinvest those profits in digital innovation, accepting smaller margins in the short run to retool for the long run. Instead, the company laid off 100 employees from its flagship property, *USA Today*, and spent billions of dollars on acquisitions, successfully boosting quarterly earnings (Gannett was still reporting record profits as late as 2004, when it earned $1.32 billion), but undermining the company's capacity for sustainable public-interest journalism.[84]

Gannett's focus on short-term profits is a common feature among today's corporate media giants—but it's not inevitable. In 1933, for example, *Wall Street Journal* owner Jane Bancroft told the newspaper's manager "to do what's best for the company" and not to "worry about dividends," and during World War II, when the United States implemented paper rationing, the *New York Times* famously turned down advertising to make more space for news content.[85] These actions came at a time when most daily newspapers were independently owned, often by families who saw operating a newspaper as a service to the community (much like endowing a public library) and who viewed profit as the reward for a service well rendered. J. N. Heiskell, the long-time owner of the *Arkansas Gazette*, captured this sentiment in the 1930s:

> He who is actually a newspaper's editor is its voice and soul and the keeper of its conscience. Choose him with care and circumspection. Arm him with freedom. Equip him with the tools of his trade. Grant him reasonable time for this work. Fortify him with your confidence. Then may you enjoy the rewards that come to a newspaper that speaks with intelligence, sincerity and conviction and that lights the way for good citizenship to follow.[86]

During the height of family newspaper ownership, in the early 20th century, newspaper owners like Heiskell were likely to bump into readers at the grocery store or to serve alongside them on the boards of local civic organizations. Today, that ownership structure has all but disappeared: after decades of corporate consolidation, less than 10 percent of daily newspapers are now independently owned, and the 25 largest newspaper chains collectively control more than half of the country's roughly 1,300 daily newspapers.[87] The result, according to critics, is that the short-run interests of investors and shareholders trump any long-term commitment to public-service journalism, especially among the industry's ascendant ownership class—Wall Street investment entities—which snatched up more than 200 daily newspapers between 2004 and 2014.[88] These investment firms "operate with a short-term, earnings-first focus," according to a report by the Center for Innovation and Sustainability in Local Media, and "are prepared to get rid of any holdings—including newspapers—that fail to produce what they judge to be an adequate profit."[89] For rural America in particular, the report warned the outcome could be disastrous:

With regional news outlets—including metro papers and television stations—pulling back coverage from outlying areas, newspapers owned by investment entities are often the only source of local news in many communities. Because they spread risk across multiple products and geographic areas, investment groups can afford to let individual newspapers fail or pursue a harvesting strategy in which they "manage the decline" of the assets in their portfolio. If their newspapers fail, and viable alternatives do not arise, many communities across the country are in danger of becoming news deserts.[90]

The stakes are made even higher by the current state of local television news, which is increasingly dominated by a small group of corporate owners, often with a clear political agenda. Thanks to decades of deregulation, including by Trump's FCC Chairperson Ajit Pai, corporations such as Sinclair Broadcast Group are now allowed to own dozens of stations across the country—a market share they can use to push out ideological commentary to millions of unsuspecting local news consumers. And this problem is only expected to get worse: in May 2017 Sinclair struck a $3.9 billion deal to acquire Tribune Media; if approved by the FCC, Sinclair would add another 42 local TV stations to its current portfolio of more than 60.[91]

With young news consumers ditching newspapers and television in favor of digital platforms, it's tempting to dismiss the significance of these consolidation trends—to write them off as steps along the path to obsolescence for legacy media. There are plenty of media critics who hold this view, but we think it's a mistake. Despite the rise of hyperlocal blogs, social media, nonprofit news, and citizen journalism, legacy institutions—especially newspapers—still carry out the vast majority of local watchdog reporting in the United States. Perhaps that will change someday, but for now the information health of communities still depends largely on the deep pockets of institutional journalism and on the expertise of professional journalists who are paid to uncover information that powerful interests want to keep hidden. As Emily Bell puts it, "Pluralism is important for a healthy news ecosystem, but so is institutional strength and guaranteed sustainability"—especially in the age of Trump.[92]

American Politics Lost Its Soul

Thomas Jefferson's famous quip that he'd prefer "newspapers without a government" to "a government without newspapers" has become gospel in American journalism, but its full significance only becomes clear in the context of a decidedly less recognizable Jefferson quote:

"I deplore," he wrote in 1814, "the putrid state into which our newspapers have passed and the malignity, the vulgarity, and mendacious spirit of those who write for them . . . As vehicles of information and a curb on our functionaries, they have rendered themselves useless by forfeiting all title to belief."[93]

Throughout his political career, Jefferson often decried the failings of the early American press, describing it as a "polluted vehicle" and lamenting its unmet promise as a democratic institution.[94] And yet, for all his misgivings, Jefferson never backed away from his belief in what the press *could* be—or what it must always be allowed to be: free. In one of his first acts as president, Jefferson granted pardons to every citizen who remained jailed under the Sedition Act, a law signed by President Adams in 1798 that effectively prohibited journalists from criticizing the government. And in 1823, even after decades of abuse at the hands of newspapers, Jefferson continued to defend the ideal of a free press, describing it to Greek scholar Adamantios Coray as one of the essential pillars of American democracy.

"This formidable Censor of the public functionaries," Jefferson wrote, "produces reform peaceably, which must otherwise be done by revolution. It is also the best instrument for enlightening the mind of men, and improving him as a rational, moral, and social being."[95]

Subsequent American politicians, despite their frequent complaints of media bias or sensationalism, have generally honored the principle of press freedom. But that precedent has increasingly come under assault in recent years, most notably by Donald Trump. On the campaign trail, Trump not only called journalists "scum," "slime," and "lying, thieving people" but also revoked the press credentials of journalists who wrote unflattering stories, threatened to "loosen up" libel laws as president, threatened a frivolous lawsuit against the *New York Times*, and even joked about the idea of murdering journalists. "Let's see," he mused at a December 2015 campaign stop in Grand Rapids, Michigan. "No, I wouldn't. I would never kill them, but I do hate them."

Any hopes that Trump would change his tone in the White House were short lived: only months into his presidency, the *New York Times* reported that Trump had urged then-FBI director James Comey to arrest journalists who published classified information, a revelation that came a week after police in West Virginia detained a reporter for his (allegedly) overenthusiastic attempts to ask Health and Human Services Secretary Tom Price a question about health care legislation.[96] (Trump did not order that arrest, but he also didn't publicly condemn it.)

So far, the American government's system of checks and balances has largely protected journalists from a full-fledged crackdown on their First

Amendment rights. However, that hasn't stopped Trump from attempting to erode the media's credibility. During the campaign, for example, Trump repeatedly responded to negative press coverage—on Trump University's unethical business practices; on the Trump Foundation's exaggerated donation figures; and on his own disparaging remarks about women, immigrants, racial minorities, and people with disabilities, to name a few examples—not by issuing apologies, but by waging a war against the messengers. "Anytime you see a story about me or my campaign saying 'sources said,' DO NOT believe it," he tweeted in September 2016. "There are no sources, they are just made up lies!"[97]

Trump also routinely picked up conspiracy theories from the alt-right blogosphere—like the theory that Hillary Clinton suffered from an undisclosed brain injury—and turned it into unofficial campaign messaging, brushing off any attempts to hold his accusations to scrutiny. Even Alex Jones, the conspiracy theorist who founded InfoWars and once peddled the myth that government officials staged the Sandy Hook massacre, seemed surprised by his newfound legitimacy during the campaign. "It is surreal to talk about issues here on air and then word for word hear Trump say it two days later," Jones said in August 2016. "It is amazing."[98]

Trump's relationship with the truth has been so tenuous that when *Politico* reviewed his public comments over a seven-day period in September 2016, the news site found that he'd made a staggering 87 false statements *in a single week.*[99] A traditional politician would have felt pressure to acknowledge some of those mistakes—or at least to provide specific rebuttals explaining how *Politico* got it wrong. But the Trump team instead doubled down, sending out senior communications advisor Jason Miller to dismiss the entire story as the product of a left-wing conspiracy.

"There is a coordinated effort by the media elites and Hillary Clinton to shamelessly push their propaganda and distract from Crooked Hillary's lies and flailing campaign," Miller wrote in an e-mail to *Politico*. "All of these 'fact-check' questions can be easily verified, but that's not what blog sites like *Politico* want people to believe. Mr. Trump is standing with the people of America and against the rigged system insiders, and it's driving the media crazy."[100]

What's especially frightening about Trump's strategy to discredit his critics is that it seems to be working, at least among his supporters. In 2015 before Trump's rise, 32 percent of Republicans had a "great deal" or "fair amount" of trust in mass media, according to a Gallup poll. A year later, that number dropped to 14 percent, the largest year-over-year change in the poll's history.[101] Meanwhile, a poll conducted two weeks into Trump's presidency found that 48 percent of Americans believe the Trump administration to be truthful, compared to just 39 percent who feel that way about the news media.[102]

Journalists might like to believe that Trump's end-around of the media is a one-time aberration, enabled by his particular brand of charisma and demagoguery. However, there are signs of a broader political culture shift afoot, from Kellyanne Conway's invocation of "alternative facts" to Greg Gianforte's assault of a reporter. This anti-media, post-truth trend has even surfaced in European countries like Italy, where former Prime Minister Silvio Berlusconi once accused the state-run broadcast network RAI of "using television as a criminal means of communication," as well as Great Britain, where Boris Johnson and Nigel Farage helped engineer Brexit with an unscrupulous campaign of untruths and misdirections.[103] "There is a global movement of minds," Richard Cohen observed in the *New York Times*. "Facts are now a quaint hangover from a time of rational discourse, little annoyances easily upended. Volume trumps reality."[104]

It is hard to imagine a more dangerous combination than the one we have now: an American public that doesn't trust journalism, economic incentives that pervert journalism, and a powerful leader who seems intent on squashing journalism.

Many observers view these trends as a prelude to fascism in the United States, citing similarities to the rise of Nazi Germany. We prefer to avoid such comparisons, if only because they can be too easily dismissed as alarmist or partisan. However, we also do not underestimate the dire reality that journalism is facing. Ken Pope is right that "journalism's moment of reckoning has arrived."[105]

The question we turn to now: how can journalists step up to meet it?

CHAPTER ONE

Reimagining Truth: Comedians, Fake News, and the Fate of "Objectivity"

"If nothing is true, then all is spectacle. The biggest wallet pays for the most blinding lights."[1]

—Timothy Snyder

"Fake news."

Jon Stewart didn't use those words, exactly, during his 2004 appearance on CNN's fiery political talk show *Crossfire*. But he came pretty close. In a moment of signature indignation, the late-night comedian and political satirist ripped into co-hosts Tucker Carlson and Paul Begala on their own program, calling them "partisan hacks" and accusing them of "hurting America" with their cheap brand of political bickering. Begala defended the show's format as "debate," but Stewart had a different name for it: "You're doing theater," he shot back. "It's not honest."[2]

The *Crossfire* duo seemed shell-shocked by Stewart's offensive, with Begala awkwardly trying to redirect the conversation as Carlson resorted to desperate appeals for mercy. "I thought you were going to be funny," Carlson pleaded. "Come on, be funny." But Stewart wasn't there to play nice, and the hosts should have seen it coming. In his then-bestselling book *America (The Book): A Citizen's Guide to Democracy Inaction*, Stewart referred to journalists as "democracy's valiant vulgarians" and blasted the press for obsessing over sex scandals and celebrity while meekly shrugging their shoulders at the "false information used to send our country to war." Writing with characteristic satirical flair, Stewart continued:

> What is the role of a free and independent press in a democratic society? Is it to be a passive conduit responsible only for the delivery of information between a government and its people? Is it to aggressively print allegation and rumor independent of accuracy or fairness? Is it to show boobies? No. The role of a free press is to be the people's eyes and ears, providing not just information but access, insight, and most importantly context.[3]

Stewart doubled down on this line of criticism during a 2004 interview with *New Yorker* columnist Ken Auletta, which aired on CSPAN less than 36 hours before his combative *Crossfire* appearance. Speaking to a room full of journalists, Stewart criticized the increasingly "symbiotic relationship" between politicians and the news media, especially on television, where pundits like Carlson and Begala provided a platform for partisan spin and packaged it as entertainment. For Stewart, this format embodied a particularly corrosive form of punditry, one that reinforced false dichotomies between left and right and amplified the loudest voices at either extreme. "To have a Democratic strategist and a Republican strategist is not a debate," Stewart explained to Auletta. "That's Coke and Pepsi discussing beverage supremacy. And it's not real."[4]

Not real. Not honest. More than a decade before Australia's *Macquarie Dictionary* named "fake news" its 2016 word of the year, Stewart made his mark on journalism by exposing the fakeness of real news. In one of his classic sketches, Stewart lampooned CNN for its vacuous wall-to-wall coverage of the post–Boston Marathon manhunt, replaying clips of on-the-scene reporters breaking such momentous news as "something just happened, we don't know what it is" and "interesting, that dog is barking." Stewart's response: "Let me tell ya a little something about canine dogs: I got one of them, and they bark a lot," he joked. "Sometimes the little f—er just stares out the window and barks, even when there's nothing out there. Sometimes he licks his own genitals. You know, you can't always read a lot into what they do, newswise."[5]

During his 16-year run on *The Daily Show*, Stewart was described as the ombudsman of television news and credited with "making media criticism funny and witty, and thus widely palatable."[6] But it didn't always seem likely to turn out that way. In 1996 Stewart was a B-list actor and failed talk show host (Paramount had cancelled *The Jon Stewart Show* a year earlier), and *The Daily Show*, then hosted by Craig Kilborn, was just finding its feet as a mock newscast that ridiculed the news media by imitating it.

Kilborn's *The Daily Show* borrowed elements from *Saturday Night Live, The Tonight Show,* and other pioneers of late-night comedy, but the program's faux news format also represented a specific response to the media culture of the 1990s, when newsmagazine shows like *Dateline* and *48 Hours* were taking infotainment to a new level and cable television's 24-hour news format was quickly becoming ubiquitous. "Every day when you woke up it seemed like there was a new 24-hour news channel," Madeleine Smithberg, co-creator of *The Daily Show,* told *DAME* in 2015. "There were too many networks with 24 hours to fill, and there really was not enough news."[7] The result was a television news landscape ripe for satire. "We were going to make fun of them by becoming them," fellow co-creator Lizz Winstead explained in 2012. "We would operate as a news organization while acting like a comedy show. It simply had never been done before."[8]

The Daily Show bolstered this faux news premise by hiring Kilborn, previously a real news anchor at ESPN, to be the show's frontman. Like most television hosts of the day, Kilborn was handsome and self-assured, giving *The Daily Show* its comedic foil to NBC's gravel-voiced anchor Stone Phillips, a quintessential 1990s news anchor whose overwrought delivery style provided comedic gold for Rob Lowe on *Saturday Night Live,* as well as for Kilborn. "My joke is always that Stone Phillips really deserves a 'created by' credit on *The Daily Show,*" Smithberg said in 2015. "We studied that guy. It became, 'Okay, we pretend we're him and mix it with stories that are much more absurd.'"[9]

Under Kilborn, *The Daily Show* forged a light-hearted comedic identity, defined by Kilborn's "frat-boy knowingness" and the content's "emphasis on celebrity mishaps."[10] The show occasionally had fun with politics, as during its coverage of the 1996 Dole–Clinton presidential debate, but Kilborn's bread-and-butter was the world of pop culture, where he found rich comedic material in royal custody battles and other tabloid fodder.

This cheap-laughs humor carried *The Daily Show* for three seasons, but when Kilborn left to host *The Late Late Show* on CBS, Comedy Central hired Stewart as his successor, ushering in a more biting brand of political satire. "I wanted [the show] to be satirical in the classic sense of the word," Stewart explained in a 2012 interview, "not the Spy magazine sense of the word where you just add adjectives like 'pepperpot.'"[11] The program's jestful imitation of the news media pivoted toward pointed criticism, and Stewart showed that he was less concerned with caricaturing 24-hour cable news shows than with highlighting their failure to perform meaningful journalism. A classic example came in 2003, when Fox News aired a segment that paired sights and sounds from the Iraq War with a soaring musical score, and Stewart cued up a biting response: "Who among us could ever forget where they were the night Fox set the war to music?" he deadpanned. "Fox, above all others, saw the war for what it was: entertainment."[12]

In January 2005, when CNN president Jeffrey Klein announced the cancellation of *Crossfire* only three months after Stewart's appearance on the show ("I agree wholeheartedly with Jon Stewart's overall premise," Klein told the *New York Times*), Stewart's media criticism landed its crowning achievement.[13] But there was always more to Stewart's magic than his searing attacks against Fox News and CNN. Indeed, for many Americans, Stewart was not only a critic of news, but also a *source* of news: in 2014, 12 percent of online Americans said they received news from *The Daily Show*, putting it on par with *USA Today* and *The Huffington Post*.[14] And when the Pew Research Center asked Americans in 2007 to name the journalist they admire most, more respondents under 30 years old chose Jon Stewart than any traditional newscaster.[15]

As Stewart's profile rose in the 2000s, the *New York Times*, *Rolling Stone*, *Newsweek*, and *Time* all took turns interpreting Stewart's cultural ascendance, and they all came to roughly the same conclusion: in an age of dishonest politics and superficial media, Stewart's secret sauce was that he gave it to people straight. No B.S. No focus group–tested spin. No straight-faced recitation of quotes he knew to be lies. Viewers of *The Daily Show* trusted Stewart to help them make sense of the news, and night after night he did that, with comedy, yes, but also with an unapologetically progressive moral compass. Stewart wore his values on his sleeve, and viewers loved it. "We live in a society now where people want to know who a journalist is before they decide whether or not to believe his or her reporting," Matt Taibbi explained in 2015. "Americans got to know Jon Stewart quickly and quickly learned to trust him even though he clearly had a point of view. It's the highest praise a journalist can get, and he deserved all of it."[16]

Of course, not everyone in journalism shared Taibbi's admiration. When Stewart and his Comedy Central partner Stephen Colbert hosted a satire-rich, quasi-political rally on the National Mall in 2015, for example, *Baltimore Sun* television critic David Zurawik derided the hosts as "fools and charlatans," and *Minneapolis Star Tribune* columnist Nick Coleman lamented that "the biggest gathering at a time of national dissension and economic decline [was] little more than an inside joke staged by cable comedians."[17] In the eyes of his critics, Stewart's ability to amass a large and devoted audience didn't make him any more worthy of J-club membership than the people uploading viral cat videos to YouTube. Journalism, they argued, is a profession with standards, rules, and ethics, and Stewart was a comedian who regularly defied them, shirking the profession's responsibilities even as he enjoyed its influence. As NPR television critic Eric Deggans explained:

> [Stewart] doesn't have to be fair in the way journalists do, so he can present his take on an issue without allowing the subject of the joke to present their side. And when he does something that seems counter to his Everyman image—like under-the-radar meetings with the president or having tough arguments with his writers about jokes on race—he can joke away the questions and insist it is not his role to explain his actions in the way he expects politicians and journalists to do.[18]

Notably, even the Pew Research Center (which rarely blends its research findings with opinionated analysis) felt compelled to push back against Stewart's supposed status as a journalist. "Are Americans confused?" a Pew report asked in 2008. "What is Stewart doing on his program . . . that might cause people to consider him a journalist?"[19]

This backlash against Stewart and *The Daily Show*'s faux news approach is an example of *boundary work*—or what sociologist Thomas Gieryn describes as "credibility contests" over "the legitimate power to define, describe, and explain bounded domains of reality."[20] These contests may seem semantic, but according to Seth Lewis and Matt Carlson, editors of the book *Boundaries of Journalism: Professionalism, Practices, and Participation*, the struggle over journalistic legitimacy is more than an academic debate. "Definitions matter," they write, "because how we think about the issue of boundaries has real consequences . . . Being deemed a "legitimate" journalist accords prestige and credibility, but also access to news sources, audiences, funding, legal rights, and other institutionalized perquisites."[21]

One can debate whether these rewards of legitimacy remain entirely relevant in the digital world, where traditional power hierarchies are rapidly eroding. But no matter the stakes, it's clear that the boundary wars aren't yet over, as comedians, citizen journalists, bloggers, and other supposed "imposters" continue to face pushback from mainstream journalists, just as television and radio reporters—the "new media" of their day—experienced resistance from newspaper journalists a century ago. "Journalists and the organizations that employ them need to be perceived by the public (aka their audience) as crucial to the provision of factual, reliable, timely, and meaningful information," media scholar Jane Singer explains. "They therefore have an interest in positioning other entities as less crucial, and an excellent way to make the point to brand them as less ethical—that is, less committed to norms that engender factualness, reliability, and so on."[22]

Mainstream journalists have criticized Stewart and his comedic ilk for encouraging cynicism in the political system, for taking quotes out of context, for trivializing serious issues, and for belittling and alienating people who disagree with them—examples of boundary work that all reflect a broader discomfort with how comedians construct and transmit *truth*. In traditional journalism, the process of truth telling is meant to be "objective," the product of impartial facts strung together by an avowedly neutral middleman. This philosophy, defined by Michael Schudson as a "faith in 'facts,' a distrust in 'values,' and a commitment to their segregation," has reigned over the profession for more than a century.[23] However, the rise of *The Daily Show* and other faux news programs is evidence that its dominance might be breaking. In this chapter, we examine how comedians like Stewart, Samantha Bee, John Oliver, and Trevor Noah are pioneering new approaches to truth telling—and how journalists in the news media are beginning to follow in their footsteps.

Jon Stewart, Glenn Greenwald, and the Truth of Conviction

In April 2001, at an event hosted by the Paley Center for Media, an audience member stepped to the microphone with a question for Jon Stewart and his colleagues at *The Daily Show*. "Since this is a political satire show," she asked, "how do you keep your own personal beliefs from showing up in the show?"

The answer must have surprised her.

"The show *is* our own personal beliefs," Stewart replied. "That's the only reason we go to work every day." A few seats down, Stephen Colbert, then a correspondent on *The Daily Show*, echoed his mentor. "I think if you try to do political satire without your personal beliefs, then you sound like a politician. You have no passion about what you're saying, and you're just spouting what the people want to hear."[24]

An early sign of *The Daily Show*'s unconventional approach came during the 2000 presidential race, when George W. Bush and Al Gore battled to a virtual tie in Florida, sparking a blitz of ballot recounts, lawsuits, and political shenanigans that ultimately gave Bush the presidency. Amid this confusion and chaos, Stewart and his team of faux news correspondents used comedy as a scythe to slice through the media noise and to capture the incredulity that many Americans were feeling. In one memorable segment, Steve Carell stood in front of a podium bearing the presidential seal and informed Stewart that he was "assuming the presidency."

"Steve, you can't do that," Stewart said in feigned disbelief.

"Bush did," Carell replied, to a roar from the studio audience.[25]

The segment was not balanced or neutral, but for many viewers it was refreshingly honest, capturing a larger truth about the political process that only a nonjournalist, unconstrained by professional standards, could deliver. "You could see the traditional media outlets struggling to cover this whole situation with some sort of dignity, and we weren't bound by that," said Chris Regan, then a writer for *The Daily Show*. "We were the only one who could approach what was going on in Florida honestly."[26] Craig Wolff, a journalism professor at Columbia University, offered a similar take: "If the election process has indeed become a circus, well, send in the clowns," he told *George* magazine. "So much coverage in the mainstream press is dishonest and manipulative. To me, the humorists are in some ways presenting the most honest coverage."[27]

The transparent conviction that Stewart brought to the news was not, by itself, an entirely new invention. (Right-wing radio hosts like Rush Limbaugh, among others, beat him to it.) However, what distinguished Stewart is that his conviction didn't cut neatly along partisan lines. In a world where everyone on television seemed to speak for either the left or the right, for MSNBC liberals or Fox News conservatives, Stewart waged a "war on bullshit" that defied these partisan framings. "I like to think of us [at *The Daily Show*] as people who sit in the center, like the rest of you, and are busy while the knuckleheads run the world on the ends," Stewart said at the Paley Center event. "It's like the old bell curve. The world is run by these people [on the ends]. And we're raising children."

Stewart's response sounded almost apolitical, but that's not quite right. As host of *The Daily Show*, Stewart understood the gravity of politics; he just didn't accept its two-party conceit—the idea that all issues could be reduced to a liberal and conservative position. "Even cartoon characters have more than left and right," he once quipped. "They have up and down."[28] In reality, Stewart didn't sit *in the center* of the political spectrum so much as he hovered above it all, serving as an independent watchdog against corruption and hypocrisy. If Republicans, for example, were going to trumpet their patriotism on the campaign trail while denying benefits to 9/11 first responders, or if Nancy Pelosi's Democrats were going to accept money from lobbyists while decrying their political influence, then Stewart was going to call them out. "He was a small-d democrat in the truest sense of the word," wrote *The Nation*'s Katrina vanden Heuvel, "always holding the powerful to account for putting the public interest behind their own."[29]

This conviction was perhaps nowhere more apparent than in his coverage of the run-up to the Iraq War in 2003. As members of both political parties, including Democratic Senator Hillary Clinton, expressed support for the war, mainstream journalism's skepticism gave way in many cases to fawning "patriotism." But Stewart was an exception. On *The Daily Show*, he carved out a rare space for unflinching dissent, booking interviews with outspoken antiwar celebrities like Susan Sarandon and Chris Rock and using the show's scripted segments to raise questions about the Bush administration's talking points and motivations for war. "Jon Stewart was really the person with the largest platform who stood up and said, 'I'm not buying it,'" Eric Boehlert of Media Matters told *The Guardian*. "He was really the only one with a national television platform that had the guts to do it."[30]

Boehlert is hardly the only journalist to express such praise for Stewart. Former NBC anchor Tom Brokaw called his friend "the citizens' surrogate"; the *New York Times* described Stewart as "a sane voice in a noisy red-blue echo chamber"; and others dubbed him "the voice of a generation," "the most trusted name in news," and "a voice of reason amid our current cacophony of partisan acrimony."[31] And yet, for all the adulation, most mainstream news organizations continued practicing journalism in *The Daily Show* era much as they always had, not daring to adopt the aggressive, fiery approach that they admired so much on Stewart's show. This contradiction seemed to puzzle Stewart as much as anyone. "I can't tell you how many times we'll run into a journalist and [they'll] go, 'Boy that's . . . I wish we could be saying that. That's exactly the way we see it and that's exactly the way we'd like to be saying that,'" Stewart told Bill Moyers in 2003. "And I always think, 'Well, why don't you?'"[32]

The answer to Stewart's question could fill an entire book (in fact, it has), but we'll keep this explanation brief: at the turn of the 20th century, the American newspaper business—defined then by strident partisanship, sensational "yellow journalism," and a loose allegiance with the facts—entered a period of rapid reform and professionalization. Fearing government regulations in the wake of the Spanish-American War debacle, news organizations adopted professional standards that called for a strict commitment to *accuracy* and professional rigor. Meanwhile, with corporate advertising quickly becoming the industry's largest source of revenue, newspaper publishers realized they could make more money if they catered to mass audiences, rather than niche audiences at the political poles. As a result, news organizations adopted an ethic of *neutrality* and embraced the idea that news should offer *balance* between competing ideologies. With the exception of the op-ed page, newspapers were to be kept free of opinion and personal bias. Together, these principles became known by what's now a familiar shorthand: objectivity.

What Stewart failed to realize is that although comedians like him can spurn the notion of "objectivity" without consequence, most mainstream journalists are not so lucky. MSNBC political commentator Keith Olbermann, for instance, was suspended without pay in 2010 for the egregious sin of making campaign contributions to Democratic candidates, an act of civic participation that supposedly undermined his ability to report on the news objectively. And when "Marketplace" reporter Lewis Wallace wrote a Medium post questioning the wisdom of neutrality in journalism, he was summarily fired by American Public Media for violating company policy. It's little wonder, then, that David Mindich described objectivity as the "supreme deity" of American journalism.[33] With few exceptions, legacy news organizations have accepted objectivity as the law of the land—and handed down punishments to those who defy it.

Late-night comedians receive much recognition for challenging journalism's norms of objectivity, but they're hardly the only ones picking that fight. Investigative reporter Glenn Greenwald, for one, has become a polarizing figure in journalism for his searing critiques of neutrality and false balance, including the one he made in a 2014 debate with former *New York Times* executive editor Bill Keller over the future of objectivity in news. Speaking for the news media establishment, Keller argued that the pursuit of objectivity (or "impartiality," as he preferred to call it) encourages fact-finding and reflects a commitment to "letting the evidence speak for itself," while disclosing a political ideology encourages journalists to seek the evidence that will support their predetermined argument. Keller explained:

> Once you have publicly declared your "subjective assumptions and political values," it's human nature to want to defend them, and it becomes tempting to omit or minimize facts, or frame the argument, in ways that support your declared viewpoint. And some readers, knowing that you write from the left or right, will view your reporting with justified suspicion. Of course, they may do that anyway—discounting whatever they read because it appeared in the "liberal" *New York Times*—but I think most readers trust us more because they sense that we have done due diligence, not just made a case.[34]

Wholly unconvinced by this reasoning ("Why would reporters who hide their opinions be less tempted by human nature to manipulate their reporting than those who are honest about their opinions?"), Greenwald argued that by trying to provide a balanced and neutral news product, journalists forgo the opportunity to hold power to account and call out their B.S. Instead, so-called objective journalists settle for placing that B.S. inside of quotation marks and transmitting it to the public unchallenged, a lazy, facile approach that amounts to transcription, Greenwald said, not journalism. He continued:

> A journalist who is petrified of appearing to express any opinions will often steer clear of declarative sentences about what is true, opting instead for a cowardly and unhelpful "here's-what-both-sides-say-and-I-won't-resolve-the-conflicts" formulation. That rewards dishonesty on the part of political and corporate officials who know they can rely on "objective" reporters to amplify their falsehoods without challenge (i.e., reporting is reduced to "X says Y" rather than "X says Y and that's false").[35]

So who won this debate between media establishment and media renegade? It depends on who you ask, of course, but one piece of evidence worth noting is that only months after his tête-à-tête with Greenwald, Keller left the *New York Times* to become editor in chief of *The Marshall Project*, a nonprofit news outlet that seeks "to create and sustain a sense of urgency about the U.S. criminal justice system."[36] This mission stops short of full-fledged advocacy, but it is "unavoidably ideological," Danny Funt observed in the *Columbia Journalism Review*. "[*The Marshall Project*] is on a crusade, however virtuous that mission may be."[37]

To say Keller has switched sides and joined Team Greenwald would be overstating the case, considering that in March 2017 he encouraged a group of university journalism students not to lose "their pose of objectivity and be partisans."[38] However, Keller's move to *The Marshall Project* is a sign of progress for those who believe journalists should stand for something and not be afraid to say so, especially because *The Marshall Project*'s transparent, pro-social justice conviction has not appeared to erode its legitimacy or soften its journalism—at least not in the eyes of its peers. The *New York Times*, *Washington Post*, *ProPublica*, and *Newsweek* have all co-published stories with *The Marshall Project*, and in 2016, the news site hauled in one of the profession's highest honors, the Pulitzer Prize for Explanatory Journalism.

The weakening of mainstream journalism's objectivity consensus became even more apparent during the 2016 presidential campaign, when Donald Trump's antics and inaccuracies elicited a more aggressive reporting style from many mainstream news organizations, including the *New York Times*, which raised eyebrows for running a front-page story with the headline, "Trump Gives Up a Lie But Refuses to Repent." The decision to use the word "lie" to describe Trump's birther theory reversal—rather than "mistruth" or "falsehood"—was scorned by some traditionalists, who argued that accusing someone of a lie is the kind of editorial judgment that belongs in the op-ed section, not on A1. However, many journalists and media critics hailed the decision as a long-overdue pivot from journalism's most powerful institutions. Jay Rosen, for one, applauded the *Times* for "saying it plainly," while Peter Beinart of *The Atlantic* encouraged other news organizations to follow the Gray Lady's lead and abandon traditional "he said, she said journalism."[39] And many of them did. CNN, for example, began using on-screen chyrons to fact-check Donald Trump's false statements (a move it made after facing criticism for its uncritical coverage of Trump during the Republican primaries). Debate moderator Martha Raddatz broke from custom to take "an unusually aggressive approach" during the second debate, according to the *Columbia Journalism Review*.[40] And Jorge Ramos of Univision repeatedly sparred with Trump on the campaign trail, while making no apologies for it. "In this case, neutrality is really not an option," Ramos explained on CNN. "I think we have to take a stand."[41]

In most cases, journalists and news organizations have invoked nonpartisan values such as "democracy" and "truth" to justify their increasingly aggressive reporting during and after the election. However, the last decade has also seen more brazen departures from the "objective" ideal. The classic example is *Breitbart*, the neoconservative news site that executive chairman Steve Bannon described as a "platform for the alt-right" political movement.[42] But explicit partisanship has also found a home on the left, including in 2017 with the launch of Crooked Media, a digital media startup founded by former Obama administration staffers Jon Favreau, Jon Lovett, and Tommy Vietor. On their flagship podcast, *Pod Save America*, the trio have fashioned themselves as informal ombudsmen of the Democratic Party, dissecting what went wrong in 2016, interviewing guests about where the party should go next, and even joining with activists to advance their progressive values, a goal that's written into the company's mission statement: "We're not journalists, we're not unbiased, we're not always serious and we're certainly not always right," the co-founders explain. "But we promise a no-bullshit conversation about politics where you can laugh, cry, scream, ridicule us daily, share your ideas, and hopefully decide that you want to help fix this mess too."[43]

By March 2017, the average *Pod Save America* episode was reaching 800,000 listeners, making it one of the top-ranked new podcasts on iTunes.[44] The company faced early criticism over its lack of on-air diversity (Favreau, Lovett, and Vietor are all white men), but it has since responded by hiring DeRay McKesson and Ana Marie Cox to host new podcasts under the Crooked Media banner. These additions have underscored an important point: in commentary, as in comedy, constructions of the truth are shaped by more than political ideology.

They're also shaped by identity.

Larry Wilmore, Samantha Bee, and the Truth of Identity

On April 8, 2015, Larry Wilmore didn't seem in the mood for joking. He looked fed up. For the ninth time in only five weeks, an unarmed black man had been shot and killed by police, this time in Charleston, South Carolina, where Michael Slager, a white officer, shot Walter Scott in the back eight times as he was running away. The aftermath followed an all-too-familiar routine: North Charleston Police Department and Slager's attorneys told local reporters that Scott had wrestled away Slager's Taser and attempted to use it against him, justifying the officer's use of deadly force in what was, authorities said, an unfortunate but unavoidable tragedy.

This explanation would normally be enough to absolve an officer of criminal responsibility, but this time the shooting was recorded by a bystander, Feiden Santana, whose cellphone video showed a very different sequence of events. Contrary to the official account, Scott was not scuffling with Slager or reaching for his Taser when the officer fired shots; he was running in the opposite direction—with no weapon and no apparent intent other than to get away.

When Santana's shocking video became public, Wilmore used his platform on *The Nightly Show* to address Scott's death and examine the broader problem of police violence against black men.[45] In the segment, Wilmore wondered aloud how many white police officers had evaded justice because their actions weren't caught on camera, and he delivered a searing critique of white privilege in the justice system, cuing up video footage of a police officer wrestling a pair of unruly beach-goers into handcuffs without ever pulling his weapon. "These two white guys jumped a police officer and they end up in a three-way sand tickle fight?" Wilmore said in exasperation. "And the brother in South Carolina was running from the cop and he's not alive today." For those three minutes, Wilmore wasn't speaking to his audience as an objective news anchor, or even as a comedian. He was talking as a black man, a black father, who had seen enough. "I've said it once before," he mustered. "I'll stop talking about this s—when it stops happening."[46]

Wilmore's authenticity gave voice to a painful truth of black life in America—one that the mainstream media paid little attention to until it was caught on tape. But what if that video didn't exist? What if the only witness to Scott's death had been the police officer who shot him? What would Americans know about Walter Scott if the story of his death had been told exclusively by local news reporters and not by Santana, and not by Larry Wilmore?

According to Ryan Grim and Nick Wing of *Huffington Post*, it doesn't take much guesswork to come up with an answer. Grim and Wing reviewed local news reports that ran within hours of the shooting—before the bystander video surfaced online—and they pieced together the quotes, police statements, and witness accounts into a composite news story. Mainstream news consumers will recognize many of the article's elements, from the credulous opening line ("A North Charleston police officer was forced to use his service weapon Saturday during a scuffle with a suspect who tried to overpower him and seize the officer's Taser, authorities said") to the police department's promise for a "complete and thorough investigation" and the story's dog-whistle reference to Scott's "lengthy rap sheet."[47]

What's sobering about this would-be news report is that it's *textbook* journalism, exactly the kind of "just the facts" reportage that journalism schools teach students and news organizations expect from reporters. Never mind that the story provides an inaccurate account of what took place. According to the logic of "objective" journalism, the reporter is not to blame for such a failure, because everything reported in the story is technically true. It's true that authorities *said* Scott tried to overpower Slager and seize his Taser. It's true that Slager's attorney *said* his client felt threatened. And it's true that Scott had prior convictions for violent crimes. The fact that these truths add up to a giant lie is not the concern of the journalist. After all, the facts are the facts. The quotes are the quotes. What's a reporter to do?

Like false balance, this contradiction represents a major thorn in the side of journalistic objectivity: whereas journalism sans conviction is blind to truths that don't exist at the partisan midpoint, journalism sans identity is blind to truths that are foreign to society's dominant culture. This news may present itself as "objective," but in fact it inherits an implicit bias—usually a white, male bias—from the institutions and people who play a part in its construction, either as sources or reporters. Cultural theorist Stuart Hall called this "the social production of news."[48] Reagan Jackson, a black author and writer in Seattle, calls it a farce. "White bias is the standard for objectivity," Jackson wrote in 2016. "The only reason we even pretend that objectivity is possible is because white culture tells us we should. I have no interest in objectivity—in fact I distrust anyone who thinks that they are somehow able to be a neutral outside observer. What are you outside of exactly? Certainly not the constructs of race, power, or privilege."[49]

Rather than chase an impossible standard of objectivity, Jackson argues that journalists should instead focus on achieving *equity* for diverse viewpoints—an area where mainstream news outlets continue to struggle. According to the American Society of News Editors, people of color represented only 17 percent of U.S. journalists in 2016, compared to 27 percent of the population as a whole.[50] This discrepancy earned the shorthand moniker #journalismsowhite, a hashtag that Jose Antonio Vargas coined in January 2016 while criticizing the lack of black newsroom leaders at the *Washington Post*, the *Wall Street Journal*, *The Atlantic*, and other major news outlets. "We are the stories we tell, and we all suffer when we can't see each other," Vargas wrote. "That's why diversity and representation in media is crucial and central."[51]

In its early years, comedy news was as white and male as the rest of the media, but it has since emerged as one of the few bright spots for diverse representation. Consider the evolution of *The Daily Show*: In 2006, five of the program's six regular correspondents, in addition to Stewart, were men, and all of them were white. But over the next eight years, Comedy Central hired Aasif Mandvi, Larry Wilmore, Jessica Williams, Hasan Minhaj, Wyatt Cenak, Kristen Schaal, and other correspondents who brought new and diverse perspectives to the show. This transformation has continued with Stewart's successor, Trevor Noah, who has worked to improve the diversity of the show's interview guests, as well as its writing and production staffs. "Since I've joined, blackness has tremendously increased at the show," said Noah, who is a biracial immigrant from South Africa. "There's been an epidemic of blackness . . . [and] we've hired additional women, as well. It's something that I'm very cognizant of."[52]

The Daily Show's diversity has become central to its appeal, but what Noah and other comedians demonstrate is that the truth of identity is more than a function of *who* is delivering the news; it's also a function of *how* that news is delivered. Unlike traditional journalism, late-night comedians are encouraged to bring their unique lens to a story, to infuse it with their anger, their indignation, their joy, or their heartbreak. That authenticity is what gave special teeth to Wilmore's segments on police violence or Jessica Williams' take on stop-and-frisk policing. In these monologues, the words don't just emerge from a black body. They emerge from a black *experience* that can only exist outside the bounds of traditional journalistic objectivity. The difference, Williams says, is not lost on viewers. "A lot of this stuff just pisses me off and makes me so mad that there's something behind the eyes," she told *Mother Jones* in 2013. "The delivery is a bit more biting, and I think people can tell."[53]

The merits of identity-infused journalism are also apparent on Samantha Bee's *Full Frontal*, the first late-night comedy news show hosted by a female anchor. Gender is a key part of the show's brand ("Watch or you're sexist" was the first season's tagline), but it is more than just a marketing ploy. Bee is authentic, Chava Gourarie writes, and she is "distinguishing herself not by virtue of being a woman, but by virtue of being herself. She certainly focuses more on reproductive rights, but coming from her, it seems obvious that these are simply issues of major importance, not women's issues."[54]

Bee's contribution to late-night comedy, as Gourarie points out, is much greater than the sum of her X chromosomes. On *Full Frontal*, Bee brings passion and serious smarts, helping viewers grapple with complex issues and exposing them to important stories around the world, from the refugee crisis in Syria to the backlog of rape kits in the United States. And in doing so, Bee is bringing another type of truth to the late-night airwaves—a *truth of analysis*—that's rooted in synthesis and sense-making, defined by depth and rigor, and made possible by time.

John Oliver, Ezra Klein, and the Truth of Analysis

In the spring of 2014, Internet service providers like Comcast and Verizon were closing in on a major policy coup. Backed by millions of dollars in lobbying money, these companies hoped to compel the Federal Communications Commission (FCC) to permit a tiered Internet infrastructure that would allow Comcast, Verizon, and other Internet service providers (ISPs) to sell faster delivery speeds to companies that can afford to pay, while relegating other online companies to the Internet's "slow lane." The proposal threatened to end "net neutrality" and undermine the Web's democratic ideals—but the U.S. media responded with a collective shrug. According to a Pew Research Center study, coverage of net neutrality was "all but absent" from television news and "sparse" in major newspapers in early 2014, as more dramatic news stories like the Malaysia Airlines crash and the outbreak of Ebola in East Africa dominated the headlines.[55]

It's no mystery why net neutrality managed to fly under the media radar, especially on television. Packed with jargon and complexity, the net neutrality debate required more untangling than a 90-second TV news package could offer, causing many broadcasters to pass over it altogether. But not John Oliver. On HBO's satirical news program *Last Week Tonight*, Oliver devoted an entire 13-minute segment to net neutrality, skillfully connecting the dots between lobbying money, Washington's regulatory revolving door, corporate monopolies, and FCC policy. Sure, Oliver's delivery lacked the staid gravitas of an *NBC Nightly News* package (at one point, he described the campaign to end net neutrality as "cable company f—ery"), but the segment was smart and insightful, and it captured people's attention. The clip on YouTube alone received more than 12 million views, and in an apparent response to Oliver's call to action at the end of his show, viewers flooded the FCC's public comment system with more than 45,000 responses—enough to temporarily crash the FCC's servers. Even academics applauded Oliver's analysis: Stanford Law School affiliate scholar Marvin Ammori told viewers they should "feel free to share the Oliver segment with full confidence that it's the truth and nothing but," and Columbia Law School professor Tim Wu, who coined the term net neutrality, tweeted that Oliver's analysis had "rendered all other explanations obsolete."[56]

Despite *Last Week Tonight*'s comedic identity (Season 1 ended with Oliver dancing goofily next to a giant costumed gecko, a white unicorn, and a pole-dancing chicken, for example), the show's deep dive into net neutrality was no anomaly. Since launching in 2014, *Last Week Tonight* has tackled issues as complex as government surveillance, mandatory minimum sentencing, border security, and police militarization, often spending 15 minutes or more meticulously dissecting thorny public policy debates and offering viewers a level of depth and nuance that's unmatched in TV comedy, if not all of broadcast news. "*Last Week Tonight* defies nearly all current norms," Brian Steinberg wrote for *Variety*. "The show surrounds soundbites with exposition, rather than letting video stand as the sole element of a segment. It trusts the attention span of its audience, believing a viewership constantly distracted by smartphones and mobile alerts will hang in there for the duration of a story, so long as it is compelling and informative."[57]

As Steinberg points out, *Last Week Tonight*'s long-form weekly format challenges the conventional wisdom of journalism in the digital age—the idea that what the public wants is more news, packaged in smaller chunks, and delivered with ever greater speed. This logic has fueled the rise of 24-hour news, push notifications, social media, and the expectation that Donald Trump's tweets will be reported the very moment they happen. This is the purest expression of news, but it's also a reminder, in Walter Lippmann's words, that "news and truth are not the same thing."[58] "News," Thomas Patterson writes, "is found in particular events rather than the underlying forces in society that create them."[59] It is the car crash that happened yesterday or the tornado that touched down five minutes ago, and it's produced by answering who, what, when, and where.

Truth, on the other hand, is constructed by answering the other 'W' question: why? According to Lippmann, "the function of truth is to bring to light the hidden facts, to set them into relation with each other, and make a picture of reality on which men can act."[60] This is a central goal of *journalism*, but it's not always achieved by *news*. As *Vox* editor-in-chief Ezra Klein writes, "We are better than ever at telling people what's happening"—the news—"but not nearly good enough at giving them the crucial contextual information necessary to understand what's happened"—the essence of truth.[61]

This distinction between news and truth has helped inspire the rise of *sense-making journalism*, an approach that places less emphasis on digging up the day's news than on piecing it all together, helping audiences connect the dots and distill meaning from the torrent of news and information that floods the digital ecosystem.[62] An early adopter of this approach was *Vox*, the digital media startup that Klein founded with a mission to help readers "understand the news." Since launching in 2014, *Vox* has experimented with innovative approaches to sense-making journalism, including its "card stacks," which use notecard-like information packages to explain "everything you need to know" about, say, Obamacare.[63] Want to find out who gets health insurance through Obamacare? That's outlined in card 4. Confused by why conservative Republicans hate the law? See card 13. Unlike other news coverage about Obamacare, which tends to focus on the latest polling numbers or the most recent legislative maneuvering, *Vox*'s card stacks try to tell a fuller story about how these news events fit together and why it all matters.

Elements of this sensemaking approach are also beginning to gain traction at legacy outlets like the *Washington Post*, which has created a new label, "analysis," to distinguish its explainer stories from hard news. The *Post*'s analysis articles generally come out hours, if not days, after a major news event, but what they sacrifice in speed they make up for depth and context. In April 2017, for example, after months of Republican promises that the Affordable Care Act (aka Obamacare) was on the verge of complete and utter failure, the *Post*'s Wonkblog reporter Carolyn Y. Johnson dug into the details of that claim and shared her findings with readers. In an analysis story interspersed with charts and graphs, Johnson explained how the Republican doomsday predictions might be proven right, but only if the government stopped making subsidy payments to insurers, triggering a "broader ripple effect" and ultimately destabilizing the health insurance exchanges.[64] Johnson didn't break any news in the story; instead, she took the time to help readers navigate a complex, nuanced truth.

Elements of sense-making journalism can now be found in *Salon*'s essays, *Slate*'s podcasts, *FiveThirtyEight*'s data storytelling, and *VICE*'s long-form narratives, to name just a few examples. However, there's arguably still something unique about *Last Week Tonight*, which airs only once a week and, thanks to HBO's business model, doesn't have to interrupt its 30-minute program with commercial breaks. This structure gives *Last Week Tonight* a luxury that's increasingly rare in journalism: time.[65] The time to build expertise. The time to cut through the bullshit. The time to deliver the news in a format that's engaging and entertaining. These ingredients, crucial to *Last Week Tonight*'s success, are afforded to Oliver and his team because, unlike almost all other media corporations, HBO is financed by paying customers, not advertising dollars. It's why Oliver can spend all week preparing a 30-minute program and crafting an explanatory report on net neutrality, whereas most other journalists, even sensemaking journalists, are stuck feeding the mass media machine, churning out content designed to maximize clicks and views for their news organizations—and thus value for advertisers.

We will return to the issue of business models in Chapter 4—but we must first ask a few more questions of comedy news. For one, what does this genre, for all its novelty and innovation, actually tell us about the future of journalism? Will we, for example, someday see a comedian sitting behind a mainstream network's anchor desk? NBC reportedly weighed this possibility in 2014, when Jon Stewart was rumored to be the network's top choice to succeed Tim Russert as host of *Meet the Press*. Stewart didn't accept the job, but what if he had? Would putting a funnyman in one of broadcast journalism's most prized positions have come at a cost? And would it have made us realize, perhaps, that we are crediting the late-night comedians of the world with too much and the nine-to-five journalists with too little?

The Limitations of Comedic Truth

In April 2009, as Vermont and New York became the latest U.S. states to embrace legal gay marriage, the National Organization for Marriage (NOM) released a TV ad warning of the dangers ahead. "There's a storm gathering," the commercial began. "The clouds are dark, and the winds are strong."

As literal storm clouds built ominously in the background, staunch opponents of gay marriage spoke fearfully of losing their freedom and their way of life. The ad received fierce criticism from progressives, but Stephen Colbert—playing his arch-conservative character on Comedy Central's *The*

Colbert Report—couldn't get enough. "I love that ad," he said proudly. "It's like watching the 700 Club and the Weather Channel at the same time."[66]

Channeling Bill O'Reilly-esque right-wing hysteria, Colbert lamented the steady encroachment of gay marriage laws from Massachusetts to Iowa to his own state of New York, where he feared it would soon become impossible for straight couples to get a wedding announcement in the *New York Times*. Colbert then criticized New York's governor for being a "perv," waxed poetic about the "good ol' days when our governor upheld the traditional definition of marriage as being between a man, a woman, and an Emperor's Club hooker," and even aired a parody of the NOM commercial, complete with purple lightning bolts and fearsome predictions about a world with legal gay marriage.[67] The segment was, like so much of Colbert's satire, a searing critique of political hypocrisy and fear mongering.

Or was it? A day after the episode aired, NOM issued a press release lauding Colbert's conservative credentials and, incredibly, thanking him for the coverage. "I've always thought Stephen Colbert was a double-agent, pretending to pretend to be a conservative, to pull one over on Hollywood," NOM president Maggie Gallagher wrote. "Now I'm sure."[68]

The generous interpretation of Gallagher's statement is that it was a work of satire itself, a tongue-in-cheek stunt designed to help NOM (and its commercial) stay in the news cycle a few days longer. But if Gallagher really did believe that Colbert was on her side, she wouldn't have been the first. According to a 2009 Ohio State University study, viewers of *The Colbert Report* interpreted its comedy differently depending on their political beliefs, with liberals viewing the show as a parody of right-wing politics and conservatives taking Colbert's persona at face value.[69] And Colbert's own experiences back up the study's findings. "I come from a fairly conservative place, Charleston, South Carolina, and people have come up to me there and said, "'Well, now I like what you do,'" he told *Rolling Stone* in 2006. "They had a little trouble with our liberal, lefty bent over at *The Daily Show*. But now they're [saying], 'Good f—ing A, man, good for you!' And I'm like, 'Well, I'm not sure . . .'"[70]

In an episode of the podcast *Revisionist History*, award-winning author Malcolm Gladwell gives a name to this contradiction: the satire paradox. The episode examines the case of Harry Enfield, a talented British comedian whose "loadsamoney" character—a "nouveau riche buffoon" who obsessed over money and status—became a cultural phenomenon in the 1990s, but not entirely in the way Enfield intended. Conceived as a critique of Britain's neoliberal turn under Prime Minister Margaret Thatcher, "loadsamoney" was nevertheless embraced as a symbol of British economic ascendance, a badge of honor worn proudly by the very people Enfield had hoped to skewer. "Everyone decided it was theirs. They made it their property," Enfield said. "It doesn't ever change anyone's mind."[71]

There are, of course, many differences between Enfield's satire-by-caricature and the more direct satire-by-evisceration (to borrow a term from the liberal blogosphere) practiced by many of today's satirists. When Samantha Bee wants to criticize Donald Trump, for example, she calls him a "demagoguing bag of candy corn" or a "tangerine-tinted garbage fire."[72] And when John Oliver disagrees with draconian voter-ID laws, he describes them as "the biggest overreaction to a manageable problem since Sleeping Beauty's father ordered all the spinning wheels in the country to be burned."[73] In either case, there's not much room for misinterpretation.

This stridently partisan approach has smoothed over critiques of ambiguity, but it has raised a new critique, namely that their ideological comedy only exerts influence within a narrow echo chamber. Among like-minded progressives, Bee and Oliver are known as heroes of the liberal movement who routinely expose the cravenness and hypocrisy of Republican ideology. But among conservatives, they're hardly known at all. "The only people who tend to see issues or politicians being 'eviscerated' by *Last Week Tonight* are ideologically liberal," Adam Felder wrote for *The Atlantic*. "If a conservative voter watched . . . he or she likely wouldn't see an evisceration, but rather an attack by a biased media."[74]

To be fair, television's faux news anchors themselves appear to have no trouble discerning the limits of their influence. When Jon Stewart stepped down from *The Daily Show*, for example, he devoted a 10-minute segment to the many social ills that his satire failed to correct.[75] And when *Time* named Oliver one of the 100 most influential people in the world, Oliver simply laughed it off. "[They] say a lot of things that are woefully inaccurate," he told the *Toronto Star*. "And that is definitely one of them."[76]

Unlike their most enthusiastic fans, comedians seem to understand that satire occupies a narrow lane in the American media ecosystem and speaks to a narrow audience. At its best, satire can untangle complicated truths, highlight diverse perspectives, and make the daily news grind slightly more palatable. But that's not all our democracy needs from journalism. It also needs journalism to facilitate a *shared conversation*, built around a common set of facts and inclusive of citizens from across the political spectrum. This may seem like an impossible challenge in the current political climate, but giving up on this democratic ideal means accepting a world where conversations about public life and public policy exist within ever smaller media bubbles, and where niche commentators feel free to use their own facts to construct their own *truths*, untethered from reality. This path is what President Obama cautioned against in his farewell speech—what he called "the splintering of our media into a channel for every taste."[77]

Democracy cannot thrive in this world. It requires news organizations that can build trust across political and cultural fissures, and that can negotiate a common understanding of fact and fiction within even our country's most polarized communities.

This starts, as it always has, with fact-checking sources, verifying information, mining public records, developing subject-matter expertise, and holding the powerful accountable. But we believe getting these fundamentals right is only half the equation. In Chapter 2, we argue that journalists must build trust in a digital world not only by doubling down on accurate, trustworthy reporting, but also by fundamentally rethinking their relationship with the people and communities they serve.

Reimagining Trust: Engaged Journalism, Open Reporting, and Listening to the Public

"If you want people to listen to you, you have to listen to them.
If you hope people will change how they live, you have to know how
    they live.
If you want people to see you, you have to sit down with them
    eye-to-eye."[1]

—Anonymous

Tasked with penning her inaugural *New York Times* public editor column in June 2016, Liz Spayd might have chosen to focus on the challenges of covering Donald Trump, the perils of false balance, or the scourge of horse-race sensationalism in the media. Instead, Spayd devoted her first column to something more fundamental, if underappreciated, in journalism: the need to listen better. "Most journalists I've worked with have a reflexive aversion to interacting with readers," Spayd wrote. "They subscribe to the view that editors and reporters have the most cultivated sense of which stories are most important, and which subjects most worthy of attention. . . . I am one of the converts."[2]

Spayd argued that news organizations can no longer afford to remain detached from the people they serve—not when digital technologies create the ability (and expectation) for journalists to listen to them. Some media commentators bristled at this argument (more on that shortly), but it wasn't long until other journalists were joining Spayd's tune. On the eve of the election, *Washington Post* executive editor Marty Baron lamented that the media had become "dominated by talk" and argued that what is "core to being a good journalist is being a good listener," before doubling down a month later.[3] "It is our job to hear all people. And to listen closely. And to give the people of America insights into each other," he said in a speech at CUNY's Graduate School of Journalism. "We will have to work harder at that."[4]

Chuck Todd, host of NBC's *Meet the Press*, warned that "remaining deaf" to the public would "only continue to fuel the anti-establishment anger and cost even more members of the media to lose credibility and eyeballs."[5]

Margaret Sullivan, the *Post*'s media columnist, shared a similar post-election diagnosis: "To put it bluntly," she wrote, "the media missed the story. In the end, a huge number of American voters wanted something different. And although these voters shouted and screamed it, most journalists just weren't listening. They didn't get it."[6]

Ditto, wrote *New York Times* columnist Nick Kristof: "We in the mainstream media are out of touch with working-class America; we spend too much time chatting up senators, and not enough visiting unemployed steel workers."[7]

And then this from *Rolling Stone*'s Matt Taibbi: "Just like the politicians, our job was to listen, and we talked instead. Now America will do its own talking for a while. The world may never forgive us for not seeing this coming."[8]

Of all the lessons for journalism to emerge from the 2016 election, perhaps none received as much attention as the importance of listening—and not only among East Coast editors and columnists. Here's just a small sample of the listening buzz that echoed across the profession during and after the 2016 presidential campaign:

- **Jeff Jarvis, director of the Tow-Knight Center for Entrepreneurial Journalism and author of *Geeks Bearing Gifts: Imagining New Futures for News*:** "Journalists are bad at listening. We think we inform the public debate when, in fact, we should be reflecting the debate by listening more carefully to the needs of the community, and then deliver context-specific journalism."[9]

- **Diane McFarlin, dean of University of Florida's College of Journalism and Communications:** "We need to spend more time listening and observing. We need to focus on the issues that really matter and not engage in vacuous stories that, while they might generate more hits, don't enlighten."[10]

- **Melanie Sill, news consultant and former executive editor at Southern California Public Radio (KPCC)**: "Journalists have the opportunity to learn from [a] collective miss. First, report *for* the people who voted, not just about them. Listen. Consider."[11]

- **Andrew Losowsky, project lead at The Coral Project**: "Journalistic culture needs to change. We need to focus more on listening, on dialog, and on building real communities of journalists and readers. If we succeed, we can increase levels of trust and engagement among the general population, find more diverse contributors to our journalism and help bridge the gap between "the media" and everyone else. We can't ignore our audiences any longer."[12]

- **Kelly McBride, vice president for academic programs at Poynter**: "Help identify the pathway forward. Give your audience a way to be heard, a way to listen to each other and concrete actions they can take."[13]

- **Josh Stearns, associate director at Democracy Fund**: "Many in the public feel like they have new avenues to make their voices heard, but often they don't feel like journalists are listening. On the other hand, many journalists feel held hostage by the analytics that drive many newsrooms. We need better ways of listening and ensuring that communities feel heard."[14]

- **danah boyd, founder of Data & Society and visiting professor at New York University's Interactive Telecommunications Program**: "We live in a moment where people do not know how to hear or understand one another. And our obsession with quantitative data means that we think we understand when we hear numbers in polls, which we use to judge people whose views are different than our own. This is not productive."[15]

- **Andrew DeVigal, chair in journalism innovation and civic engagement at the University of Oregon's Agora Journalism Center**: "A lot of people come into journalism because they want to give voice to the voiceless, but the fact is they aren't voiceless, it's just that no one listens, they just don't have the platform."[16]

- **Andrew Haeg, founder and CEO of GroundSource**: "I believe we need to start teaching journalism as a more humble profession, one which seeks not to be the smartest person in the room, but the best listener. One that sees audiences as people, as teachers, as sources of inspiration and expertise."[17]

Listening to the public is not exactly a new idea in journalism. In fact, the push for greater public participation in news has been underway for nearly three decades now, existing under different banners—"public journalism," "civic journalism," and "engaged journalism," among them—but always emphasizing, as the *American Journalism Review* wrote in 1994, the need for news organizations to "listen more closely to their audiences."[18]

Advocates of this approach argue that journalism's tradition of fierce independence from the public is incompatible with the open, connected, participatory culture of the Internet. Jay Rosen famously made this case in his 2006 essay "The People Formerly Known as the Audience," which described a "shift in power" that occurred when blogs, podcasts, social media channels, and pocket-sized cameras democratized the means of media production: "Think of passengers on your ship who got a boat of their own," Rosen wrote. "The writing readers. The viewers who picked up a camera. The formerly atomized listeners who with modest effort can connect with each other and gain the means to speak—to the world, as it were."[19]

No longer could these citizens be merely counted as "eyeballs" and sold to advertisers, Rosen argued. In the new media ecosystem, citizens gained access to the tools of reporting, storytelling, curation, and publishing, and they stopped relying on a "media system that ran one way, in a broadcasting pattern."[20] This differed from past technological disruptions (like the ones caused by radio and television, for example) because it represented more than just a changing of the guard. According to Jarvis, "the net's real victim was not one medium or another. What it killed was the idea of the mass," leaving publishers with no viable option but to embrace a model of journalism that's less transactional and more *relational*. He explains:

> Relationships—knowing people as individuals so we can better serve them with more relevance, building greater value as a result—will be a necessity for media business models, a key to survival and success. Yes, of course, we will still make content. But content is not the end-product. It is only one tool we will use to inform and serve our communities and their members. Content may still have intrinsic value as something to sell. But now it also has value as a means to learn about a person: what she is interested in, what she knows and wants to know, where she lives, what she does—all signals that can enable a news organization to deliver her greater relevance and value and earn more loyalty, engagement, and revenue in return. That is how Google, Facebook, and Amazon operate.[21]

But relationship building is more than just a revenue play for journalism. It's also a strategy for earning back the public's attention and trust. As All Digitocracy founder Tracie Powell points out, "news organizations have been indifferent toward communities and audiences for so long that now communities and audiences are indifferent toward [them]." The fix, she writes, is "all about relationships"—about figuring out who news consumers are, and then tailoring news products to meet their needs.[22]

Joy Mayer, an independent engagement strategist, compares this trust-building process in journalism to the trust-building process in dating: both take time and effort, as well as a commitment to putting your partner's (or customer's) needs first. "Relationships involve caring whether you're meeting the needs of the other party—and being willing to adjust if you're not," Mayer explains. "They involve knowing what people need from you and whether you're meeting those needs . . . You earn trust by being there consistently, and by listening."[23]

Building relationships will not happen overnight, especially in minority communities where distrust for institutional journalism often spans generations. Bridging these chasms will take time—but Haeg believes news organizations are already beginning to understand both the need and the payoff. "A few key newsrooms [next year] will make a journalistic and business argument for listening," he predicted in 2016, "even though it's hard to measure cleanly on Chartbeat. They'll do it because they know that building loyalty and trust requires tuning into the concerns and voices of the whole community."[24]

Of course, what all these arguments for relationship-driven journalism share is the basic assumption that citizens are worth listening to, that they have something valuable to contribute to journalism, and that they are fundamentally decent people whose voices deserve to be heard. In certain circles, it's heretical to suggest anything less. But many journalists who interact with the public on a daily basis might offer a different response: *Have you read the comments lately?*

The Case for (and against) Listening to the Public

Spayd's inaugural public editor column marked an important victory for the pro-listening movement, but it didn't take long for the skeptics to strike back. A day later, *Slate* published a scathing rebuttal by staff writer Isaac Chotiner, who dismissed Spayd's thesis as "terrible advice" and "phony populism." He continued:

> You might think that amid a general dumbing down of news coverage and with local newspapers losing circulation, the *Times'* commitment to quality journalism is all the more necessary and urgent (and even strategically sensible). But Spayd essentially argues that the *Times* needs to become more focused on the desires of its readers, whatever those desires may be. She seems unaware that there is a difference between giving readers what they want and ensuring that readers receive the best news coverage possible—the latter being the purpose of a newspaper, including a digital one.[25]

Many of the comments posted to Chotiner's article featured equal disdain: "If 'listening to the readers' means hanging out with riff raff like us in places like this, then this is terrible advice," one commenter wrote. "Personally, I look forward to the *Times*' new All About Cats section," snarked another. "Liz L" summed it up this way: "Ugh, the whole consumer model. First higher ed, now journalism. As if it's just a new Doritos flavor to be focus-grouped and then mass marketed."

The pushback against Spayd's column reflects a broader resistance to the idea that listening to the public might actually result in stronger journalism. Many journalists prefer to see themselves as society's noble gatekeepers, delivering the news and information that democracy needs to function—while viewing the public as an unenlightened mob that would turn the news media into a celebrity gossip service if given half a chance. Haeg described this scornful attitude in a post on Medium:

> I had a colleague who referred to the audience as the "great, unwashed masses." It was always said for laughs, and it was funny in a hard-bitten, grizzled news veteran kind of way. But that always stuck in my craw, and I realized that he was actually expressing what many, maybe most journalists felt. Spend any time in a newsroom, and listen to the tone with which people refer to the public—whether they're commenters, or tweeters, or callers to talk shows. It's as if we're the sentries at the gate, keeping the zombies from overtaking the little civilization we've built.[26]

Before the Internet, journalists didn't have much trouble walling themselves off from the citizen-zombies, or at least isolating any engagement to narrow and discrete channels, like the newspaper's letters-to-the-editor section. But that changed in the early years of the social Web, as comment sections became ubiquitous and social media platforms like Facebook and Twitter created new channels for public participation. Suddenly, news consumers could talk back to the newsroom, or even talk among themselves *without* the newsroom, requiring journalists to accept a new role as participants in a conversation, rather than leaders of a lecture.

If news organizations had fully embraced this digital revolution and optimized their news routines for public participation, then journalists' first experiences with online engagement may have been more universally positive. However, most organizations instead treated engagement like an add-on to traditional news routines, confining it to troll-ridden comment sections where journalists, especially female journalists, were subjected to a steady stream of hate speech and vitriol. As British journalist Laurie Penny lamented in 2011: "An opinion, it seems, is the short skirt of the Internet. Having one and flaunting it is somehow asking an amorphous mass of almost-entirely male keyboard-bashers to tell you how they'd like to rape, kill and urinate on you."[27]

Sadly, Penny's account is neither hyperbolic nor particularly uncommon. According to a 2014 Pew Research Center study, 40 percent of all adult Internet users have personally experienced online abuse, including stalking and sexual harassment. The problem has become so severe for women that many journalists, including *The Guardian* columnist Jessica Valenti, are making the case for abandoning comment sections altogether. "On most sites—from YouTube to local newspapers—comments are a place where the most noxious thoughts rise to the top and smart conversations are lost in a sea of garbage," Valenti wrote. "For writers, wading into comments doesn't make a lot of sense—it's like working a second shift where you willingly subject yourself to attacks from people you have never met and hopefully never will."[28]

In addition to eroding journalists' support for comment sections, experiences like these have contributed to a broader ambivalence toward engagement with the public. For many journalists, the hate-mongering trolls on the Internet are not just a shadowy subset of the public; they *are* the public, and the idea of "listening" to them falls somewhere between naive idealism and sheer lunacy. This mindset helps explain why Chotiner responded to Spayd's column with such dismissiveness, as if (and he actually suggested this) listening to the public is no more important for a journalist than it is for an "investment advisor or a plumber." After all, he concluded, "if the reporters and editors at the *Times* don't know journalism better than the average person, then why are they being paid to make journalistic decisions?"[29]

Chotiner's rebuttal is evidence of what Hearken co-founder and CEO Jennifer Brandel describes as a "culture war" in journalism over the merits of public participation. On one side, Brandel argues, are critics like Chotiner who represent "the traditional, conservative 'journalists know best, audiences don't know what they want, they're an ignorant mass' idea."[30] This camp views public participation in journalism as a threat to editorial independence—a slippery slope leading invariably to tabloid fodder—and believes the role of journalists is to give the public not the news and information they *want*, but rather the news and information they *need*. (And who better to make those judgments, the argument goes, than journalists themselves, who are paid to do just that?)

This isolationist logic is deeply embedded in the DNA of many legacy newsrooms, but there are increasingly signs of evolution afoot, from the pro-listening buzz that emerged after the 2016 election to the surge of newsroom "engagement" positions that have listening built right into the job description. When *ProPublica*, for example, set out to hire an engagement reporter in 2015, the investigative news outlet listed "conceiving and executing a plan to pull our readers into the reporting of the story itself" as one of the position's most important responsibilities. "We assume you know how to do a Twitter collection and why social video is important," the job posting explained. "What we're looking for is somebody who will find and reach the people actually impacted by a story, get them to inform our work and be a central player in the storytelling on all platforms to maximize the resonance of the project."[31]

Meanwhile, similar engagement positions have appeared at the *Texas Tribune*, the *Los Angeles Times*, the Center for Investigative Reporting, and Southern California Public Radio; engagement-focused conferences and workshops have popped up in Chicago; San Francisco; Portland, Oregon; Macon, Georgia; and other cities across the country; and even university journalism schools—not always known for breaking with tradition—have started retooling their curriculum to catch up with the engagement trend. In 2014 the University of Oregon's School of Journalism and Communication founded the Agora Journalism Center to promote "innovation in communication and civic engagement," and in 2015 CUNY launched a new master's program that prepares students for "listening to a community, hearing and discerning its needs and then thinking about how best to help it meet those needs."[32]

So what explains this surge of interest in engagement? We believe one factor is news organizations' growing recognition that citizens, when excluded from journalism's conversation, can now build their own. We are, after all, living in a world where self-made YouTube stars Destin Sandlin, Ingrid Nilsen, and SWooZie can score an exclusive interview with the president of the United States, where @sockington, a Boston-area cat's Twitter persona, can amass twice as many followers as the *Boston Globe*, and where anyone with a smartphone and Internet access can publish content to the Web in seconds. This is what Rosen meant by "the people formerly known as the audience." He realized that when citizens are only one click away from streaming to the world on Facebook Live or publishing a hot take on Twitter, they don't depend on the media to "give them a voice." They have a voice, and they now have the means to share that voice with the world, with or without legacy journalism.

A stark reminder of this new reality came in 2015 at the University of Missouri, where protesters occupied the campus quad and attempted to block freelance photographer Tim Tai and other journalists from accessing the encampment. Journalists rushed to decry the incident as a violation of First Amendment freedom, and they were right. But it was also a sign of the shifting relationship between journalists and the communities they cover. Whereas past protest movements and dissidents have often pleaded with news organizations for coverage, the protesters in Missouri didn't think they needed journalists to communicate their message. They had a Twitter account with thousands of followers, and they had the ability to tell their own stories on Medium, Snapchat, and Facebook. So instead of welcoming Tim Tai and other reporters, they pushed back. "There's a power shift happening," observed Mike Fancher, former executive editor of the *Seattle Times*. "Journalists need to understand that it's happening with or without them."[33] Media critic Mathew Ingram made a similar diagnosis. "If you have the tools and resources and platforms with which to craft your own message and tell your own story, you're much less likely to look favorably on the traditional media's ability to do that for you," he wrote following the Tim Tai incident. "That's a painful lesson the mainstream media are going to have to swallow sooner or later."[34]

If the rise of citizen media making is one factor behind journalism's embrace of engagement and listening, another is the disruption of the industry's business model. Before the Internet, circulation revenue generally accounted for less than a quarter of most news organizations' total revenue, and advertising provided the rest. But the tables are starting to turn, writes Jake Batsell, a journalism professor at Southern Methodist University, "as digital ad rates continue to fall and the connection between page views and revenue proves ever more tenuous." In this media landscape, "the relationship with loyal, paying, *engaged* customers becomes increasingly important. . . . Online news consumers, with myriad choices at their disposal, will pull out their credit cards to subscribe only if they feel truly engaged."[35]

Thanks in part to these business incentives, news organizations increasingly understand that listening to and engaging the public is critical for survival. And unlike a decade ago, they now have the tools and technology to do it effectively. This technological revolution—a third force behind the rise of engaged journalism—has been headlined by new companies and platforms such as Hearken, an "engagement management system" that helps journalists involve the public in choosing and reporting stories; GroundSource, an SMS messaging tool that facilitates two-way conversations between newsrooms and the public; The Coral Project, a collaboration between the Mozilla Foundation, the *Washington Post*, and the *New York Times* to create open-source tools for engagement; and Civil Comments, a platform that uses the power of the crowd to moderate comment sections.

Together, these tools demonstrate that the quality of public engagement is largely a function of the systems and processes that enable it. A decade ago, when citizens felt like they needed to yell to be heard, they yelled. When they were only invited to react to news, they were reactionary. When they were treated like a faceless mob, they behaved like one. That's what many journalists experienced in first-generation comment sections, which facilitated the worst kind of engagement with the worst elements of the public. But today's technology is reshaping the infrastructure of public participation, and it's winning over converts like Batsell, a former skeptic of engagement who is now one of its most forceful champions. In his book *Engaged Journalism: Connecting With Digitally Empowered News Audiences,* Batsell describes his evolution:

> Too often back then I considered readers—my paying audience—to be an afterthought. Like many newspaper reporters, for much of my career I wanted to hear from readers only when they had a scoop or tip to offer or perhaps some kudos I could share with my editor. Sure, I aggressively sought out sources of all stripes while reporting a story, but it didn't occur to me to make a habit of proactively engaging the readers who consumed my journalism . . . Perhaps to a fault, I idealized the role of the journalist as a beacon for American society. I was the reporter. I was the expert. Readers were merely people who had the privilege of beholding my brilliant informative prose. And most readers who called or e-mailed were crackpots anyway, right?[36]

But Batsell's attitude changed as he began to see the value that citizens could add to his work. He recalls a pair of assignments for the *Dallas Morning News* that helped topple his initial skepticism:

> As I covered controversial toll road proposals during the 2007 Texas legislative session, I learned that breaking news on the Web and blogging about my beat could elicit valuable real-time reactions from reader and sources, better informing my coverage for the next day's paper. A few months later, when I blogged from a fan's perspective about a quixotic quest to upgrade my nosebleed seat for a sold-out Dallas Cowboys game, readers rooted me on and offered tips and suggestions about how to navigate the sea of eBay hawkers, Craigslist scammers, and game-day scalpers. Over time I realized that having an ongoing dialogue with readers could be both practical and fun while helping me to build trust and better connect me as a journalist with the community I covered.[37]

The growing ranks of converts like Batsell and Spayd, as well as the profession's collective response to the 2016 election, are evidence that journalists are warming to the *idea* of listening to the public. But what exactly should that listening look like? And how is it supposed to work when thousands, even millions, of digitally empowered citizens are all talking at the same time? In the remainder of this chapter, we examine three approaches that have gained particular traction in journalism: listening for story ideas, listening for news leads, and listening as conversation.

Hearken, GroundSource, and Listening for Story Ideas

"I wish Macon would . . ."

In 2015 Georgia Public Broadcasting (GPB) used GroundSource to send this message to participants in Macon's Listening Post experiment and invite them to finish the sentence. In response, the newsroom received dozens of text messages from local residents, including one from a woman who said she wished Macon would resume Sunday bus service. GPB reporter Michael Caputo saw that message, and he followed up with a story that explained why Macon's Sunday bus service had ended and what it would take to bring it back.[38]

This feedback loop—a consumer expressing a need and an organization fulfilling that need—would seem obvious for almost any other public-facing enterprise. But it's not how journalists have traditionally approached their work. In the pre-digital age, news stories were instead chosen in closed-door editorial meetings, where journalists pitched ideas that they'd come up with themselves and believed to be newsworthy. Journalists ostensibly pitched these stories with reader needs and interests in mind, but short of sending out surveys or counting up the number of letters-to-the-editor submitted in response, there were few ways to determine whether they were hitting the mark.

That problem seemed to find a solution with the rise of advanced audience metrics, which allowed journalists to start tracking clicks, "likes," time spent on a page, and countless other proxies for audience interest. However, what these quantitative metrics obscure is the complex web of factors that produce them. News organizations tend to assume that clicks, likes, retweets, and other engagements are positive endorsements of their content, but that's not always the case. People might click on a story because they're sucked in by a clickbait headline, leave a comment because they're angry, or share a post on Facebook because they're dumbfounded by its absurdity. Take *The Oregonian's* story in 2016 about a single Yelp review alleging racial insensitivity on the menu of a minority-owned cupcake shop.[39] The article on *The Oregonian's* website received more than 800 comments from readers, and it was shared more than 6,000 times on social media—numbers that might lead an audience engagement editor to conclude that the article was a huge hit with *The Oregonian's* audience. But the substance of those 800-plus comments told a different story. Readers described the article as "one of those useless sidebar articles found on Facebook" and as "a fugitive story from _The Onion_," and in a comment that perfectly cap-tured metrics' fatal flaw, "Sunny" wrote that the story was "too stupid to continue commenting on." The catch: Sunny had already commented more than 35 times.

Techno-optimists will argue this is a technical problem with a techni-cal solution—and that with better engineering, algorithms will be able to distinguish between positive and negative consumer experiences, allow-ing publishers to weight metrics and evaluate content accordingly. But if the ultimate goal is to give news consumers the journalism they need and want, there is another, more direct option: _asking them_, a proposal perhaps best articulated in an open letter to news publishers drafted by participants at The Engagement Summit in 2016:

> We want to know: As your customers, why don't you seem to care about us? Why do you think you know what's best for us without even asking us? The truth is, the issues that we care about are not reflected in your stories . . . The amount of real and useful news is shrinking while an avalanche of mis-information, sensationalism and chatter surrounds us. We see what you are doing: you care more about your metrics and your advertisers than you do about us.[40]

Although traditional audience metrics continue to exert tremendous influ-ence in many newsrooms, engagement-minded journalists around the country are starting to demonstrate the merits of a more public-powered approach to story selection. This trend started in 2012 when Brandel, in collaboration with WBEZ and the Association of Independents in Radio, launched _Curious City_, a program that invited listeners to submit their burn-ing questions about Chicago, vote for their favorite submissions, and then tune in to hear how WBEZ reporters tracked down the answer. This pro-cess led to stories about Chicago's "secret" network of underground rail-road tunnels, the challenge of making ends meet as a minimum-wage worker, the amount of road salt that ends up in Lake Michigan, and hun-dreds of other fascinating news features—and all without a single segment about subjects many journalists fear the public will want if allowed to ask, like Kim Kardashian gossip pieces or cat videos.[41]

Encouraged by _Curious City_'s success, Brandel left WBEZ in 2014 to launch Hearken, a civic tech company that offers consulting and tools to help newsrooms produce similar works of journalism that engage readers throughout the story's full life cycle. The early results have been positive: in less than three years, the company has partnered with more than 90 news organizations, including the _Chicago Tribune_, St. Louis Public Radio, and the BBC, and its model has spawned everything from deep-dive investigations, like Michigan Radio's award-winning reporting on the condition of an oil pipeline under Lake Michigan, to quirky news features, like WUWM's quest to find out why the rules for bar dice are different on the south side of Milwaukee.[42] Meanwhile, even for those who insist on subjecting this public-powered journalism to the metrics test, there's a lot to like: at WBEZ, the Hearken approach netted 41 percent of the station's most popular stories in 2014; at KUOW in Seattle, six of the station's ten most popular stories that year came from Hearken; at Michigan Radio, Hearken stories received about 12 times more unique page views in 2015 than other Web content; and at Bitch Media, a 2017 analysis found that Hearken content helped boost time-on-page numbers and more than double the site's membership conversation rate.[43]

Alongside Hearken's success, tools offered by The Coral Project and GroundSource have contributed to similar public-powered success stories, including GPB's radio feature about Sunday bus service in Macon. However, despite these signs of progress, public-powered reporting still remains a fringe movement within journalism, not yet embraced by the industry's rank and file. Price sensitivity is likely one reason for the slow adoption (Hearken's services currently cost news organizations about $8,000 a year, for example), but Brandel says an even bigger obstacle is journalism's lingering culture of disdain for the public. In a post on Medium, she explained:

> In about two-thirds of the meetings I've had with newsrooms, someone in the room, often a manager, editor or some other higher-up says something along the lines of, "If we gave the audience what they wanted, they'd ask for crap!" Or "Our audience isn't very smart, they probably wouldn't have any good ideas." Or, the big doozy, and the inspiration for this post, said by a manager during a meeting at a highly respected, hugely award-winning news outlet: "Our audience is a bunch of idiots and assholes. Why exactly would we want to hear more from them than we already do?"[44]

This question—why listen?—remains one of the biggest barriers to engagement in journalism. In 2017, however, a Pulitzer Prize–winning investigation by the *Washington Post* made answering it a whole lot easier.

David Fahrenthold, *ProPublica,* and Listening for News Leads

David Fahrenthold, a veteran reporter for the *Washington Post*, likes to say he started his investigation into Donald Trump's charitable giving with a simple goal: to prove Trump right. Specifically, he wanted to verify a claim made by Trump's then-campaign manager Corey Lewandowski, who told Fahrenthold in May 2016 that Trump had already delivered on his promise to donate $6 million, including $1 million of his own money, to veterans' groups around the country.[45] (The Donald J. Trump Foundation raised that $6 million during a January 2016 fundraising event that Trump hosted instead of attending Fox News's Republican presidential debate.)

The norm in journalism is to keep investigations like this one close to the vest so that another newsroom can't swoop in and steal the "scoop." But Fahrenthold did something unusual: he conducted the investigation in public, reaching out to veterans' groups on Twitter to see if they'd received donations from the Trump Foundation—and giving a shout out to @realDonaldTrump, Trump's personal Twitter handle, with every tweet. The result: Fahrenthold couldn't find any veterans' groups that had received money, because, as it turned out, Trump had *not* given it away.[46]

This revelation contradicted Lewandowski's initial claim to Fahrenthold, and it set off a deeper examination of Trump's charitable giving, again with the stated goal of proving him right (Trump claimed to have donated "tens of millions" of his own dollars over the years) and again conducted publicly on Twitter. Over the next three months, Fahrenthold called more than 400 charities to ask about Trump's history of charitable giving, documenting the outcome of each call on a new line in his reporter's notebook. Once a page was full, Fahrenthold then snapped a photo and posted it on Twitter, allowing his audience to follow the investigation in real time and make suggestions about other charities he should call.

This open-reporting approach established trust in Fahrenthold's reporting, since the public could see it unfolding in front of their eyes. And it also helped Fahrenthold land his biggest scoop of the campaign: in September, he learned that Trump had purchased a six-foot-tall portrait of himself nine years earlier using money from his foundation. To figure out if that purchase violated federal laws against "self-dealing," Fahrenthold needed to know if the portrait was hanging at one of Trump's homes or businesses, so he started searching for the painting and documenting his quest on Twitter. "Soon," Fahrenthold explained, "I had attracted a virtual army, ready to join the scavenger hunt. I had begun the year with 4,700 Twitter followers. By September I had more than 60,000 and climbing fast."[47]

Fahrenthold never located the original portrait, but with help from two Twitter followers, Allison Aguilar and Enrique Acevedo, he eventually located a second painting that Trump had purchased with foundation money. It was hanging up at Trump's golf resort in Doral, Florida, in plain sight. But without his "virtual army" on Twitter, Fahrenthold admits he "never would have found it."[48]

Fahrenthold's investigation, which earned the Pulitzer Prize for National Reporting in 2017, demonstrated that the public not only can ask good questions (the Hearken model), but also help journalists track down important answers. Another example is *De Correspondent*'s Shell investigation, which began when the Dutch news site surfaced evidence that Shell had known the risks of climate change as early as 1986—and yet done almost nothing about it. Like Fahrenthold's investigation, Jelmer Mommers' reporting for *De Correspondent* began with a call-out to the public: "Do you know something outsiders don't?" Mommers asked in an open letter directed to Shell employees. "Do you think society—and journalists like me— misunderstand what's required for making the transition to clean energy? If so, email me and we'll set up a meeting. I'm especially interested in meeting with you if you think I'm asking the wrong questions entirely, or if you think I'm just another journalist who doesn't understand Shell. Please set me straight."[49]

Mommers interviewed more than 19 Shell employees and posted the transcripts on De Correspondent's website, creating what co-founder and publisher Ernst-Jan Pfauth called a "flywheel effect" for the outlet's work. "The updates [Mommers] published amplified his reach and trust," Pfauth wrote. "They brought in new readers and new sources."[50] Eventually, one of those sources handed Mommers the mother lode: a box of Shell's internal company documents, including a 1986 report that acknowledged the possibility of "fast and dramatic" changes to the climate that "could have major social, economic, and political consequences."[51] This report, along with a 1991 public information video produced by Shell, helped show that the company knew about the risks of climate change decades ago, even as it doubled down on exploration for oil and natural gas.

Fahrenthold's collaborative Twitter sleuthing and Mommers' public callout are both examples of "crowdsourcing," a term defined by the Tow Center for Digital Journalism as "the act of specifically inviting a group of people to participate in a reporting task—such as newsgathering, data collection, or analysis—through a targeted, open call for input; personal experiences; documents; or other contributions."[52]

Many journalists have experimented with crowdsourcing in one form or another, but few news organizations have integrated it into their work as consistently or comprehensively as *ProPublica*, a nonprofit news outlet specializing in long-term investigations with national reach. *ProPublica* has distinguished itself in part by assembling a full-time engagement team, which works to strengthen the newsroom's reporting and maximize its impact through crowdsourcing and public participation. "We don't want to just write a story and then distribute it," explains engagement editor Terry Parris Jr. "[We] want our engagement team to find the ways in which those who are impacted by that investigation can participate in it, contribute to it, and ideally shape that story."[53]

An example of this approach in action is *ProPublica*'s Agent Orange project, which began in June 2015 with a public call-out: "Are you a veteran of the Vietnam War era?" senior reporter Charles Ornstein asked in a post. "We're interested in talking to all veterans who served in Vietnam and the wider Western Pacific area during that time, including those stationed in Korea. You can help us learn more about this issue by completing the short survey below, which includes questions about your service, family and health."[54]

Within a week, more than 1,000 veterans had completed *ProPublica*'s 35-question survey about Agent Orange exposure and side effects; by 12 months, that number had eclipsed 6,000, a remarkable response made possible in large part by Parris's engagement work. Instead of sending out the survey and simply hoping veterans would find and complete it, Parris instead spent months building trusted relationships on social media—mainly on Facebook, where he interacted with veterans' groups and introduced them to the project, shared the survey and explained how responses would be used, and provided periodic updates about the investigation's progress. According to Parris, this sustained engagement helped *ProPublica* earn the credibility and trust it needed for a crowdsourcing project of that scale. "[Veterans] know I'm not just some random [reporter] parachuting in," Parris said. "They know I'm Terry from *ProPublica*. They know that name."[55]

In the case of *ProPublica*'s Agent Orange investigation, Parris and his colleagues were listening to the public for a very clear purpose: to discover the extent of Agent Orange exposure during the Vietnam War and to understand its impact on veterans. However, there are also occasions when journalists listen with less specific aims, or even for the sake of listening itself. What results from this work often is not a news article, but instead something less common in journalism: a conversation.

'Under Our Skin,' Discourse Media, and Listening as Conversation

On July 5, 2016, a cell phone video posted to YouTube showed Alton Sterling, an African American man, being wrestled to the ground and shot in the chest by police. He was the 129th black man that year to die during an encounter with law enforcement.[56] A day later, 32-year-old Philando Castile became the 130th. Castile had notified the officer that he was carrying a licensed concealed weapon, but when he reached for his wallet, the officer fired seven shots into his arm.[57] The two men's deaths sparked protests across the country, including in Dallas, where an otherwise peaceful Black Lives Matter rally ended with an unaffiliated sniper opening fire and killing five white police officers. The act of retaliatory violence inflamed an already bitter racial divide, and it led to a familiar refrain in the media about the need for a "national conversation on race."

The challenge for journalists, of course, came in determining what that conversation should look like and what role the news media should play in convening it. For the most part, news organizations slipped into old habits. On television, cable news hosts filled hours of airtime with rancorous debate between the "two sides"—Black Lives Matter and Blue Lives Matter—that produced little more than rhetorical fireworks. In one segment on CNN, anchor Don Lemon sat idly by as two panelists shouted over each other ("You're the one fomenting violence that resulted in cops' death last night," Jeff Roorda accused his co-panelist) and resorted to personal insults ("Why don't you be quiet? Why don't you listen? You're so arrogant you can't even hear," Angela Rye fired back).[58]

Meanwhile, newspaper coverage of the racial unrest followed an equally predictable pattern, with reporters dutifully covering the symptoms of racial division—the shootings and protests—while leaving the causes unexplored. In a story typical of this approach, *Minnesota Star Tribune* reporter Randy Furst wrote about four police officers who walked off the job at a women's basketball game where players protested the deaths of Castile and Sterling. Furst provided readers with a who-what-when-where overview of the basic facts, and he quoted representatives from both the basketball team ("We are highlighting a longtime problem of racial profiling") and the police union ("I commend them for [walking out]")—an approach that media scholar Todd Gitlin described as an act of stenography, not the start of a conversation. "A conversation jostles assumptions," Gitlin wrote. "A conversation seeks to grasp and explore more than two points of view. It investigates why people say what they say, and whether any of them change their minds because they might have heard—if they were listening—something other than what they expected to hear."[59]

Although the mainstream media rarely met this mark during the explosive summer of 2016, there was at least one sign of progress for engaged journalism and the country's conversation on race. In June 2016 the *Seattle Times* launched "Under Our Skin," a multimedia documentary project that featured interviews on race with 18 community members, including

Greg Rickel, a white Episcopal bishop; Varisha Khan, a Muslim American college student; and Tariqa Waters, a black artist and small business owner.[60] By asking each respondent to explain their perspective on loaded terms like "microaggression" and "white privilege" and then cutting their responses into four- to seven-minute video segments, the *Times* created a medley of voices that represented the messy middle of America's conversation on race. There was disagreement without argument, 18 sides instead of 2, and a rare opportunity to understand how the conversation on race is shaped—and often limited—by the ambiguity of its language. "A lot of these terms are constantly used but never really unpacked," said Louis Chude-Sokei, an English professor featured in the project. "And people are interpreting them in quite different ways than the people who are speaking them."[61]

Instead of amplifying voices at the extremes, these videos helped bring more diverse and more nuanced perspectives into the conversation—as did the community engagement that followed. After the project's public launch, the *Times* invited the public to share responses in the comments section, on social media, and even at a mobile booth set up at the BAAMFest festival in Rainier, and within weeks, the *Times*' staff had reviewed and published hundreds of readers responses in a custom-built comments feed that accompanied the videos. For community members, this final step was crucial. "The comments are what inspired me," one commenter wrote. "The video did not actually discuss anyone trying to address and prevent their own microaggressions or how to go about doing so. The comments were uplifting because [they] acknowledge that it's a struggle to constantly check yourself and that everyone, regardless of race or ethnicity, needs to do it."[62]

The project's impact even stretched beyond the Web, with local schools, churches, and government agencies asking the *Times* if they could use "Under Our Skin" as an instructional tool, and the head football coach at the University of Washington inviting one of the interview subjects, Bishop Rickel, to address his entire team. "It definitely made us uncomfortable," one player said after Rickel's presentation. "But I liked it. He forced us to think like real men."[63]

Projects like "Under Our Skin" became more common after the 2016 election, which set off a wave of journalism projects aimed at facilitating conversations across political divides. Among the notable examples are:

- **"The Run-Up" dialogues**: In its podcast "The Run-Up," the *New York Times* aired a series of conversations between pairs of voters who discussed their stark political differences.

- **The Alabama/California Conversation Project**: Spaceship Media partnered with Alabama Media Group to hold online conversations between women in Alabama who voted for Trump and women in California who voted for Clinton.

- **#AirTalkItOut**: Southern California Public Radio's talk show *AirTalk* broadcast a town hall with four Trump voters and four Clinton voters, who reflected on the election and their expectations for the next four years.

- **Melting Mountains**: *The Evergrey* organized a day-long "rural-urban gathering" between voters in King County, Washington, and Sherman County, Oregon, which voted for Clinton and Trump in opposite proportions.[64]

In these projects, the role of journalists is primarily to *listen*, not for quotes or sound bites, but for experiences and insights that inform the journalist's next steps. *Discourse Media* reporter Brielle Morgan employed this approach for an investigation into Canada's child welfare system, which she launched by hosting a series of "listening events" with affected youth and their allies. Before writing a single story, Morgan spent months developing expertise on the issue and building relationships with the people whose insights, stories, and connections would be crucial to her work. "People close to the system . . . are tired of tragedy-driven coverage that does little to inspire hope or illustrate ways forward for young people and families," Morgan wrote. The listening tour "was about building trust and creating opportunities for others to tell their story."[65]

By putting engagement and listening at the heart of its work, *Discourse Media* CEO Erin Millar says the company is specifically trying to connect with millennials, a generation she says often feels "misunderstood, pandered to, disrespected or outright ignored."[66] Of course, Millar isn't the first to make that diagnosis, nor is she the first to propose a bold plan for reaching young news consumers, a challenge that has confounded media executives for more than a decade. In Chapter 3, we examine the different ways that news organizations have chased this goal, starting with a look at one of the fastest-growing and hippest brands in journalism: *VICE*.

Reimagining Reach: *VICE,* Snapchat, and Journalism's Quest for Digital-Native News Consumers

"If there's not a rebellious youth culture, there's no culture at all. It's absolutely essential. It is the future. This is what we're supposed to do as a species, is advance ideas."[1]

—John Lydon

"Twelve months from now we'll be on the cover of *Time* magazine as the guys who brought millennials back to TV," *VICE* co-founder Shane Smith boasted to the Hollywood Reporter in February 2016, claiming he was on track to build "the biggest f—ing media company in the world."[2] His cocksure tone was familiar to media industry analysts—and arguably it was justified. Six months earlier, Rupert Murdoch bought 5 percent of the company for $70 million dollars, raising its value to $1.4 billion. And after negotiations that same month unraveled with Time-Warner, the A&E Networks (a joint venture between Disney and Hearst) bought a 10 percent stake, raising *VICE*'s valuation to $2.5 billion.[3]

"Shane Smith is one of the best salesmen ever," said Doug Herzog, former president of Viacom Music and Entertainment Group in a personal interview.[4] Before occupying the top executive suite, Herzog was president of Comedy Central and paved careers for Jon Stewart, Stephen Colbert,

Samantha Bee, and *South Park* creators Trey Parker and Matt Stone. And before running comedy, he developed and greenlit many of MTV's most iconic programs, including *The Real World*, *Beavis and Butt-Head*, and the *MTV Music Awards*.

Co-author Ed Madison and Herzog met 40 years ago at Emerson College in Boston, where they learned to make television together as classmates. In this chapter, we break from academic tradition—and third-person voice—to provide a transparent account of that enduring 40-year friendship and, most importantly, the lessons learned along the way.

Launching CNN's Entertainment News

Doug Herzog was the first person I called when I was hired as a founding executive producer and director at CNN in 1980. We launched *People Tonight*, the fledgling network's nightly entertainment news program. I was 22, Doug was 21, and we were the first national talk show to interview Tom Hanks, Pee Wee Herman, Tom Cruise, and many rising stars of that era. After CNN and a run at *Entertainment Tonight*, Doug was the chief architect behind *MTV News*. He offers a keen perspective for this chapter on reaching young audiences.

"I think it's fair to say that *VICE* has taken a page out of the MTV playbook, but they've done it their own way. Hats off to them," Herzog said while noting that HBO's Pay TV model allows *VICE* some additional liberties in terms of running risqué content. "They've gone places that we weren't going to go, and couldn't because of being advertiser supported."[5]

VICE Media's pursuits are influenced by the life experiences of the founders, who bring *how they live* and *who they are* to the brand—the unbridled rawness of life sometimes overlooked or overly packaged for consumption by traditional outlets.

VICE's founders are not what one would expect. BBC broadcaster Mark Coles' profile on Smith described him as "a hard-partying, tattooed former Ottawa punk rocker who turned a community magazine into an international multi-media empire" and noted *VICE*'s appeal to millennials disillusioned with mainstream media.[6]

WIRED characterized the founders as "a recovering heroin addict and two welfare cheats," and *VICE* magazine as a "caustic cocktail of provocation, hedonism, and arrogance." Headlines such as "The *VICE* Guide to Shagging Muslims," "Latino Is the New Black," and "A Guy Who Was on Acid for a Whole Year" made the publication a "hipster bible."[7]

That street-savvy nature led the team to abandon accepted approaches and experiment in ways traditional executives might never consider. Yet many of their gambles have paid off.

Estimates of *VICE*'s value continued to skyrocket as the company announced one new deal after another, including partnerships with Verizon to produce and disseminate exclusive content to the carrier's mobile customers and with Snapchat to distribute news and entertainment. Over time, *VICE*'s eclectic portfolio of properties grew to include a record label, marketing agency, clothing line, and film production company.[8]

In 2015 *Inc. Magazine* placed the company's worth at $4.5 billion, dwarfing the valuation of the *New York Times* ($2.5 billion) and *BuzzFeed* ($1.5 billion). Smith speculated that if *VICE* went public, it could be worth up to $20 billion.[9]

VICE is cultivating buzz and market share among millennials by being brash and provocative. Out of the gate, *VICE* was prolific, generating more than 70 original news-oriented video series and serving more than 36 countries.[10] HBO renewed the Emmy Award–winning *VICE* series for an additional four years and agreed to add a nightly news series and a dedicated channel on its HBO Now app. It was described by HBO as the "most expansive programming deal ever."[11] It is an impressive trajectory for an unbridled media brand that Smith and co-founders Suroosh Alvi and Gavin McInnes launched two decades earlier as an obscure Canadian music magazine.

At a time when legacy media empires appeared to be crumbling, *VICE* Media was a conundrum. Onlookers were attempting to deconstruct the recipe for the company's secret sauce. *The Spectator*'s deputy editor Lara Pendergast said:

> *VICE*'s strength is getting younger audiences to join conversations about important international topics in a way traditional media have not. Its videos may fail every rule in the BBC impartiality book. But they are brilliantly edited and, often, utterly compelling. *VICE* News has found young, fearless foreign correspondents to serve a youthful audience who are bored stiff by traditional outlets but are quite prepared to watch videos on their mobile phones.[12]

Other critics were less flattering, suggesting that *VICE* was far from groundbreaking, not worthy of emulation, and was essentially nothing new. Several argued that the company's rise relied on sordid practices reminiscent of the yellow journalism that plagued the profession around the turn of the 19th century when William Randolph Hearst and Joseph Pulitzer waged headline wars.

"Like the flash press, *VICE* defines itself oppositionally to mainstream culture, burying its nose into stories that 'classier' outlets would reject as too unsettling," wrote *Reuter*'s Jack Shafer.[13] For example, as if lifting a reel from Mondo Cane, *VICE* online ran a piece about a Chinese dog-meat festival, complete with photos of a dead and slaughtered hound and links to a similar piece from last year ("I Ate a Dog in Hanoi").[14]

In a candid moment captured in the 2011 documentary *Page One: Inside the New York Times*, media critic David Carr confronts *VICE* executives as they portray mainstream media as being in a state of financial free-fall for failing to engage millennials. "Print as a medium continues to nose dive; publications like *Newsweek* and *Time* are going down fast," one of Smith's executives interjected, emphatically stating that the biggest media companies were now courting *VICE* with open checkbooks. One of those companies was CNN.[15]

In a later gathering, Carr was blunt: "What the f—k is going on with you doing business with CNN?" Undeterred, the executive asserted that *VICE* knew how to speak to younger viewers, claiming, "They listen to us; we're a trusted brand for them."[16]

The executive further suggested that *VICE*'s renegade style of coverage in parts of Africa rivaled the *New York Times*. The documentary then cut to a scene of a *VICE* report on Liberia where a camera panned a beach littered with human excrement. "People here don't have toilets," a Liberian man explained, "and because they don't have toilets, they use the beach." A second segment featured villagers boasting about cannibalism while holding up human organs. Smith told Carr these were legitimate stories that the *New York Times* wasn't willing to cover. Instead, the *Times* preferred to write about surfing.

Carr wasn't having it. "Just a sec. Timeout; we've had reporters going there to report on genocide after genocide. Just because you put on a f—ing safari helmet and looked at some poop doesn't give you the right to insult what we do."[17]

Smith backed down and apologized.

Style and depth of coverage aside, it is fair to say that Smith had a point. Like many legacy media companies, the *New York Times* was slow to embrace digital. *WIRED* reported extensively about what became known inside the company as the "Timesian" way, an institutional philosophy that was a barrier to innovation.[18] It resulted in an bureaucratic, top-down management structure perpetuated by smugness.

In 2014 *BuzzFeed* leaked an internal *Times* Innovation Report revealing several unflattering secrets about the company's corporate culture:

> What *Timesian* means or doesn't mean often depends on who's defining it, but it's typically in the same general neighborhood as authoritative, or maybe stuffy. Editors are infamous for their lengthy divinations on whether new

headline styles are sufficiently *Timesian*, and, per the Innovation Report, nothing slowed down a new initiative more than when management deliberated on just how Timesian it was or wasn't.[19]

However, the *New York Times* appears to have turned the corner on new media revenue, more so than many of its rivals. In 2016 it generated nearly $500 million in digital revenue, far exceeding competitors such as the *Washington Post*, whose digital products brought in $60 million in 2016. *BuzzFeed* generated $170 million. Meredith Kopit Levien, the *Times*' chief revenue officer, stated: "Today we have the largest and most successful pay model for journalism in the world."[20]

Those numbers counter a prevailing alternative-fact-based narrative about "the failing @nytimes"—perpetrated via Twitter by President Donald Trump. In fact, the *New York Times* reached a significant milestone in February 2017, surpassing 3 million paid and print subscribers.[21]

Media analyst Ken Doctor observed: "Trump, of course, has become the greatest source of lead generation the American press has ever seen, his campaign and then election inspiring hundreds of thousands of Americans to rush to buy digital news subscriptions and memberships." Other publications also experienced a post-election surge. January 2017 was *The New Yorker*'s largest month ever. Doctor reported a 230 percent increase in subscriptions for the 92-year-old publication, saying that, "The magazine now has its largest circulation ever, at more than a million."[22]

The *Times* has also shown a willingness to foster new media initiatives, such as its recent partnership with Spotify. For $5 per week, *Times* subscribers receive a one-year all-access digital subscription to the *New York Times* bundled with Spotify's premium music streaming service, which would otherwise cost $120 annually.[23]

Accessing and interpreting accurate metrics about *VICE* Media gets complicated. Digital publishers bear the constant burden of demonstrating massive and continual growth, specifically with attracting much sought after and yet elusive millennials. This constant pressure incentivizes content providers to employ questionable tactics that can essentially massage the numbers and provide data that makes certain audience segments falsely appear younger. A common strategy is bundling independent site traffic results. comScore charged Vice.com of inflating its audience metrics by combining its numbers with those of other online properties it manages but does not operate. In December 2016 Vice.com alone had 25.4 million unique visitors, but *VICE* Media allegedly took credit for 58.8 million.[24,]

"Traffic assignment" is legal, but the practice can backfire when the volatility of lesser known sites sinks aggregate performance.

One can better understand the rise and impact of *VICE* by stepping back and examining the "playbook" written by Herzog and his MTV creative team 35 years earlier.

MTV and News for Generation X

MTV was the first media network brand to capture the ethos of American youth culture. Debuting in August 1981, MTV (short for Music Television) was created by media executive Bob Pittman, whom *Adweek* dubbed "the jack of all media" and former MTV executive Tom Freston called "the wonder boy of branding."[25]

Freston's praise acknowledged that his former boss was a bona fide prodigy. Pittman began his media career at age 15 as a radio DJ. By age 23, he was programming NBC's premiere New York radio station, WNBC-AM.

Cable television brought the innovation of niche networks that could cater to specific categories of audience interests. Herzog reflected:

> I always try to explain to my kids, when I grew up there were just three television networks and PBS, and you just watched what they put on. Cable broke that open, but then you watched what cable put on. It wasn't like today with 500 channels, there were 20, maybe. MTV was revolutionary. There was just nothing else like it. Young people flocked to it, the brand was strong, we created a community, and it was a certain time and place.[26]

Print publications matured similarly. As the 20th century ended, so, too, did the prominence of general-interest magazine stalwarts such as *Life* and *Look*. They were eclipsed by niche publications such as *People* magazine, which appealed to readers specifically interested in pop culture trends and celebrity tribulations. ESPN was *Sports Illustrated* for sports enthusiasts, and CNN was *Time* magazine for news junkies. An interesting footnote is that even with the legacy credibility of its *Sports Illustrated* brand, Time Warner failed with CNN/SI—its attempt to compete with ESPN.[27]

Pittman and his team positioned MTV to appeal to a specific demographic of music fans who were underserved by mainstream media and difficult to target: 16- to 24-year-old males. Marketers have referred to consumers born between 1965 and 1980 as Generation X and suggest they are the ignored generation. Pew Research characterized Gen Xers as the "neglected middle child," stuck between bolder Baby Boomers and more conspicuous millennials. "From everything we know about them, they're savvy, skeptical, and self-reliant; they're not into preening or pampering, and they just might not give much of a hoot what others think of them," Pew reported.[28]

Pittman welcomed the challenge of feeding this audience's needs. "Someone told me early on when you are trying to solve a problem it's the mix of math and magic," Pittman stated at a French festival on creativity.[29]

However, Pittman's premonitions didn't prosper overnight. Conservative cable operators initially shunned MTV, and it was only available to an audience of 10,000 viewers in northern New Jersey. However, his vision for what MTV would become was spot on. After the network signed on with the simple statement: "Ladies and Gentlemen, rock and roll," it would take another year for MTV to seal carriage deals with major cable companies in New York and Los Angeles.[30]

Under Pittman and Herzog's leadership, MTV emerged as the era's most profitable cable network. In its prime, MTV reached 387 million households worldwide, and analysts considered it to be the #1 media brand in the world.[31]

"We had them held captive," Herzog recalls. "There was no Internet. There was radio, limited television, and there was print."[32]

Pittman negotiated deals with record labels that essentially provided the network with free content in return for promoting songs and bands, and that became part of MTV's magical dominating strategy. Pop culture analyst Linda Holmes observed, "They [record companies] were always irked that they had to pay for a video that was almost entirely made to be played on MTV."[33] Despite this, the channel's quick rise in prominence gave it an upper hand. MTV was the perfect platform for the masterful theatrics of emerging artists such as Madonna, Prince, and Michael Jackson.

"Part of MTV's impact—for better or worse—was that it transformed music into a multi-sensory medium. It wasn't enough to sound good; suddenly bands had to be hypersensitive to their visual image—whether that meant shooting videos in Sri Lanka, a la Duran Duran, or playing up their oddball looks, such as ZZ Top," wrote *USA Today*'s Jim Lenahan. Once rock icons including Mick Jagger, David Bowie, and Pete Townsend joined the "I want my MTV" promotional campaign, the network emerged as an indisputable force.[34]

"There was not much there in the way of news when I got there," Herzog recalls. "Just two or three people ripping stuff out of *Billboard*, rewriting it, and sending it down to the studio." MTV's on-air VJs had always offered audiences tidbits about their favorite artists. However, the network saw the potential of news and tapped Kurt Loder to become its first formal journalist and host of "This Week in Rock," which grew to become *MTV News*. As former *Rolling Stone* editor, Loder brought credibility and a wealth of relationships to the fledgling network.

"That was a big deal at the time," Herzog said. "We started expanding staff, and going out into the field and shooting stories, which I had learned to do at CNN."

MTV's first substantive foray into news came with its "Choose or Lose" campaign coverage of the 1992 presidential election. Having owned up to prior experimentation with pot and marital challenges, Bill Clinton was the perfect candidate for the MTV generation. One of *Time* magazine's Top 10 Presidential Pop Culture Moments is during an MTV town hall where Clinton did not flinch when asked "Boxers or Briefs?" Clinton smiled and responded, "Usually Briefs."[35]

"It was a planted question," Herzog laughingly said. "It was still television. We wanted to make sure it was going to feel like MTV."

Loder speculated that MTV might have played a role in George H. Bush's defeat to Bill Clinton in his bid to reclaim the presidency. "I think there's some statistic somewhere that it did. The idea that you get young people involved is sort of revolutionary. I mean, it was just a joke. George Bush was laughing even as we waved goodbye down the tubes. He just couldn't imagine why he should talk to MTV," Loder told Annenberg Media.[36]

"Bill Clinton came out [and] literally thanked MTV at the inaugural ball we threw for him," Herzog said. "I remember my colleague Judy McGrath falling out of her chair when he did that."

MTV's management soon realized it could not rely solely on music videos to build a sustainable brand. Soon Herzog was rising through the ranks and was entrusted to experiment with game shows, including *Remote Control* and the breakthrough reality series *The Real World*.

To target its key demographic—young males—the company developed *MTV Sports*, a high-octane series profiling radical athletics, hosted by Dan Cortese. It also began producing news specials. "We did specials about drugs, sexuality, and social justice through the prism of young people," Herzog said. "*VICE* is [also] focused on young guys."

While *VICE* Media emerged by replicating MTV's playbook, Viacom's properties, especially MTV, seemed to be losing their way. Media analysts began speculating about whether the parent company would even exist in a decade. Bloomberg reported that its properties' Nielsen ratings were sliding, "including Comedy Central, BET, VH1, Nickelodeon, Spike, and TV Land."[37] MTV's prime-time audience dropped 21.7 percent, following a 25 percent dip the previous season in the target 18- to 34-year-old demographic.[38]

Rather than embrace YouTube's disruptive innovation, Viacom in 2007 demanded the removal of 100,000 unauthorized videos and issued the parent company, Google, a $1 billion lawsuit. The companies settled a year later, and Viacom aggressively pushed its content to its own branded platforms. However, legacy media companies such as Viacom missed the point. When YouTube users indiscriminately uploaded their favorite programs to the service, they considered it acts of piracy, rather than an opportunity.[39]

Free-for-all video sharing introduced new audiences to vintage content. Monty Python's DVD sales soared 23,000 percent in 2014 after excerpts were widely circulated. Collective thinking at the corporate level was that Comedy Central would succeed with its own digital initiative, but it suffered a blow when two of its top stars, Jon Stewart and Stephen Colbert, left the network.[40]

"Legacy media companies clearly had difficulty navigating where they were in the world with the advent of the digital space," Herzog said. "On one hand you had Viacom, which sort of ignored it all, and Disney tried to embrace it. And some were successful and some not."

Viacom's dramatic downturn came as Comcast's NBC Universal division infused $200 million in the nimble news innovators *BuzzFeed* and Vox Media. *BuzzFeed* was awarded a Pulitzer and bolstered its investigative news operation by partnering with the BBC. By summer 2017, Vox .com's global unique visitor stats had grown to 116 million.[41]

Praying for a Linear Media Renaissance

Hope still exists for linear real-time television networks. For *VICE* Media, its A&E deal came with the keys to H2 (its second History Channel) and prayers that Smith could lure elusive millennials to a new channel that would be journalism's second coming. What emerged in 2016 was *VICELAND*, a 24-hour news and lifestyle network reminiscent of the company's successful HBO series. With series such as "Weediquette" and "Gaycation," Smith was thumbing his nose at broadcast media's safe and predictable conventions, confident that younger viewers would want a whiff.

Thus far, the network's fortunes have not risen nearly as fast as the company's valuation. In its first three weeks, *VICELAND*'s audience averaged just 60,400 viewers, which is 77 percent lower than H2's 241,000 viewers during its final three weeks.[42] What happened? One possibility is that millennials just aren't coming back to scheduled television. Mobile devices untether us from cables and prescribed ways we can access media. Apart from breaking news, competitive sports, and special events, linear real-time television watching is arguably obsolete.

As of the publication date of the book, a final verdict remains to be handed down about whether *VICELAND* can emerge as sustainable.

"It's been a few years since they started this," Herzog said. "I'd be surprised if they were to launch *VICELAND* today. However, they are building a library, using somebody else's money and I think it is a good play for them."

VICELAND's more popular programs appear to draw more viewers via its YouTube channel, racking up an estimated 166,000 views for the second installment of "Gaycation" and 6.3 million for the premiere of "Weediquette."[43] However, *International Business Times* reporter Oriana Schwindt wrote, "Any comparison between online video 'views' and TV viewers is bunk; TV ratings are calculated as the average number of viewers per minute for a given program while the standard for what's considered a 'view' online [varies] widely, depending on the site or app being used."[44]

Online bliss also appeared to be waning for *VICE*'s signature website, which took a 17 percent traffic hit in March 2016.[45] A company spokesperson countered that comScore's measuring methods failed to capture the totality of *VICE*'s multiplatform presence accurately.

Its alleged online decline coincided with other ethics-related controversies. News reports surfaced that *VICE*'s corporate culture was rife with bad habits that were hurting business. Several freelancers revolted, claiming the company failed to compensate them for services rendered.

VICE Media has grown so quickly that Smith told *Digiday*, "I don't know a lot of stuff we're doing." The company produces a staggering 7,000 pieces of media content each day. He acknowledged he doesn't personally or professionally care for some of the stories *VICE* publishes, claiming: "The brand isn't me anymore. I think the greatest success of *VICE* is that we revamped the brand, giving it over to the interns and said, 'Have at it.' Sometimes that's unpleasant or not pretty."[46]

For talented young multimedia producers, getting a gig at *VICE* was the fulfillment of a dream. Positions sometimes offered travel to exotic places, free license to challenge the conventions of broadcast news, and bragging rights that you held an enviable job. Whether it was reporting about the effects of climate change on ancient rainforests or the perils of sweatshops in Bangladesh, *VICE* allowed millennials who were lucky enough to get the gig to report on global injustices and tell stories with the power to move and influence their generation.[47]

However, in recent years, several employees and freelancers offered a counternarrative about what it is like to work for *VICE*. Job recruiting sites became populated with anonymous unflattering posts. "Hipster sweatshop that would make Aldous Huxley roll in his grave," read a headline on Glass Door.com.[48]

The post listed several pros:

Cool company creating cool content. Lots of cool parties and perks. Lots of opportunity for advancement if you like inflated job titles and meager salaries for 70+ hours of work a week.

And a litany of stinging cons:

Low pay, poor organization. Open workspace means you have 18" of personal space on your "desk;" literally a MacBook Pro sweatshop. Loud, chaotic, disorganized. Feels like a college computer lab during finals. Except that's every, single, day. Expect an inflated job title for 50+ hours of work every week for bad pay. People put up with the slave labor because *VICE* is "cool" so they feel privileged to make Shane Smith more money. Modern day serfdom. Love your servitude.[49]

Gawker reporter Hamilton Nolan wrote about the disconnect between how much investment capital the company had accumulated and what *VICE* was paying its employees, saying: "The company pays shitty wages to low-level employees, 'compensating' them instead with the sheer coolness of working for *VICE* Media." One employee told Nolan, "The appeal is street cred, lots of free parties/booze and the hope that one earns a coveted *VICE* ring." (Literally, a ring that said "*VICE*," given to lucky employees.)[50]

Smith responded that the company offered employees a generous stock option plan, making 250 of them millionaires in 2015 and another 2,000 millionaires in 2016.[51]

Although employee benefits at *VICE* are a matter of dispute, it clearly has invested in expanding its reach. In 2013 *VICE* News invested $50 million into strengthening its international news presence, hiring 60 reporters worldwide.[52]

VICE is not the first media brand to misjudge millennials' appetite for cable networks. In 2005 former Vice President Al Gore and a team of investors launched Current TV, touted as an "independent voice" for a target audience of people between 18 and 34 "who want to learn about the world in a voice they recognize and a view they recognize as their own."[53] Despite collaborations with Google, Yahoo, and Twitter, Current was behind the times in terms of content delivery. Netflix and other on-demand streaming media services were addressing the public's unwillingness to wait around to watch scheduled television. Current withdrew plans to raise $100 million dollars through an initial public offering because of "market conditions," and by spring 2011 the network had laid off 80 staffers. Two years later the network's assets were acquired by Al Jazeera for a reported $500 million.[54]

What emerged was Al Jazeera America, Qatar-based Al Jazeera's ambitious attempt to compete with CNN, Fox News, and MSNBC. However, the network never gained traction. On a good night, it attracted only 34,000 viewers. Audience levels were so dismal at times that Nielsen could not track it. Chief executive Al Anstey confessed in a memo to staff that the parent company was closing Al Jazeera America "driven by the fact that our business model is simply not sustainable."[55]

In 2013 Participant Entertainment, the source of high-profile socially conscious films, including *Spotlight*, *Lincoln*, *Food Inc.*, *The Help*, *An Inconvenient Truth*, and *CITIZENFOUR*, also attempted a cable channel aimed at millennials. Participant founder and chairman Jeff Skoll characterized himself as a social entrepreneur. Winnings from his stewardship of eBay allowed his Skoll Foundation to invest approximately $400 million in social justice causes worldwide.[56]

Participant's 75+ films have garnered Academy Award nominations and 11 wins and have grossed in excess of $2 billion.[57] Few management teams were better positioned to meet the challenge of addressing interests and viewing patterns of millennials.

However, the company failed to rally a consistent following and therefore was not sustainable. In summer 2016 CEO David Linde announced it would pull the plug, stating, "As the media landscape changes, we have been evaluating how we fulfill our mission to entertain and inspire social action around the world's most pressing issues. That process has led us to the decision to move away from owning and operating a cable network. While this conclusion was not an easy one, it is ultimately in the best interest of all our stakeholders, and allows us to allocate more resources toward the production of compelling content across all platforms."[58]

"The challenge of starting a new linear channel these days is really tough," Herzog said. "And, building a digital business is also tough."

Of the upstarts, Al Jazeera has had more success with AJ+, its direct-to-online digital offering that targets millennials through YouTube, Facebook, Instagram, Twitter, and Medium. To date, AJ+ has 9.6 million "likes" on Facebook and 550,000 Twitter followers. In June 2015 *Variety* reported that AJ+ became Facebook's second largest news video producer, followed by NowThisNews. They were the ninth largest video producer on the platform overall.[59]

Another news upstart to watch is RYOT Media. To several media critics, RYOT emerged as a *VICE* wannabe. Yet it has oriented itself around civics first and commerce second. Its online manifesto reads:

> RYOT is a citizen, not an enterprise. We're creating a movement that people want to be a part of by building a community around protecting the beauty

in our world. We know the revolution isn't finished until it moves out of the speakeasy and into the tailgate. We're not looking for the "new" beat, we're looking for permanence. We don't pretend to hide behind neutrality. We care about what happens to the world.[60]

With much fanfare, on April 20, 2016, Arianna Huffington announced HuffPost's acquisition of RYOT. The company was an innovator in documenting news using immersive 360-degree video and virtual reality technology. A year before the acquisition, RYOT partnered with Huffington Post to produce *The Crossing*, a VR film that documented the refugee crisis in Greece. It also collaborated with the *New York Times* and the Associated Press. "Our focus has been on 360-degree and virtual-reality video because you can really bring people inside the story," said co-founder Bryn Mooser. "Now we're bringing that storytelling and tech expertise to the global audience of the Huffington Post."[61]

However, Huffington and Mooser made it clear that HuffPost RYOT's technological edge would not be its greatest asset. There was a grander purpose for combining the companies. In a joint statement, they said: "We tell stories of resilience that move audiences to take action. And maybe it's media karma, but RYOT's mission—to 'Inform, Entertain, and Activate to Ignite Change Through Next Generation Storytelling'—even overlaps with HuffPost's own: to 'Inform, Inspire, Entertain, and Empower.'"[62]

The digital upstarts have gained traction by providing news and information in bits and spurts, rather than trying to program a 24/7 linear network such as *VICELAND*.

What RYOT, and particularly *VICE*, get right is an unapologetic willingness to assault broadcast news conventions. No "stand up" story introductions in front of (insert your choice of routine institutional backdrops). No handheld microphones. And absolutely none of the broadcast-speak presentation style that many millennials at the University of Oregon tell us projects a false sense of authority.

It is that predictable intonation where sentences end on an up note with a forced sense of deliberateness that many young people assess as fake.

"It's cheesy," said one our University of Oregon undergraduate journalism students. "You know they're going to say something really lame, and try to make lame puns. They exaggerate just to get your attention. It's too corny."[63]

When pushed to describe a more favorable way to present broadcast news for millennials, he said, "I'd prefer something more realistic, less big smiling faces. I like the underdogs, the people that just give it to you like they are trying to be your friend."

VICE and RYOT have boldly broken the broadcast news mold. Their reporters seem more like friendly guys or women you would like to hang out with on a Friday night. They don't talk at you. They come across as though they are talking with you. Reporters dress casually, the men are rarely closely shaven, and the women are not heavily made up. The result is a heightened sense of authenticity.

Whereas CNN correspondents predictably suited up in flak jackets and tear gas masks in 2014 to cover civil unrest in Ferguson, Missouri, following the fatal police shooting of Michael Brown, *VICE* reporters were working the back alleys, knocking on doors, and interviewing the community's real residents, who offered a counternarrative.

WIRED magazine noted that *VICE* "stage-dives into its coverage, dispatching amateur reporters—armed with little more than a camera, designer sunglasses, and a pair of steel cubes—to travel to the places that more-seasoned correspondents wouldn't be caught dead in for fear of . . . well, being caught dead. Like the streets of Baghdad, way outside the Green Zone. Or a black-market arms bazaar in Pakistan. Or the toxic remains of Chernobyl."[64]

VICE has also dispensed with the notion that news stories should conform to prescribed length and format limitations. Although the popularity of *VICE's* full-length documentaries might suggest otherwise. *VICE's* news stories run as long as they remain compelling—and are typically personable.

The relationship between newsrooms and advertising suites has historically been characterized as the separation of church and state. The intent was to not have advertisers influence editorial decision making. However, rather than shy away from working with brands, *VICE* and RYOT embrace the practice.

Recent *VICE*-branded content campaigns have included "Culture of Kong," a text and video series developed with Warner Bros. to boost *Kong: Skull Island*, and *15 Years of SB Dunk*, a 20-minute documentary short film created for Nike. *VICE* Media predicted that the majority of its 2016 revenue of $750 million to $850 million was from sponsored content and agency work.[65]

Like *VICE*, RYOT's largest revenue source is branded content. Walgreen's contracted with RYOT to help chronicle its work with Vitamin Angels, a nonprofit nongovernmental organization (NGO). And PepsiCo commissioned the company to produce content about its recycling initiatives in Central America.

Legacy Media Can Learn by Listening

The "Ira Glass effect"—that's how a radio industry analyst characterized the phenomenal way the public radio host of *This American Life* (*TAL*) and a legion of *TAL* alumni producers have brought millennials back to radio and long-form audio storytelling.[66]

TAL reaches approximately 2.2 million radio listeners weekly and broadcasts on more than 500 stations. It is also among the most popular podcasts in the country, with another 2.5 million people downloading each episode. "We crossed this line where we now have just as many people listening to us as a podcast as on the radio. The radio part is not going away, but the podcast audience is younger and all over the world," Glass told the *Denver Post* in 2016.[67]

Glass is transparent about his formula for effective storytelling, stating that the best stories lead up to a moment of reflection. "There's always a time where you ask yourself 'Why the hell am I listening to this?' This is your other biggest tool in storytelling," Glass said in a widely shared YouTube video series on storytelling tips. "If there isn't some point, or purpose, that your piece is driving toward, you're running the risk of the reader feeling disappointed with your work."

Glass shared some of his time-tested secrets for achieving dramatic effects in narrative journalism:

> Unanswered questions create a "tension" in the reader's mind—almost like an itch you have to scratch. This is why you'll see techniques like cliffhangers used on TV shows (or "Continued on P12!" in magazine and newsprint stories). This is something you want to manipulate when you're telling stories. You should *constantly* be raising and answering questions.[68]

Glass has leveraged his company's success with several spinoffs. Listeners were transfixed by *Serial*, a multi-episode long-form podcast by *This American Life* producers that examined a contested 1999 murder case in Baltimore. It was the fastest podcast to reach 5 million downloads in iTunes history, according to Apple.[69] Glass's team followed with *S-Town*, a seven-episode series about an Alabama man's life and death in what he described as a "shit town." The program was downloaded more than 40 million times, topping previous records set by *Serial's* second season, and far surpassing *This American Life's* podcast audience.[70]

TAL alums have launched their own entrepreneurial enterprises. One of the most prolific is Brooklyn-based Gimlet Media. The company produces more than a dozen popular podcasts—including *StartUp*, *Crimetown*, and *Reply All*—and is downloaded more than 7 million times a month by audiences in 190 countries.[71] Gimlet co-founder Alex Blumberg learned his craft at *TAL*. He was previously a co-founder of *Planet Money*, another NPR hit.

TAL and Gimlet's successes are antithetical to conventional thinking about how to appeal to millennials. "Twitter-panel-pundit-verse will tell you, the mandate to publishers is obvious: create shareable, short, catchy— 'snackable'—content," said Chris Giliberti, a Gimlet executive.[72] However, the company's long-form programs outperform its shorter offerings. He points to the negative impact of social media and 24/7 Internet connectivity. "Many posit that in this age of omni-connectedness we are lonelier than ever, as social media provides an illusion of togetherness that functionally serves to drive us further apart. What better way to fill the void than long form, immersive content experiences?" Gimlet said.[73]

Social scientists also express concerns about the long-term impact of being tethered to our mobile devices. MIT Professor Sherry Turkle said:

> These days, always connected, we see loneliness as a problem that technology should solve. Afraid of being alone, we rely on other people to give us a sense of ourselves, and our capacity for empathy and relationships suffers. We see the costs of the flight from conversation everywhere: conversation is the cornerstone for democracy and in business it is good for the bottom line. In the private sphere, it builds empathy, friendship, love, learning, and productivity.[74]

Long-form narrative podcasts are presented with candor and authenticity, two traits our millennial students at the University of Oregon tell us they want from mainstream media. Relatable presentation styles resonate with young people. In an informal gathering with undergraduate journalism majors, one told us, "I like how easy podcasts are to consume, and how they seem kind of straightforward." Another said long-form audio "can take you to a place, and you can actually hear the sounds or hear the person's voice, and it transplants you to that place."[75]

In 2007 Glass and his creative team briefly ventured into television, producing two seasons of *This American Life* on Showtime. Like Smith, Glass was committed to challenging broadcast conventions. However, rather than toss them out, Glass and his production team decided to parody them. Early on they deliberated about where to position the host. When recalling their creative process for the show's archives, director Chris Wilcha said they "had to confront the suffocating history of TV host clichés. It seemed like every imaginable way to film a TV host had been done: in a black void like Charlie Rose; on a fake living room set; strolling down a street with an interviewee, nodding meaningfully."[76]

Wilcha opted to embrace the clichés rather than avoid them. They took the *Tonight Show*–styled desk, so associated with late-night talk shows, and placed it on location in unconventional settings. "One week the desk is on the salt flats in Utah, one week in a garage, one week by nuclear cooling towers. It embraces TV conventions, while kind of winking at them," Wilcha recalled.[77]

Then they discovered that Monty Python had beat them to positioning a desk in odd places. So they "ditched the desk," Wilcha said, "and filmed Ira's bits for the show with a little Flip camera [they] bought at Best Buy for $149." [78]The team determined that Glass had earned a level of credibility with his audience that transcended the need for a traditional prop. The desk, with Glass behind it, potentially placed a barrier between him and the program's viewers.

The Showtime series was well received. However, the rigors associated with producing quality television far exceed radio's requirements. In addition to getting good sound, television producers have to consider lighting, space for cameras, additional crew, logistics, visual titling, and other effects. Convinced they didn't have the bandwidth to continue producing a high-quality radio series and a television series, Glass and his team shut the television series down in 2009. The series garnered three Emmy Awards and significant critical acclaim for effectively replicating the authentic storytelling that made the radio series an enduring brand, and the DVDs remain a collectible item.

It is important to note that *This American Life*'s decision to ditch the desk is symbolic for where journalism finds itself at this particular point in history.

Once Upon a Time It Was All About the Desk: The Trivialization and Tabloidization of Broadcast News

What Henry Ford was to the auto industry, Edward R. Morrow and Walter Cronkite were to the founding of broadcast journalism. Cronkite told the world a president was assassinated and that a man had walked on the moon. Cronkite symbolized authority in broadcast journalism, and in his era, serious news was delivered from behind a desk. It was the "anchor" that helped define the gravitas of an anchorman, and later anchorwomen. Sitting behind *the desk* was among the highest honors in broadcast news, and who would inherit each network's perch was the subject of much speculation.

Late-night talk show hosts also present from behind desks; however, they share their platforms with guests. During the early days of broadcast, news anchors were the sole arbiters of credible television journalism.

The significance and symbolism of the news anchor desk changed with Roone Arledge's appointment to head *ABC News* in 1979. Arledge made a name for himself pulling the network's sports division into prominence with the creation of *Monday Night Football* and *Wide World of Sports*.

However, he had no prior credentials in hard news. Arledge used the same playbook of flashy graphics and dramatic music to create ABC's *World News Tonight* and the news magazine *20/20*. The latter was ABC's answer to CBS network's *60 Minutes*—primetime television's perennial cash cow.

Arledge developed the concept of serializing "special reports" that transformed real-life tragedies into TV dramas with narrative arcs. He perfected the art of interrupting primetime programming with "breaking news updates" to build audiences and buzz. The successful formula led to the creation of ABC's *Nightline* in 1980, hosted by Ted Koppel.

Persona was always a factor for succeeding in broadcast news. On *Saturday Night Live*, Gilda Radner regularly lampooned Barbara Walters, and Stephen Colbert acknowledged that Bill O'Reilly was his Comedy Central character's alter ego. Morrow and Cronkite all had a distinctive repartee that played well on television.

NBC got into the news magazine game with *Dateline NBC*, hosted by news anchor Stone Phillips and former *Today* show host Jane Pauley. However, the program had a credibility problem. "How can you take a story seriously when the anchor/reporter's name is Stone Phillips?" wrote one critic. A *Radar* magazine article stated: "It may come as a shock, but pretty boy Stone Phillips . . . graduated with honors from Yale . . . sources insist he's 'very smart' . . . despite his robotic on air persona."[79]

A double-standard surfaced for women journalists who asserted ownership of their femininity and dared to ask tough questions. Before inheriting the anchor desk at CBS, Katie Couric was labeled "perky."[80] She pushed back, saying that the characterization had sexist overtones. "Bob Costas is short and cute, but nobody calls him perky. Perky is just slightly demeaning, and I think that is why it [has] always kind of irked me," she told producers of *Makers*, a series that profiles accomplished women.[81]

Before Couric, Jessica Savitch emerged as one of the first women to claim the seat behind the anchor desk. While earning her stripes Houston, Savitch recalled that when she reported on a storm without makeup, the station's switchboard lit up with 60 callers inquiring about whether she was ill.[82]

Roger Ailes reportedly had a mini-skirt dress code for women on-air talent at *Fox News*[83] Fox's afternoon opinion series, *The Five*, reportedly had a "leg cam" that focused on women's lower limbs. Rupert Murdoch's unauthorized biographer, David Folkenflik, reported that "they sort the women they have by the degree of attractiveness, and particularly the degree of attractiveness of the legs. I believe it's the seat on the front right where, having arranged this hierarchy, they put the woman with the best legs there, and they have a camera that goes directly for the legs."[84] Shortly after Ailes was let go by *Fox News* and subsequently died, reports surfaced that women journalists at Fox were suddenly wearing pants."[85]

Forced to compete against Fox, CNN, and MSNBC, several mainstream media organizations tarnished their credibility for the sake of expediency and ratings. In 1993 *Dateline NBC* acknowledged it had rigged a fiery test crash of a GM pickup truck for dramatic effect and agreed to an out-of-court settlement. "We deeply regret we included the inappropriate demonstration in our '*Dateline*' report," read *NBC News* co-anchors Jane Pauley and Stone Phillips, the result of a settlement negotiated just minutes before. The confession reversed the network's emphatic denials of any impropriety just days earlier and came at a time when NBC was experiencing significant revenue and ratings decline.[86]

Dateline NBC's "To Catch a Predator" series employed a simple, provocative format that resonated with audiences. The program partnered with Perverted Justice, a social justice group whose members impersonated minors and engaged in Internet conversations with suspected sexual predators. Producers coordinated sting operations at private homes involving law enforcement where *Dateline*'s hidden cameras awaited alleged perpetrators. At an appropriate moment, host Chris Hansen emerged from the shadows to confront suspects. The formula proved effective for ratings and bringing many criminals to justice. In 2006 50 men were arrested and charged with felonies during a three-day show-related sting in Riverside County.

On face value, the show's premise was ethical: capturing heinous villains. Yet claims soon surfaced that the series engaged in entrapment. *Dateline* anchor Stone Phillips acknowledged that ". . . in many cases, the decoy is the first to bring up the subject of sex." Phillips defended this, saying ". . . once the hook is baited, the fish jump and run with it like you wouldn't believe."[87] In a 2007 sting, charges were dropped against 23 online suspected predators because of insufficient evidence. Collin County District Attorney John Roach later shared his concerns about the series: "We were in the law enforcement business—not show business." The series ran for three years and resulted in numerous localized and international spinoffs.[88]

Presentation of broadcast news was further trivialized during the late 1980s and early 1990s era of tabloid television. Rupert Murdoch's acquisition of 20th Century Fox expanded his empire to become a platform for inexpensive faux news formats that had proven successful in Australia. Americans were already rabid consumers of supermarket tabloid publications, so translating the formula of sensational headlines to television was a safe bet. *A Current Affair*, hosted by Maury Povich, debuted in syndication in July 1986 and featured scandals and celebrity gossip from the start.

Sensing an opportunity to leverage the success of its syndicated series *Entertainment Tonight*, Paramount launched *Hard Copy*, an edgier tabloid show designed to run adjacent to local news. King World/CBS entered the genre with *Inside Edition*, and both programs benefited from co-opting the symbolism of the anchor desk.

Fueled by unabashed sensationalism, tabloid television programs thrived on the kind of stories people sheepishly glance at while in line at supermarkets. Because the programs aired next to traditional newscasts, tabloid television shows blurred the distinction between mainstream and faux news.

Paramount's decision to enter the tabloid market ran afoul with a number of its "A-List" stars, including actor George Clooney and director Steven Spielberg, who responded to surveillance of their personal lives by boycotting *Hard Copy* and *Entertainment Tonight*.[89]

Bill O'Reilly worked for several networks and anchored *Inside Edition* before Roger Ailes elevated *The O'Reilly Factor* to the flagship position at Fox News. Allegations of sexual harassment eventually cost Ailes and O'Reilly their jobs at Fox, but not before, according to critics, they contributed to the trivialization and tabloidization of broadcast news. Sophia McClennon at *Salon* was quick to write the *O'Reilly Factor*'s obituary, stating: "O'Reilly's attitude toward women was directly connected to his attitude about our nation in general. It was a caustic, aggressive, egotistical, bullying mentality that infected O'Reilly's fans and brainwashed them from being able to see the truth."[90]

PolitiFact found that only 10 percent of O'Reilly's utterances were true and that 53 percent were significantly false. A content analysis of the show's "Talking Points Memo" segment, conducted by Indiana University researchers, revealed that on average the host reverted to name calling every seven seconds. "If one digs further into O'Reilly's rhetoric, it becomes clear that he sets up a pretty simplistic battle between good and evil," said Associate Professor Maria Elizabeth Grabe.[91]

McClennon went further, offering her explanation of why Stephen Colbert chose O'Reilly as his Comedy Central character's alter ego. "Calling him 'Papa Bear,' Colbert emulated O'Reilly's bloviating punditry. While the character would draw on a range of pundits including Glenn Beck and Rush Limbaugh, Colbert still favored O'Reilly as the prime model because O'Reilly had basically defined the modern pundit persona."[92]

Colbert's character mocked O'Reilly's use of the anchor desk by accentuating certain passages of his faux news script with a raised brow, a pointing finger, and a dramatic pivot to face a second camera angle.

Mining for Millennials

A common narrative paints young people as reluctant followers of current events and disengaged civic actors. However, polls contradict that assertion. "The idea that young people are not interested in the outside world, I think, was wrong," said Tom Rosenstiel, executive director of the American Press Institute (API) at a 2010 conference on millennials. "Young people were not interested in the old delivery systems, in appointment viewing, in having to consume your news at breakfast only . . . Now that they have a delivery system that meets their behavior, their needs, their personality, they're avid consumers."[93]

Eighty-five percent of the millennials surveyed by Rosenstiel's API researchers said keeping up with the news was at least somewhat important to them, and 69 percent reported following it daily. As our focus group of millennials told us earlier, young people prefer authenticity more than rigid formalities or formats.[94]

To attract these young audiences, mainstream news needs a significant reboot. But it has been slow to happen. At the local level, broadcast news executives remain committed to having reporters produce "news packages," which do not greatly differ from the model established by broadcast icons Edward R. Murrow and Walter Cronkite. Broadcasters also demonstrate minimal imagination when it comes to story assignments. Recycling rather than reinventing is the norm. How many more ribbon-cutting ceremonies must audiences endure? Especially for millennial audiences, these stories are formulaic, predictable, and downright dull.

Real stories that touch, inspire, and engage audiences involve "characters." We do not mean fabricated reality show caricatures, but rather real human narratives. As an example, Pulitzer-winning writer Héctor Tobar captured the compelling story of 33 Chilean miners who were trapped underground for 69 days and emerged to become international heroes. Tobar chronicled their story in the book *Deep Down Dark*, which became the basis for the motion picture feature *The 33*.

We are not suggesting news stories have to rise to the level of epic feature films in order to gain audiences. Small community stories can be just as compelling. Often, it is a matter of approach that makes the difference. A story on health care legislation can be localized and made more meaningful by focusing on how a real person confronts the challenges of a shift in public policy.

Rather than exploring how real people are affected by public policies, many news organizations instruct their reporters to stick with interviewing policy makers. They rely on a "go-to" list of experts who, predictably, spew prepared talking points. Paying political surrogates to pontificate is a sure recipe for monochromic monotony, and millennials tune out.

In fairness, most gatekeepers of broadcast journalism are not tone deaf. However, they need only look at their aging audience to see that business as usual will not suffice. Reluctance to innovate is often driven by fear. It can seem risky to change course when you're already struggling to make quarterly numbers and maintain market share. Additionally, the ongoing pressure to "feed the beast," as the 24/7 news cycle is referred to by journalism professionals, is constant. Reporters can feel as though they live in a perpetual sense of playing catch-up in order to meet its demands. "Such is the state of the media business these days: frantic and fatigued," wrote Don Irvine for Accuracy in Media. "Young journalists who once dreamed of trotting the globe in pursuit of a story are instead shackled to their computers, where they try to eke out a fresh thought or be first to report even the smallest nugget of news—anything that will impress Google algorithms and draw readers their way."[95]

While many newspaper staffs are dwindling, more broadcast news is being produced at the local level. However, long gone are the days when news crews include a separate sound person to monitor audio. In smaller markets, reporters travel without a dedicated videographer, requiring they shoot and edit their own news stories. Watching a reporter set up a tripod, set the camera on auto-focus, and attempt to frame a shot of themselves with any degree of aesthetic quality saddens industry veterans who experienced and cherished the value of teamwork. After shooting and editing one's work, which can add up to several stories in one day, local news reporters are expected to blog, tweet, and post to Instagram and Facebook. Little wonder that innovation takes a backseat to the daily grind. The cutbacks are a result of smaller budgets, forced by audience fragmentation.[96]

However, experimentation is not confined to major media companies. On college campuses, students now produce journalistic work that approaches the quality of traditional professionals in the industry. These students make use of $400 digital SLR cameras that accommodate interchangeable lenses, bringing a cinematic quality to storytelling that rivals Hollywood-caliber aesthetics and provides the same rich level of storytelling younger audiences have come to expect.

Trailblazer David Dunkley Gyimah calls himself a *cinema journalist*. Based in the UK, Gyimah built a reputation for himself by challenging the profession's conventions. His work was influenced by *Primary*, an award-winning Cinéma vérité-style documentary that captured impromptu moments of candidate John F. Kennedy's successful 1960 presidential bid against Richard M. Nixon. The film employed handheld camera techniques to follow Kennedy through backroom corridors and as he approached podiums along the campaign trail, immersing viewers in evocative moments as Kennedy himself experienced them.[97]

Gyimah interviewed Robert Drew, one of *Primary*'s key filmmakers, and asked why traditional news failed to adopt these more compelling storytelling methods. "Cinéma vérité requires a degree of time and artistry that news people don't have time for," Drew answered. Drew's methods were groundbreaking and archived because he cajoled Time-Life into investing in the development of nonexistent shoulder-mounted camera gear. Drew and his colleagues broke the rules of conventional storytelling and made a few of their own. "No interviews. Tell the story through action, not narration. Don't interfere with what's happening, just observe. In *Primary,* the cameras follow the candidates as they meet voters on the street, catnap in cars, and confer with aides in private rooms," wrote Thom Powers who curates documentaries for the Toronto Film Festival.[98]

We are not suggesting that storytelling, regardless of what we call it, does not benefit from reporter mediation. From the time of the earliest scribes, journalists have served as information gatherers who contextualize complex topics for broader audiences. Topics such as health care can be so complex that they are incomprehensible. An effective reporter serves as a guide.

However, traditional *narration* in broadcast storytelling often comes across as ominous and impersonal. Reporters can appear to talk at audiences rather than talking with them in a conversational style.

It is problematic that many legacy media companies still define themselves as "broadcasters" rather than as storytellers. To remain relevant, media companies will have to abandon or more broadly define the term *broadcasting.*

Originally, the word referred to over-the-air transmission of signals in an era of "rabbit ear" antennas that had to be fiddled with to secure adequate picture quality. Viewers who lived in obstructed areas were out of luck unless they were willing to incur the added expense of a rooftop antenna. Stronger access to over-the-air signals still was not guaranteed.

Today, only 17 percent of American households view programs over-the-air. An intriguing side note is that antenna usage was as low as 7 percent before a resurgence in recent years as consumers have sought to cut the cable cord and free themselves from the considerable expense of paid access. Also, to "broadcast" connotes a one-way, producer-centric process of communicating with audiences, which disregards the participatory impact of social media.[99]

Audiences, especially millennials, are more inclined to consume media on mobile devices than via televisions. In fact, when we informally poll our University of Oregon students, only a small percentage even own a TV. And if they do, it is most often used to watch live sports.

Companies that still consider themselves broadcasters not only missed the DSLR cinematic technological revolution, but also that *stories* compel audiences to watch media, more so than conventional *reports*. There is a subtle yet significant distinction between the two. As previously noted, stories have characters. Reports are most often filled with faceless facts. This does not negate the importance of solid fact-based news reporting. In fact, we need more of it. More so, we're speaking of how stories are told, regardless of the medium.

The Takeaway is one of public radio's more innovative news programs, carried on approximately 200 stations nationwide. In comparison to the packaged-style storytelling heard on NPR's flagship program "Morning Edition," *The Takeaway*'s stories are intentionally conversational. Former host John Hockenberry describes the show as the experience of listening to two women with strollers walking together through a park. "All of a sudden they happen upon two other people engaged in a conversation, and you feel drawn to walk over and join."[100]

Prominently featured as well are audio clips provided by audience members, who reflect on relevant issues presented during the course of the program. Hockenberry relishes the fact that narrative storytelling is bringing millennials back to radio, mostly via podcasts. Yet he worries that this trend is not extending into consumption of hard news.

"If you listen to *Radiolab* or *Serial*, they are personally powerful but they don't give a broad view of what's going on in the world," Hockenberry said during a visit with journalism students at the University of Oregon. "Feature stories are not the drivers of the cycle of political or economic news."[101]

While covering spot news in Middle East conflict zones, Hockenberry developed a knack for crafting stories with richer narratives than traditional journalism, narratives with scenes and characters.

"I am a person who does daily news, and who passionately believes that daily news has every bit as much the opportunity to deliver the immersive narrative experience that you get from longform pieces," Hockenberry said. "The same rules apply: create a scene, deliver a sense of place, create characters, make sure that the characters have a sense of movement within the story that is somehow relevant to the news that you are trying to deliver. All of that is possible in daily production."[102]

Traditionalists fear that embracing storytelling may rob broadcast news of its legitimacy. They worry that it all becomes entertainment—and therefore ceases to be news. It is a legitimate concern, and there are areas that are still open for debate.

Another factor regarding presentation is the tools available to capture and disseminate news. Smartphones and mobile apps have transformed the ways in which media is consumed and shared.

Engaging Millennials in a Snap!

Mark Zuckerberg leveraged the power of relationships and the desire to feel connected to one another with Facebook. However, once parents and grandparents took to using the platform, its fashionable factor was greatly diminished. "It's hard to look cool when you're hanging out with mom and dad," said David Ebersman, the company's former chief financial officer.[103]

The permanence of Facebook posts was also a negative facet. Parents may have enjoyed sharing one of their kid's cutest antics, but few kids want their most awkward middle school moments to follow them into high school and college. The conundrum set the stage for an opportunity in social media.

In April 2011 a group of friends who were students at Stanford huddled to discuss a final project and turned a classroom assignment into a potential threat to Facebook's dominance. Snapchat capitalized on many millennials' desire to soften their social media footprint by extinguishing unflattering photos and mindless text messages—yet still stay connected.

Evan Spiegel, Bobby Murphy, and Reggie Brown saw a potential opportunity that Facebook, Google, Apple, and Microsoft missed. What started as an insignificant assignment was shaping up to become much more. The purpose of the app was to make the exchange of images and communication ephemeral, where whatever was sent or said would quickly vanish.[104]

Spiegel realized that existing forms of social media compelled users to curate a perfect online persona, which was labor intensive and sometimes led to regrets. "People are living with this massive burden of managing a digital version of themselves," Spiegel said. "It's taken all of the fun out of communicating."

Fundamentally, Snapchat would be about communication, but in a way that allows people to break from the burden of having to carefully construct an image. When Spiegel first shared the idea, several of his classmates doubted that a platform based on impermanent content would have any appeal. "Everyone said, 'That is a terrible idea,'" Spiegel remembers. "Not only is nobody going to use it, they said, but the only people who do, will use it for sexting."[105]

Nevertheless, it was Snapchat's vanishing message feature that made the app distinct. "Snapchat isn't about capturing the traditional Kodak moment. It's about communicating with the full range of human emotion—not just what appears to be pretty or perfect," said CEO Evan Spiegel when describing the company's goals and purpose in his first blog post. He went on to explain that Snapchat functions as a stress-free alternative to platforms such as Twitter and Facebook, where you don't have to worry about "emergency detagging of photos before job interviews or photoshopping blemishes out of candid shots before they hit the Internet."[106]

The company subsequently began tinkering with features to be more competitive and alluring, and it began reaching out to potential partners to appeal to a wider audience. In partnership with PayPal, it offered a digital wallet. It also began to allow users to choose how long messages would last.[107]

Snapchat reported a 415 percent increase in users for the first quarter of 2014, and by 2017 it had more than 100 million daily active users.[108]

"Snapchat has grown from a marketing question mark to a marketing must-have in a relatively short time," wrote Hootsuite social media blogger Dara Fontein. And Snapchat's gains did not go unnoticed by the company's competitors.[109] When Snapchat's founders turned down Facebook's $3 billion acquisition offer, Bloomberg characterized the older company's response as: "If we can't have you, we'll create our own versions of you."[110]

When Snapchat released its Stories function, which allows users to create a flipbook-style narrative themed around events such as birthday parties, copycats began to appear. Facebook-owned Instagram soon offered a disappearing story feature, helping the app reach 150 million daily users by winter 2017. Then came vertical video Twitter Moments, featuring curated collections of tweets and branded advertising, reminiscent of Snapchat.[111]

Snapchat co-founder and CEO Evan Spiegel responded: "If you want to be a creative company, you have got to be comfortable with and basically enjoy the fact that people copy your stuff."[112]

Despite tough competition, Snapchat has managed to rise to prominence since its advent in early 2011. Like MTV and *VICE*, the company has partnered with numerous entities to innovate and bring about original content. In a similar fashion, it also targets the 14- to 28-year-old demographic. However, whereas MTV and *VICE* target mostly males, Snapchat has a more evenly gendered user base.

Snapchat is becoming ever more popular as a platform for viewing certain events, so much so that more people watched the 2015 MTV Video Music Awards on Snapchat stories than on cable.[113]

Viacom, MTV's parent company, and Snapchat have now partnered to produce content, which is fitting because Snapchat and MTV have the same desired audience—the elusive millennials.

"Their influence in undeniable. It is part of the landscape. Snapchat is impacting storytelling and how people communicate with one another,"

Doug Herzog observed. "Now, what the future is? No one knows. The question is: Are they having their moment? Are there more moments to come?"

Other brands, networks, and shows working with Snapchat include "The Voice," E! News, and *ESPN.* Discovery Communications plans to bring Shark Week to Snapchat. In 2017 *Saturday Night Live* producers launched "Boycott," an original Snapchat series.[114]

One of the backers helping to drive Snapchat's ambition is Elisabeth Murdoch, daughter of media mogul Rupert Murdoch. She remained in the shadows after leaving her father's empire in the wake of *News Corp.*'s 2014 phone-hacking scandal. With those troubles behind, Murdoch began to position vertical networks to maximize Snapchat's potential far beyond its ephemeral messaging service roots.

"I don't think there are many other people at the vanguard of this platform creating content," Murdoch said. "But it's hard to deny the momentum and success Snapchat has with such a huge audience."[115]

Snapchat's foray into programming began with journalism. *Good Luck America* was produced by former CNN correspondent Peter Hamby who now heads the company's news initiatives. The program drew 5.2 million viewers each episode during its second season, a 53 percent increase from its first season.[116]

In spring 2017, Snapchat and *NBC News* announced plans to partner in the production of a four- to five-minute newscast. The platform's transition to series production began with one program per week, then expanded to five. The company announced it would feature 20 different weekly shows by the end of 2017, including a mix of documentaries, news, reality shows, and dramas—intending to emerge not just as a competitor, but as the next standard in entertainment.[117]

"We're still in the learning phase but we're very encouraged by the response to these shows," said Sean Mills, head of original content at Snapchat. "It's a huge opportunity considering the tens of billions of video views on Snapchat every day, and we're at the very early stages."[118]

The potential revenue from advertising attracts significant partners, which is what Snapchat needs to keep filling its pipeline. And seeking more than just money, legacy networks are coming to Snapchat in hopes of connecting with TV's lost generation, the millennials. Snapchat has attracted 41 percent of 18- to 34-year-old Americans across its growing services. For comparison, only 6 percent of that demographic is spread across the top 15 TV networks.[119]

"We are getting a lot of interest from networks, studios and production companies, and from talent directly," explained Mills. "I think we're being pretty open minded about how it's all going to evolve or work. We think all these can be great partners."

Snapchat desires to do what *VICE* failed to do—have millennials watch television, but on mobile devices rather than on big flat screens. And so far, it is working.

New York Times writer Farhad Manjoo said, "Snapchat has quietly become one of the world's most innovative and influential consumer technology companies." He went on to explain that Snapchat "is pushing radically new ideas about how humans should interact with computers. It is pioneering a model of social networking that feels more intimate and authentic than the Facebook-led ideas that now dominate the online world. Snapchat's software and hardware designs, as well as its marketing strategies, are more daring than much of what we've seen from tech giants, including Apple."[120]

However, despite the enthusiasm and growing array of features available through Snapchat, the mobile app only has an eighth of the daily users as the current king, Facebook. Snapchat's revenue per user is also only 20 percent of what Facebook makes per user.[121]

Snapchat faces additional challenges that can accompany rapid growth in the tech sector. To handle the millions of users chatting and sending images everyday, the company expects to spend more than $2 billion on Google cloud computing services over the next half decade.[122]

Between 2015 and 2016, costs swelled by 148 percent. Advertising revenue increased 157 percent during that period, but it was still $30 million lower than anticipated. Overall, the company fell well short of Wall Street's first-quarter predictions, announcing a shocking $2.2 billion loss.[123]

However, Snapchat's appeal to the public and partners has increased with a pronounced upward trend despite increasing operation costs. As of this book's publication, Snapchat has more than 158 million daily users, which far exceeds that of Twitter when it went public. And although this number is well below what Facebook possessed when it went public, Snapchat has proven to be a formidable contender.[124]

CHAPTER FOUR

Reimagining Revenue: Paywalls, Crowdfunding, and the End of the Advertising Age

"The future does not fit in the containers of the past."
—Rishad Tobaccowala

The summer of 2012 was an unlikely time for optimism in the U.S. newspaper business. In the prior decade, print advertising revenue declined more than 50 percent; media companies' stock prices plummeted; daily newspapers folded in Cincinnati, Seattle, Baltimore, and Denver (not to mention dozens of small towns around the country); and more than 13,000 reporters lost their jobs.[1] Circulation was dropping, and experts were predicting that newspapers would soon be obsolete.

If there was any escaping this downward spiral, nobody in the industry seemed to have it figured out. But that's what made Aaron Kushner's purchase of the *Orange County Register* in 2012 so tantalizing: *Kushner wasn't from the industry*. The Stanford economics and organizational analysis graduate had made his fortune during the dot-com boom, when he launched (and later sold) a successful Web company. At no point in his career had Kushner even worked in a newsroom, let alone owned a newspaper. But if what the news business needed was fresh thinking, the logic went, then perhaps Kushner was the perfect guy for the job.

There was, of course, plenty of cause for skepticism. Only five years earlier, billionaire real estate magnate Sam Zell had taken the helm at

Tribune Co., the parent company of the *Chicago Tribune* and *Los Angeles Times*, amid hopes he could stabilize revenue and "revive a media empire;" instead, he saddled Tribune Co. with debt and led the company into Chapter 11 bankruptcy.[2] That memory made some journalists wary of the *Register*'s new owner—but others believed Kushner was different. Unlike Zell and other deep-pocketed businessmen who'd swooped into the newspaper industry with more bluster than vision, Kushner actually had a plan, and it was a plan that journalists loved: instead of cutting costs by laying off reporters and scaling back the newspaper, he wanted to make the *Register* a must-read publication again by *expanding* the newsroom and doubling down on deep-dive reporting. It was, according to local journalist Gustavo Arellano, a "field of dreams" strategy for journalism: "If you build it up, readers will come," Arellano summarized. "Discourage web hits for the sake of web hits, and reporters will come. Erect a paywall on your website and beef up the print edition, and people will subscribe. Then advertisers will pay. Then the revenue comes in, and journalism is saved."[3]

Within a year of Kushner's takeover, the *Register* had hired 200 newsroom staff, added dozens of new print sections, created a trainee program to cultivate young talent, and even improved the quality of the paper stock.[4] The changes endeared him to journalists inside the newsroom ("Frankly, I still have to pinch myself every morning to remind myself Kushner is for real," one reporter marveled) and enchanted those on the outside.[5] "Can Aaron Kushner save the *Orange County Register*—and the newspaper industry?" asked Ryan Chittum of the *Columbia Journalism Review*.[6]

"Just amazed at what's happening at OC Register right now," tweeted Mark Katches, a former *Register* editor. "If the OC Register can pull off this major hiring spree and show that it works, it will be amazingly great for print journalism."[7]

The hitch in this fairytale story is that Kushner's plan didn't work. In fact, it never came close. Despite the huge investment of resources, weekday circulation for the *Register* grew less than 3 percent during Kushner's tenure, and advertisers never came rushing back, forcing the company to lay off hundreds of employees and cut back its print offerings.[8] Meanwhile, the *Los Angeles Register* and *Long Beach Register*—two other daily newspapers launched by Kushner's company, Freedom Communications— both failed within two years, and in March 2015, Kushner resigned from his CEO post. Eight months later, Freedom Communications filed for bankruptcy.

The reason for starting the chapter with this reinvention-story-gone-wrong is not to suggest that commercial newspapers—or commercial journalism, for that matter—are doomed to fail. (In fact, we hope to demonstrate otherwise.) Rather, we begin here because the fate of Kushner's grand experiment underscores several important realities that inform the analysis in this chapter.

The first reality is that money matters. Blue-sky visions for journalism's future have their place, but the *Register*'s unraveling demonstrates that quality journalism cannot exist without a smart business model. Revenue questions invite no easy answers, of course, but we believe a thorough examination of journalism's future cannot exist without them.

The second reality is that medium matters. Kushner's print-centric strategy might have worked in a world of Boomers, but a growing share of today's news consumers have never read a hard-copy newspaper in their lives. Kushner, by looking for journalism's future in its rear-view mirror, failed to recognize that it's these younger readers—not their parents—who will ultimately shape what works and what fails in the new media ecosystem.

Finally, the third reality is that legacy institutions matter, even when their traditional news products become obsolete. The reason for this is simple: despite the rise of citizen journalism and digital startups on the Internet, institutions like the *Register* still employ the vast majority of this country's investigative journalists and beat reporters. As former *Los Angeles Times* editor John Carroll reminds us, you can "take any story in a blog and trace its origins, [and] about 85 percent of it can be traceable to newspapers. They break nearly all of the important stories. Who's going to do the reporting if these institutions fade away?"[9] Maybe digital startups or foundation-backed nonprofits will eventually shoulder that load, but for now legacy institutions still do the majority of the heavy lifting, making it as important as ever to seek answers to journalism's most elusive question in the digital age: who's going to pay?

The (False) Promise of Digital Advertising

In 2011 media critic and author Dean Starkman described an emerging intellectual consensus about the "Future of News"—or FON, for short.[10] This anti-institution, pro-disruption consensus, championed by the likes of Jeff Jarvis and Clay Shirky, mostly sidestepped thorny business-model questions, like how journalism's future would pay for itself. But to the extent that FON adherents muddied their boots with matters of revenue, they seemed to agree on at least one thing: paywalls would never work. According to the FON consensus, news and information were destined to be free on the Internet, and news organizations that did not yield to this logic would inevitably be toppled by it, a premise seemingly validated in

2007 when the *New York Times* ended its TimesSelect paywall experiment following disappointing results. If the *Times* couldn't pull off a paywall, the argument went, then what mainstream newspaper *possibly could*?

The FON consensus was famously short on proposed alternatives ("Nothing will work, but everything might. Now is the time for experiments, lots and lots of experiments," Shirky wrote in 2009), but its resistance to paywalls and digital subscriptions implied at least some measure of faith in *digital advertising*.[11] As Jarvis wrote in response to the Times-Select shutdown: "The *Times* killed the service in 2007 and freed its content again for a few simple reasons: First, it increased the audience to the paper's site . . . Second, the *Times* could make more money on the advertising shown to its additional audience. Third, opening up improved the paper's Googlejuice by bringing in more clicks and links, which in turn yielded more traffic"—and more digital ad revenue.[12] The *Times*' own statement on the decision similarly hinted that audience and advertising growth were major factors. "We believe offering unfettered access to *New York Times* reporting and analysis best serves the interest of our readers, our brand and the long-term vitality of our journalism," senior vice president Vivian Schiller wrote. "We encourage everyone to read our news and opinion—as well as share it, link to it and comment on it."[13]

The *Times*' pivot away from reader support and toward digital advertising revenue seemed like a sign of the times. Aside from the *Wall Street Journal* and a handful of other niche publications with successful paywalls, most news organizations in the late 2000s were settling for a strategy of giving away content for free and trying to cobble their way to profitability through some combination of digital advertising and editorial cost cutting. Even Starkman, a staunch believer in subscriber-supported journalism, acknowledged that the industry's momentum was moving in the opposite direction. "Let's face it," he wrote, "the FON crowd has had the upper hand. The establishment is gloomy and old; the FON consensus is hopeful and young (or purports to represent youth). The establishment has no plan. The FON consensus says no plan is the plan. The establishment drones on about rules and standards; the FON thinkers talk about freedom and informality. FON says 'cheap' and 'free;' the establishment asks for your credit card number."[14]

Starkman's "establishment" thinking seemed on the ropes back then, as news organizations placed their bets with digital advertising and ditched efforts to charge for content. But that soon changed. In 2010 and 2011 subscription models came roaring back across the news industry—and this time they showed signs of promise. In Minnesota the *Minneapolis Star Tribune* quickly enrolled 18,000 digital subscribers after launching a "metered paywall" that gave readers access to 20 free articles each month before requiring them to pay.[15] In South Carolina, the *Post and Courier* boosted circulation revenue by $1.6 million within only nine months of adding a digital-only subscription option and pricier print-plus-digital bundle.[16] And at the *New York Times*, a new-and-improved metered paywall reversed the results of its failed TimesSelect experiment. By July 2012 the *Times* had amassed more than 500,000 digital subscribers (and counting), helping push total circulation revenue past total advertising revenue for the first time in its parent company's history.[17]

As paywalls started to show results, dozens of other news organizations joined the bandwagon, including some that had fiercely resisted the idea. The *Washington Post* added a paywall in June 2013 after years of holding out, and five months later, Digital First Media CEO John Paton, who'd previously dismissed digital subscription revenue as "a stack of pennies," announced that his company would be launching its own paywall experiment.[18] With Paton's defection, media economist Ken Doctor estimated that more than 40 percent of all U.S. newspapers in 2013 were employing some form of digital-subscription model. "Even the paywall contrarians," Doctor wrote, "are coming around."[19]

This trend can be explained in part by improvements in the mechanics and implementation of paywalls, which started to become more sophisticated after the TimesSelect failure. However, the other half of the equation is that digital advertising, the main alternative to paywalls, fell well short of expectations. Between 2003 and 2013, newspaper revenue from digital advertising inched up from $1.2 billion to $3.5 billion, while print advertising revenue dropped precipitously from $44.9 billion to $16.4 billion, leaving a hole of $26.2 billion.[20] Digital advertising may continue to grow for newspapers, but there's cause for skepticism.

For one, millennials are downloading digital ad blockers at a staggering clip, and increasingly so are their parents. In the United States, 18 percent of Internet users are now blocking ads online, according to 2017 data, including 15 percent of users over 55 years old.[21] This ad-blocking trend has mostly happened on desktop browsers, but mobile devices are quickly catching up: in May 2016 the *New York Times* reported that mobile ad-blocking adoption had doubled over the previous year, with one in five smartphone users worldwide now blocking ads on their mobile devices.[22] News organizations that depend on advertising revenue for survival are rightly concerned. According to a 2016 report by AOL, 49 percent of publishers identified ad blockers as a "primary mobile challenge for publishers," ranking it ahead of all other prospective pitfalls. "We're probably in the first inning of ad blockers in mobile," AOL executive Matt Gillis said, "[but] I think publishers are concerned about it because they've seen it creep into other mediums."[23]

Another foreboding sign for advertising-supported digital publishers is that the global ad market is increasingly dominated by middlemen. In 2015 five tech companies—Facebook, Google, Yahoo!, Verizon, and Twitter—accounted for more 65 percent of all digital advertising revenue, including 80 percent of the year-over-year growth.[24] It's not clear exactly how much money trickles down to U.S. news publishers, but credible estimates range from $5 billion to $12 billion.[25] That's not a pittance, but it's not likely to support growth in the industry, especially as print advertising revenue—still a multibillion-dollar business—continues its decline. "This is going to get worse," Alan Rusbridger, former editor of *The Guardian*, said in 2016, citing Facebook and Google's growing market share. "They have a means of distribution which we simply can't cope with."[26]

There are still a *few* slivers of promise in the digital advertising world. In 2016 podcast advertising revenue grew 72 percent, from $69 million to $119 million—with revenue projected to grow another 85 percent in 2017.[27] Some publishers have also found early success with "affiliate linking," an emerging form of native advertising that allows publishers like *The Wirecutter* to receive a kickback whenever consumers buy a product featured on their site. (In 2016 the *New York Times* purchased *The Wirecutter* for $30 million, joining national outlets such as *Gizmodo* and Vox Media that have already embraced affiliate linking.) And then there's the most ballyhooed growth opportunity of all: mobile video advertising, a market that grew 145 percent in 2016, generating $4.2 billion in total revenue.[28] Many news organizations are scrambling to capitalize on this trend by beefing up their video teams or partnering with automated video-production companies such as Wochit and Wibbitz to churn out video at scale. "Right now, we're doing a couple hundred videos a day," Tronc chairman Michael Ferro said in 2016. "We think we should be doing 2,000 videos a day."[29] Ferro's enthusiasm for video is an extreme example, but he's not alone. When Reuters asked news publishers about their plans for online video, 79 percent said they planned to invest more than the year before, reflecting the industry's broad optimism about its prospects for revenue growth.[30]

So, will video be the magic bullet that finally makes digital advertising viable for publishers? Even amid the current hype, it doesn't seem likely. The reality is that ad-blocking software poses the same threat for video as for display advertising, and Google and Facebook still control the primary means of distribution, making it difficult to envision a path to sustained revenue growth. In addition, industry analysts say news organizations shouldn't expect the video market's high advertising rates to stick around as supply increases and as less engaging formats become the norm. "There's a stampede toward video because that's where the high [cost per thousand (CPM) impressions] are," Gershon Media president Bernard Gershon said. "But you get the high CPMs in high-quality environments like a scripted drama or live TV. You're not creating that environment while someone scrolls through their Facebook feed with the mute on."[31]

The generally bleak outlook for journalism's digital advertising future has contributed to a reversal in the "future of news consensus," according to Starkman, who claimed victory for the pro-paywall argument only three years after declaring it on the ropes. "The intra-journalism debate that has unfurled over the last couple years has been heated and often angry, sometimes surprisingly enlightening, sometimes deeply stupid," he explained. "But now, it shows signs of abating. I see a consensus taking hold, one that, all in all, is much, much healthier for public-interest reporting than the old one."[32]

Ryan Chittum, one of Starkman's colleagues, stated the case even more forcefully: "The war is over," he declared in 2012. "The evidence is in. Newspapers, large and small, premium and not, gain additional revenue through subscriptions and lose little if anything in digital ads."[33]

The growing consensus behind reader-supported journalism now also includes Twitter co-founder and Medium CEO Ev Williams, who announced plans in 2017 to nix Medium's advertising business and replace it with a member-supported subscriber model. "Ad-driven systems can only reward attention," Williams told the *New York Times*. "They can't reward the right answer. Consumer-paid systems can. They can reward value. The inevitable solution: People will have to pay for quality content."[34]

None of this is to suggest that paywalls have been an instant or universal success. They haven't. Paywalls still "generate only a small fraction of industry revenue," according to a 2016 research study, and dozens of paywall experiments have come and gone with only modest success.[35] However, despite these setbacks, the trend line remains clear: news publishers in the United States increasingly agree that paywalls are a vital part of journalism's revenue future. The only question now is how to best implement them—and after more than a decade of experimentation, the answer is finally coming into focus.

The *New York Times*, the *Boston Globe*, and Solving the Paywall Puzzle

Although the failure of TimesSelect in 2007 was widely interpreted as a sign that news consumers wouldn't pay for journalism on the Internet, it's clear now, 10 years later, that the naysayers spoke too soon. As of

April 2017 the *New York Times* had added 2.2 million digital-only subscribers since launching a new-and-improved paywall in 2010, and executive editor Dean Baquet was projecting even stronger growth on the horizon.[36] "We think that there are many, many, many, many people—millions of people all around the world—who want what the *New York Times* offers," he told *WIRED*. "And we believe that if we get those people, they will pay, and they will pay greatly."[37]

The *Times* owes at least some of its recent revenue growth to President Trump, whose attacks on the media coincided with a sharp rise in subscriptions following the 2016 election. However, the newspaper's paywall success is also a testament to the lessons the *Times* learned from its first paywall experiment and the changes it made for Round 2, including its pivot from a "hard" paywall to a metered approach. With the TimesSelect service, readers were required to pay $7.95/month before they could read even a *single* article from the paper's opinion section or archives. About 135,000 digital-only subscribers signed up within the first two months, but growth quickly slowed to a trickle, in part because nonsubscribers never had the chance to see what they were missing.[38] Meanwhile, the hard paywall also cut into the newspaper's ad revenue as stories by popular columnists like Maureen Dowd and Paul Krugman reached fewer readers than before the paywall.

The *Times* responded to these flaws by adopting a metered approach, allowing readers to access up to ten articles each month before running into the paywall. Additionally, the newspaper began to experiment with market segmentation and targeted pricing, creating new product offerings catered and marketed to specific audiences, such as college students and crossword enthusiasts. By identifying these audience segments and designing products with their specific needs and price points in mind, the *Times* has been able to generate additional revenue from unlikely sources, while also cultivating brand loyalty that may pay further dividends down the road.

Together, these innovations have turned digital subscriptions into the cornerstone of the *Times*' business model and its plans for the future. In 2016, CEO Mark Thompson set a goal of reaching 10 million digital subscribers, a reader-centric vision echoed by the company's "2020 Report," which detailed the newspaper's strategy for growth leading up to 2020.[39] The report concluded:

> We are, in the simplest terms, a subscription-first business. Our focus on subscribers sets us apart in crucial ways from many other media organizations. We are not trying to maximize clicks and sell low-margin

advertising against them. We are not trying to win a pageviews arms race. We believe that the more sound business strategy for the *Times* is to provide journalism so strong that several million people around the world are willing to pay for it.[40]

The *Times* is often cited as Exhibit A in the argument for paywalls in journalism, but as skeptics point out, the paper's deep pockets, international reach, and global reputation are not luxuries enjoyed by most other newspapers trying to implement digital-subscription models. For these organizations, a more apt example for comparison is the *Boston Globe*, a metropolitan daily newspaper that increased its digital subscriber count to roughly 84,000 in 2016, up 29 percent from the year before.[41] Like the *Times,* the *Globe* initially launched with a hard paywall before pivoting to a metered approach, which currently gives readers access to two free articles per month. This two-article threshold is one of the stingiest in the news business, but it appears to be working: in 2015 the *Globe* was able to raise its base subscription price to nearly $7/week—one of the highest rates in the country—without sacrificing subscriber growth. "It wasn't just luck," said Daniel Burstein, director of editorial content at MECLABS. "Peter [Doucette, vice president of consumer sales and marketing] conducts a lot of testing to learn about his customers, and he really looks at the data."[42]

Although there is no one-size-fits-all solution for implementing paywalls, a few common themes are starting to emerge from the most successful experiments. For one, paywall-protected content must be worth paying for, because no rational consumer is going to cough up money for unoriginal, formulaic content that looks exactly like what they receive from other sites for free. Consumers need unique value, and that's only created when news organizations invest in quality journalism. Consider the case of the *Washington Post*, which has hired dozens of reporters and spent millions on digital innovation initiatives since Amazon CEO Jeff Bezos purchased the struggling newspaper in 2013. The *Post* was a late adopter of paywalls, but in July 2016 the paper reported 145 percent year-over-year growth in digital subscriptions—a sign that the investments were paying off.[43] "Be riveting, be right, and ask people to pay," Bezos said of his advice for news organizations. "You can't shrink your way to profitability."[44]

Bezos's pro-growth philosophy is shared by editors at the *Globe*, where the "Spotlight" investigative team and the paper's innovative "Ideas" section continually produce some of the best metro journalism in the United States. According to Kathleen Kingsbury, who until recently served as the *Globe*'s managing editor for digital, these types of premium content drive the highest share of subscription conversions because they provide readers with insight and information that they can't access anywhere else. "If you're doing high-impact journalism, which we really try [to] do every day, then that drives subscriptions," Kingsbury said. "That makes people want to subscribe to the *Globe*."[45] Industry-wide numbers appear to back her up. According to Ken Doctor, the average U.S. daily newspaper spends 12.5 percent of its annual budget on content creation; at the *Times*, the *Globe*, and the *Minneapolis Star Tribune* (another metro newspaper with a successful paywall) that number is closer to 20 percent.[46] "Readers know quality, depth, and breadth when they see it, and they're willing to pay for it," Doctor wrote in 2015. "There's a lesson in that for the industry."[47]

Another important lesson is that the mechanics of paywalls matter almost as much as the content behind them. The TimesSelect experiment is a perfect example. Between 2007 and 2011, the *Times* did not reinvent its journalism, nor did readers suddenly become more inclined to pay for digital news content. What changed was the paywall itself, which became broader and more porous, allowing the *Times* to successfully navigate the delicate balance between audience growth and conversion rates. As executive vice president for product and technology Kinsey Wilson explains: "We're a general interest publication. We need to create a great experience for subscribers, but we want a great experience for people who are consuming it lightly, too."[48]

Finally, a third lesson from successful paywall experiments is that the "newspaper" is no longer a single product; rather, it's a loose digital *bundle* that can be broken into separate news products and marketed and sold to niche audiences. The *Times* utilized this product differentiation strategy to acquire 200,000 paying customers for its crossword-only subscription option. Meanwhile, news consumers elsewhere have shown they're willing to pay for products as small as a single investigation or one-time storytelling project, giving rise to a new revenue trend in journalism: crowdfunding.

The Guardian, De Correspondent, and Crowdfunding the News

One side effect of Donald Trump's bluster during the 2016 presidential campaign is that journalists paid relatively little attention to the Republican Party's policy vision, which happened to include one of the most unconventional land-use proposals in modern times: the defederalization of public lands. "Congress should give authority to state regulators to manage energy resources on federally controlled public lands within their respective borders," the Republican Party platform stated. "Congress shall immediately pass universal legislation providing for a timely and orderly mechanism requiring the federal government to convey certain federally controlled public lands to states."[49]

Despite being overshadowed in the mainstream media by health care coverage and Russia-related scoops, the Trump administration's public-lands policy continued to matter a great deal to hunters, fishermen, ranchers, environmentalists, and other rural Westerners—and *The Guardian* sensed an opportunity. "Today, the Guardian US launches This Land is Your Land, a new series to hold politicians and corporate interests accountable for their environmental policies," the news organization announced in June 2017. "We're asking our readers to join us in this project, by helping us raise $50,000 to support our coverage throughout the year."[50]

The campaign raced past its $50,000 target within 36 hours, and by late July, *The Guardian* had raised nearly $100,000—more than the cost of a full-time reporter's annual salary. This success story was only the latest sign of crowdfunding's growing footprint in journalism, where news organizations are increasingly looking to raise revenue around specific projects or initiatives. Other recent examples include:

- **In the Shadow of Liberty**: In 2016 the Center for Cooperative Media used Beacon, a now-defunct crowdfunding platform for journalism, to raise more than $31,000 of funding for In the Shadow of Liberty, a reporting series about immigration policy and immigrant communities in New Jersey.[51]

- **Trumpocracy: The Russia Connection**: With the Trump administration's entanglements with Russia growing ever murkier, *Mother Jones* launched a crowdfunding campaign in May 2017 to support additional investigative reporting on the Russia story. It took only 72 hours for the campaign to raise $15,000 in new monthly donations and $100,000 in one-time gifts, surpassing its initial goal. "We weren't sure how you, our readers, were going to respond to the idea of doubling down on this beat," CEO Monika Bauerlein and editor-in-chief Clara Jeffery wrote in a May 15 update. "But now we know you think it's enormously important—and that you want us to go as hard as humanly possible."[52]

- **Statehouse News Project**: In 2015 nonprofit news outlet InvestigateWest raised nearly $3,000 from 53 donors to support its Statehouse News Project, an initiative to improve public-accountability news reporting on the Washington State legislature. A year later, InvestigateWest raised $6,170 from 72 funders to repeat the project.[53]

- **The Ferguson Fellowship**: After the Black Lives Matter protests in Ferguson, Missouri, the Huffington Post raised more than $40,000 to keep Mariah Stewart on the ground as a reporter for 12 months. Huffington Post successfully crowdfunded the Ferguson Fellowship again a year later.[54]

- **Investigating Internships**: In 2013 *ProPublica* crowdfunded an investigation into the ethics and equity of the internship economy. The campaign raised about $24,000, which *ProPublica* used to hire an intern to lead its investigation.[55]

- *Boston Review* **website**: In 2012 *Boston Review*, a nonprofit magazine, raised more than $13,000 with Kickstarter to upgrade its website.[56]

Crowdfunding still makes up only a small slice of journalism's total revenue pie, but its share is getting larger. According to a Pew Research Center study, the number of journalism projects successfully funded on Kickstarter grew from 64 in 2010 to 173 in the first nine months of 2015. The total funding also grew significantly during that period, from less than $300,000 to more than $1.7 million.[57]

In addition to funding specific projects, crowdfunding has emerged as a viable option for getting startups off the ground. Among the most notable examples is *De Correspondent*, a Dutch news site that raised $1.7 million in 2013 to "uncover, explain and highlight deep-lying structures and long-term developments that powerfully shape our world, rather than reporting on the latest hype, scare, or breaking news story."[58] The crowdfunding campaign received 5,000 individual contributions in the first hour and surpassed its initial fundraising goal within eight days, but what's even more remarkable is that funders contributed their money without knowing exactly what they were buying: *De Correspondent*'s campaign articulated a general vision for the outlet, but all the details were to-be-determined.[59] "When you try to sell an idea, it's very easy to refer to what people know—'the platform looks like this, and you can compare the writing style with that,'" editor-in-chief Rob Wijnberg said. "We didn't want to do that, because we really wanted to be able to create something new—start with a clean slate."[60]

De Correspondent's $1.7 million campaign set a record for crowdfunding in journalism, but two other European startups have since come close to or surpassed that total: *El Español*, a Madrid-based digital news site that crowdfunded 3 million euros in 2015, and *Krautreporter*, an ad-free German magazine that raised $1.38 million in 2014. According to Khari Johnson, founder of the *Between the Cracks* blog, what all three campaigns shared was an emphasis on "attracting an initial audience, not just money"—an insight also shared by *De Correspondent* co-founder Ernst-Jan Pfauth: "Crowdfunding in journalism is not so much about 'selling' a product, but much more about 'growing a community,'" Pfauth wrote. "That makes it important to focus on aspects that strengthen the feeling of belonging to a movement, rather than on 'offering the best deal.' People who back journalism projects aren't in it for 'a deal;' they're in it because they want to support something they deem important."[61]

Gabe Bullard, a 2015 Nieman Fellow, reached a similar conclusion in a 2016 report for Nieman, arguing that crowdfunding is less a "business model that will save journalism" and more "part of a philosophy." According to Bullard, "[projects] that succeed, whether they're in Texas, St. Louis, or the Netherlands, come from journalists who want something besides a paycheck, and who are willing to use their support and supporters to produce reporting that's innovative, engaging, and about much more than money."[62]

Arguably, the real value of crowdfunding is the opportunity it provides news organizations to better tell their story. Instead of a purely transactional pitch (e.g., "send us $5 a month, and we'll deliver the Sunday newspaper to your doorstep"), what crowdfunding encourages is a more compelling, thoughtful statement of value to the community. Effective crowdfunding pitches say, "We believe that digging into municipal corruption (or environmental pollution, or Donald Trump's entanglements, etc.) serves the public's interests, and we need your help to do it"—an ask that speaks to people as altruistic supporters, not merely as consumers.

Donald Trump's presidency has provided much low-hanging fruit for journalistic crowdfunding, but news organizations should already be thinking about life beyond the current administration. What happens when the White House is occupied by a less divisive president whose policies are less offensive to mainstream news consumers? What happens when the freedom of the press is no longer under daily attack, or when the public reverts to taking journalism for granted? To sustain the momentum generated by Trump's presidency, news organizations will need to craft a message that's focused less on what journalism is *against* and more on what it's *for*. With respect to the *Washington Post*, "democracy dies in darkness" is probably insufficient. The pitch for journalism must be more compelling and more personal, making the promise to serve *you*, to raise *your* voices, to report on *your* interests, to strengthen *your* communities.

If news organizations can deliver on this promise, then we expect the opportunities for revenue growth through crowdfunding to long outlive the Trump presidency. But even alongside digital subscription growth, this won't be enough. As advertising revenue continues its long-term slide, news organizations will also need to explore other monetization strategies that can complement donations, subscriptions, and memberships. One good place to start? Live events.

Live Events, Big Data, and Journalism New(s) Events

A light-hearted comedy "roast" in Minnesota raised $160,000.[63] A live storytelling series in Arizona landed a $100,000 sponsorship.[64] A slate of politically themed events in Texas brought in $1.2 million.[65]

These are just a few of the success stories from journalism's ascendant events business, which has emerged as a key revenue stream for dozens of news organizations across the country, from digital startups to legacy newspapers. Many of these organizations view events primarily as an editorial initiative—an innovative new way to reach audiences with compelling content—but the revenue is nothing to sneeze at: *The Atlantic*, the *Texas Tribune*, the *Chattanooga Times Free Press*, and *MinnPost* have all built robust event businesses that account for 10 percent or more of their annual revenue, while at the digital news site Billy Penn, that number has eclipsed 80 percent.[66] "Events are a proven way to diversify revenue that, if done right, are significantly harder to disrupt than other revenue models," Kevin Loker wrote in 2014. "They deepen connections with audiences and sponsors. They reinforce multiple values of a publishing brand. And they can grow."[67]

Events come in a wide range of styles and formats, and they feature a number of different monetization strategies, including ticket sales, sponsorships, and vendor fees. Critics have raised questions about the ethics of accepting corporate money to sponsor events, but defenders argue that accepting sponsorships for an event is no different than running advertisements in a print newspaper. (In both cases, companies pay news organizations money for access to an audience; all that changes is the delivery format.) Additionally, news organizations have tried to address ethical concerns by disclosing the sponsors of their events and by setting clear restrictions on those sponsors' influence. The *Texas Tribune*'s code of ethics, for example, states that event sponsors "do not determine the panelists, the subject matter or the line of questioning."[68]

Ultimately, any qualms about the ethics of sponsored events do not seem to be slowing down the sector's rise in journalism. The *Tribune* netted nearly $1.2 million from events in 2013, and the list of news organizations hosting annual events has grown to include *Willamette Week*, an alternative weekly newspaper that stages TechFestNW and MusicFestNW in Portland, Oregon; the *New York Times*, which organized 16 conferences around the world in 2013; the *New Yorker*, which hosts the annual New Yorker Festival; and dozens of other publications, big and small, across the country.

Celeste LeCompte, vice president of business development at *ProPublica*, says the growth of live events is indicative of a broader philosophical pivot in the industry—from viewing journalism as an "article business" to viewing it as an "information-finding, knowledge-making, storytelling, community-building business."[69] According to LeCompte, stepping back and understanding the source of journalism's value will help news organizations come up with innovative new ways to deliver that value to consumers. "Events are one part of that," she explained in a phone interview. "I suspect we'll see more ideas about how to capture that value over time."[70]

One example from LeCompte's own work is the ProPublica Data Store, which repackages data compiled by *ProPublica*'s reporting team and then sells it to external clients, including other news organizations. Launched in 2014, the Data Store generated more than $200,000 in its first two years, inspiring LeCompte and *ProPublica* to expand its offerings and start selling data sets provided by other organizations.[71] "So many news organizations have these kinds of datasets, but don't have the resources to build out a marketing channel or sales support system to do anything with them," LeCompte told Nieman Lab in 2016. "We want to offer that support."[72]

Product development is still a relatively new trend in journalism, but there are already promising signs of progress, from the *Washington Post*'s investment in audience-management and AI software under Bezos to the innovations by RYOT Media and the *New York Times* in virtual reality storytelling, a long-hyped technology that finally seems poised for a breakthrough.

None of these revenue opportunities are likely to be a magic bullet that replaces advertising revenue in one swoop, but they should offer hope that Aaron Kushner's dream to rebuild journalism's business model through high-value, public-interest news reporting isn't a fantasy. The vision he tried to implement at the *Register* can happen; it just needs more time, more experimentation, and more capital.

And a whole lot less paper and ink.

CHAPTER FIVE

Reimagining What's Next: Enduring Questions for the Future of Journalism

"In a time of drastic change, it is the learners who inherit the future. The learned usually find themselves equipped to live in a world that no longer exists."[1]

—Eric Hoffer

Imagine for a moment that it's January 1, 2030, and journalism is dying. Or maybe it's already dead. Since the Big Recession of 2020, more than 700 legacy news outlets have either filed for bankruptcy or sold out to Algorithm Media Group, a multinational corporation that uses artificial intelligence and geolocation technology to generate "trendy" content and deliver it directly to people's mobile phones—all without human journalists. Hyperlocal news sites, community bloggers, and nonprofit news organizations still exist, of course, but their content has become harder to find online since the end of the open Internet, which suffered a pair of fatal blows during the Trump administration: first, the decision to roll back Obama-era net neutrality regulations, and second, the landmark mergers between Google and Verizon and Facebook and AT&T. These mega-corporations now serve as gatekeepers of the modern Internet, charging publishers for the right to "be discovered" on their platforms and taking an ever-growing cut of the digital ad revenue generated by publishers' content. In this landscape, the only hope for survival is volume, an economic reality brazenly exploited by hyperpartisan outlets like *Breitbart*, which is now the top "news" source for conservatives, and Progressive Media International, a digital media conglomerate with more than 200 news sites, each speaking to its own narrow identity group on the Left. Unsurprisingly, this fracturing of progressive media has been mirrored by a fracturing of progressive politics. For the last decade, liberals have routinely split their votes between three minority parties, helping Republicans maintain control of Congress and allowing Steve Bannon to claim an electoral majority in the 2028 presidential race, despite winning only 29 percent of the popular vote. (Three progressive candidates and one mainstream Republican split the other 71 percent.) On November 7, 2028, *Breitbart* offered this summary for its 80 million daily readers: "DESPITE MAINSTREAM MEDIA LIES, BANNON WINS IN A LANDSLIDE, RECEIVING MANDATE FROM REAL AMERICA."

Conversely, imagine that it's January 1, 2030, and journalism is thriving. It's been nine years since President Elizabeth Warren signed the Restoring Democracy Act, a sweeping reform package meant to insulate American democracy from demagogic leaders. Among other measures, the act established the country's first nationwide tax to support public-interest journalism, generating billions of dollars each year to fund local nonprofit news outlets across the country.[2] Together, these local newsrooms have helped turn the engaged journalism movement's vision into a reality, with journalists now routinely using digital tools and in-person convenings to facilitate conversation across ideological, racial, and cultural divides. Meanwhile, even the dynastic social media world has undergone a transformation: following a string of public-relations snafus, including the fallout from a scathing FCC report on fake news, Facebook has lost 50 percent of its market share in the United States, where a majority of millennials now prefer CiviSquare, a mission-based nonprofit founded by three former Facebook engineers who wanted to make social media more, well, social. Neighborhood groups, local governments, community activists, and public schools all use the platform for grassroots organizing, and millions of news junkies visit the site for its curated stream of reliable, fact-checked content from across the political spectrum.

So, what path are we heading down? In reality, of course, journalism's future probably won't conform to either hypothetical, at least not perfectly. But we find these extremes useful as a way to consider the potential consequences of political and social decisions being made today—and to illustrate what's at stake, both for journalism and democracy.

Our analysis in this book has focused so far on broad issues of truth, trust, reach, and revenue in journalism. But we recognize that many of the forces shaping the future of news don't fit neatly into such categories. In this chapter, we try to connect some of the missing pieces, starting with perhaps the timeliest of all: the fate of Donald Trump's war against the media.

Will Donald Trump Squash the News Media or Be Squashed by It?

We should start by acknowledging the elephant in the writer's studio: by the time you read this sentence, Donald Trump may no longer be president of the United States.

In the months before this book went to press, we learned that Donald Trump Jr. and high-level campaign staff secretly met with a Russian lawyer who promised dirt on the Clinton campaign; that Michael Flynn and Jared Kushner attempted to establish "backchannel" communications with Russia prior to Inauguration Day; that President Trump shared highly classified information with Russian diplomats during a meeting in the West Wing; that Attorney General Jeff Sessions had two undisclosed meetings with Russian Ambassador Sergey Kislyak during the 2016 campaign; and that Trump asked FBI Director James Comey for his "loyalty" and encouraged him to back off from the investigation into Michael Flynn before unceremoniously firing Comey weeks later.

These remarkable scoops were all first reported by the news media— and mostly by two newspapers: the *New York Times* and the *Washington Post*. During a one-week stretch in early 2017, these two rivals seemed to break major news almost every day, adding new layers to an increasingly unseemly narrative surrounding Trump's relationship with Russia. By May, even Republican members of Congress were beginning to float the phrase "obstruction of justice"—and to raise the specter of impeachment. "Any effort to stop the federal government from conducting an investigation, any effort to dissuade federal agents from proceeding with an investigation, is very serious and could be construed as obstruction of justice," Florida Republican Carlos Curbelo said. "Obstruction of justice—in the case of Nixon, in the case of Clinton in the late 90s—has been considered an impeachable offense."[3]

After years of layoffs and industry turmoil, legacy journalism appears to have regained some of its swagger during the Trump presidency, despite the president's efforts to slow it down. In October 2016, for example, Trump threatened to sue the *New York Times* for libel if it didn't retract a story about his alleged sexual assaults, but the *Times* stood its ground ("We welcome the opportunity to have a court set him straight," the company's attorneys wrote), and a lawsuit never came.[4] Similarly, Trump's campaign promise to "open up libel laws" showed no signs of progress during the administration's first 100 days, nor did his tweets about "fake news" prevent watchdog journalism from forcing real-world consequences, including Jeff Sessions' recusal and "drug czar" nominee Tom Marino's withdrawal.

The resilience of the First Amendment is good news for journalism—and an affirmation of the U.S. government's system of checks and balances. However, it doesn't mean that Trump's war against the news media has failed. In fact, when it comes to the media's credibility, there are troubling signs that Trump is winning. A poll by Emerson College Polling in February 2017 found that 49 percent of Americans considered the Trump administration to be truthful, compared to just 39 percent who felt that way about the news media.[5] And the trust gap also appeared in relation to specific issues, such as Trump's unsubstantiated claim that he was wiretapped by the Obama administration during the 2016 campaign. Despite extensive news reporting debunking this charge, a CBS poll found that nearly half of all Americans, including 74 percent of Republicans, considered it "very likely" or "somewhat likely" that the allegations were true.[6]

Meanwhile, Trump's war on the media has also contributed to a broader culture of disdain toward journalists—a culture that allowed Greg Gianforte to get elected to Congress one day after physically assaulting a reporter, and that has emboldened Internet trolls to ruthlessly heckle and abuse journalists online. Take the case of Julia Ioffe, a Russian-born journalist whose family emigrated to the United States when she was seven years old to escape anti-Semitic persecution. In April 2016, following the publication of a Melania Trump profile story that Ioffe wrote for *GQ* magazine, neo-Nazi blogger Andrew Anglin wrote a post on The Daily Stormer calling for readers to "go ahead and send [Ioffe] a tweet and let her know what you think of her dirty kike trickery. Make sure to identify her as a Jew working against White interests, or send her a picture with the Jude star from the top of this article."[7] Anglin's followers responded en masse to this call to action, swarming Ioffe's e-mail with personal insults and threats, including a cartoon that showed a Jew being shot in the head. "From my inbox," Ioffe wrote when she posted the cartoon on Twitter. "Subject line: 'They know about you!'"[8]

Trump has not explicitly endorsed these attacks, but critics argue his fingerprints aren't hard to miss. *Washington Post* executive editor Marty Baron, for one, cited Trump's "outright assault on the press" as a major cause of the growing abuse of journalists. "It is no wonder that some members of our staff at the *Washington Post* and at other news organizations received vile insults and threats of personal harm so worrisome that extra security was required," he said in November 2016. "It is no wonder that one Internet venue known for hate and misogyny and white nationalism posted the home addresses of media executives, clearly inviting vandalism or worse."[9]

What these developments suggest is that the struggle between President Trump and the news media may not end with a clear winner. Sure, it's possible that the muckraking work of investigative journalists will eventually force Trump's removal from office. (Maybe it already has.) But even resignation or impeachment would not solve the larger problem of public mistrust, which threatens to undermine journalism's credibility even if its constitutional freedoms remain intact. Jeff Jarvis aptly calls this conundrum the "Trump paradox."[10] He explains:

> In failing, [Trump] would succeed in killing the press . . . The enemy of the people convinces the people that we are the enemy. The press that survives, the liberal press, will end up with more prizes and subscriptions, oh joy, but with little hope of guiding or informing the nation's conversation. Say the *New York Times* reaches its audacious dream of 10 million paying subscribers. So what? That's 3 percent of the U.S. population (and some number of those subscribers will be from elsewhere). And they said that blogs were echo chambers. We in liberal media will be speaking to ourselves—or, being liberal, more likely arguing with ourselves.[11]

We believe journalists can still fend off this mutual destruction, but they'll need to start by recognizing that citizens don't implicitly value journalism's watchdog role in the same way they do. (A 2017 Pew Research Center poll found that only 42 percent of Republicans believe the media "keeps politicians from doing things that shouldn't be done," whereas 56 percent believe criticism "keeps politicians from doing their jobs.")[12] Instead of resting on their laurels as the "fourth estate," journalists need to actively and aggressively *make the case* for nonpartisan watchdog journalism, and they need to demonstrate to citizens how that watchdog role serves the *public* interest, not just the interests of Democrats or Republicans. This will be an uphill battle in today's polarized America, but that shouldn't stop news organizations from taking a few first steps:

- **Be transparent:** Journalists love to cite the saying that "sunshine is the best disinfectant," but they're often less eager to apply that logic to their own work. To build support for watchdog journalism, news organizations must pull back the curtains and start explaining decisions and distinctions that might seem obvious inside the newsroom, like the difference between an opinion column, a news story, and a news analysis feature. Many news organizations use these labels to distinguish content types online, but they rarely communicate to readers what the labels mean. The same is true of major editorial decisions, such as granting anonymity to government sources. Journalists assume that the logic guiding these decisions is self-evident when in reality most people don't have a clue. It's the responsibility of *journalists* to fix that.

- **Involve the public:** In addition to showing the public how sausage is made, news organizations must involve citizens in the sausage making itself. Whether it's by allowing the public to vote on story ideas, inviting them to contribute personal stories to a crowdsourced investigation, or recruiting them to participate in a scoop-sleuthing scavenger hunt on Twitter, news organizations need to establish trust in their work by encouraging a sense of collective ownership. This participatory logic has been widely embraced in the civic tech world, where designers and coders regularly talk about *building with* consumers and not just *for* them. But journalists have instead maintained a distance from the public, an approach that's incompatible with the participatory nature of the Internet and unconducive to trust. Ultimately, if news organizations hope to build trust in their *output*—the news—they'll need to give citizens *input* into how it's made.

- **Tell a better story about journalism:** For better or worse, people's perceptions of products and brands are largely shaped by marketing. It's why companies will spend millions of dollars for a 30-second ad spot during the Super Bowl or hire a six-figure marketing consultant to help them craft an edgy brand identity. Ever since the 1920s PR campaign that helped make smoking cigarettes socially acceptable for women, companies big and small have poured money into improving public perception of their brands. News organizations would benefit from adopting a similar approach. To be clear, we're not suggesting that news organizations can rebrand their way out of their current trust crisis. Obviously, journalists need to walk the walk before they talk the talk. But the two shouldn't be mutually exclusive. As news organizations take steps to build more trustworthy journalism, they should toot their own horns, highlight their successes, reaffirm their commitment to serving the public, and invest in developing brands that connect with consumers. If news organizations get their pitch right, they might be able to pull off a public-opinion turnaround like the one Steve Jobs orchestrated at Apple in the 1980s. If not, journalism will continue to be defined by its detractors, who don't always tell the truth about the news media, but who at least tell a compelling story.

Finally, surviving the Trump era and its aftermath will also require journalism to become more honest about one of its core values: objectivity. For decades, journalists have tried to convince the public that they're neutral observers who merely serve as conduits for "objective" reality. But this position has always been a false promise. Like the people they serve, journalists are complex, dynamic, and opinionated creatures. Openly acknowledging this human subjectivity does not preclude fairness, and it does not prevent journalists from applying consistent standards of verification and analysis to a rigorous, if imperfect, pursuit of truth. The public may still find fault with the finished product, of course, but that shouldn't stop journalists from establishing methodological rigor as their professional benchmark or from making an honest, authentic case about how they apply that rigor to their work. Ultimately, we believe that if journalists make that case, a majority of Americans will buy it.

And Trump might not topple journalism after all.

Will Digital Gatekeepers Accept the Responsibility That Comes with Their Power?

"Gatekeeping" is a term used by media theorists to describe the function news organizations have traditionally filled in determining which stories were covered and their level of prominence in any given mass media publication or broadcast.[13] However, today's gates are computer algorithms that, although invisible to the eye, regulate access to massive amounts of information. Facebook has been called the "most powerful newspaper on Earth," reaching nearly 2 billion people each month and "driving more traffic and attention to news than anything else on earth," said Joshua Benton, director of the Nieman Journalism Lab.[14]

Critics have charged Facebook with ignoring the adage that "with great power comes great responsibility."[15] Founder Mark Zuckerberg's initial response to the explosion of propaganda and misinformation on Facebook in 2016 did little to quell those concerns. "We're a technology company. We're not a media company," Zuckerberg told an audience in August 2016, just as attention was turning to Facebook's potential role in the dissemination of false information.[16]

"Our democracy has a lot of problems," Benton writes, "but there are few things that could impact it for the better more than Facebook starting to care—really *care*—about the truthfulness of the news that its users share and take in." If it doesn't, Benton warns, "the forces that drove this election's media failure are likely to get worse." [17]

In the wake of fallout from the 2016 election, Facebook has started to show signs of newfound responsibility to the public, including an updated mission statement. Previously, it stated that Facebook sought "to give people the power to share and make the world more open and connected." Now, it is "to give people the power to build community and bring the world closer together." [18]

"We used to have a sense that if we could just do those things, then that would make a lot of the things in the world better by themselves," Zuckerberg told CNN Tech. "But now we realize that we need to do more too. It's important to give people a voice, to get a diversity of opinions out there, but on top of that, you also need to do this work of building common ground so that way we can all move forward together." [19]

Facebook is also working to fight misinformation in substantive ways by forming and funding alliances with established nonprofits and universities. In January 2017 it formally announced the Facebook Journalism Project, which promised collaborative development of news products, training, and tools for journalists and the public. [20]

What more could Facebook do? For one, it could take the lead in helping users distinguish the difference between news reporting and commentary—whether the media in question originates from a conservative or liberal perspective. Many young people are now raised without newspapers, and therefore without a sense that publications have dedicated sections: hard news, opinions, sports, and lifestyle. On television, these distinctions are often discernible by program scheduling. Heated commentary tends to generate clicks but not necessarily ad revenue. Advertisers like heat, but not fire. Major sponsors generally prefer to avoid controversy, as demonstrated when several dropped their support of Bill O'Reilly, and earlier Glenn Beck.

It is easy to conflate straight news with commentary, which is likely why the public, when polled, says it distrusts the media. People easily confuse the two.

Additionally, Facebook could place more constraints on baseless clickbait. During the run-up to the 2016 presidential election, many blatantly fraudulent stories circulated on Facebook's platform. One of the most egregious was a report that the Pope had endorsed Donald Trump. [21]

"Fake news" has become such a salient topic and issue of concern that many organizations are publishing methods and apps to help discern the quality and veracity of a source. Maggie Farley, a veteran journalist, designed and built an app to test people's ability to identify false information. In an interview with NPR by Tennessee Watson, she explained that although fake news and misleading material have always been part of the digital landscape ("People have always been trying to manipulate information for their own ends"), the sheer amount of it cropping up is startling, and how it can influence people even more so. [22]

Will Legacy Media Learn from What's Now Considered the Fringes?

Today's fad can evolve into tomorrow's institution. As we've noted, few observers took Ted Turner seriously when he announced plans to launch CNN—the world's first 24-hour news network—in 1980. Nearly 40 years later, "Chicken Noodle News" (as sneering legacy journalists dubbed it) is a $10 billion enterprise by some analysts' accounts.

Ezra Klein turned to blogging after his college newspaper rejected his efforts to join their staff. However, the setback allowed him to hone his journalistic voice through Wonkblog and to eventually launch Vox, which is now a leading online news source. He landed an exclusive interview with President Barack Obama in the weeks before he left office. Klein is transparently unapologetic about Vox's progressive political perspective.

At the opposite end of the political perspective is blogger Matt Drudge, who was not taken seriously by many in mainstream media before he scooped every other news organization with revelations about former President Bill Clinton and Monica Lewinsky. According to one Quantcast assessment, the site has more than 3 million page visits per day.[23] Authors Mark Halperin and John Halperin dubbed Drudge "the Walter Cronkite of his era."[24] They went on to claim, "If Drudge says something, it may not lead everybody instantly in the same direction, but it gets people thinking about what Matt Drudge wants them to think about."

YouTube allows anyone to create an instant news channel, and some of its personalities draw significant millennial audiences. Although edging more towards commentating than news reporting, Philip DeFranco's vlog (video blog) claims to have amassed 2 billion views and 5 million subscribers with several "current event" and pop culture–themed channels and shows.

Consider Drudge's and DeFranco's followings within the context of the fact that MSNBC's Rachel Maddow on her best nights attracts only 1.5 million viewers, and among those only 350,000 are the targeted 25- to 54-year-old demographic.[25]

To be clear, we are not casting Drudge, or even the less ideological DeFranco, as exemplars for journalism's way forward. As with Sean Hannity and Bill O'Reilly during his run, they tend to only trumpet political perspectives to people who share their beliefs. They are commentators, offering audiences distinct flavors of journalism that should not be confused with the work of news anchors or correspondents.

However, mainstream media can learn from how Drudge and DeFranco have cultivated followings by connecting with citizens who have otherwise felt marginalized. DeFranco lived in his car for a period before discovering he had a knack for presenting "newsie type stuff, and things that matter" with the launch of his *sxephil* YouTube channel in 2006.[26] A year later, his fortunes began to turn when, as a lark, he uploaded a crude video commentary that quickly garnered 1.8 million views. Next came funding and promotional support from YouTube. His *Philly D* and *SourceFed* channels spun off gaming and sketch comedy verticals, plus a merchandise line.

DeFranco's staccato style of news story delivery is accomplished by tightly editing out the breaths between sentences, which accentuates the jump cuts that are reminiscent of television's iconic Max Headroom animated character from the 1980s. DeFranco makes a comfortable living as a news entertainer and has expanded his team of researchers and editors to more than a dozen professionals.

Fans voted him *WIRED* magazine's Sexiest Geek in 2008.[27] A self-identified Libertarian, DeFranco says he politically stands as "fiscally conservative and socially liberal, for the most part."[28]

In 2013 he sold his media properties to Discovery Digital Networks, only to regain control in 2017 with his announcement of "The Philip DeFranco Network," which is fan funded. His promotional video featured construction shots of his new production studio and a promise that he would be an authentic voice for his core millennial audience. He's also been called "the Walter Cronkite for the YouTube generation," by the *Los Angeles Times*. Fast Company dubbed DeFranco "this generation's Jon Stewart."

Several legacy media brands are also bringing a fresh perspective to journalism, such as NPR, which continues to be a pioneer of innovation. Kinsey Wilson, the network's former chief of content, led the development of "NPR One," a Pandora-style app launched in 2014 that allows listeners to access live and archived audio news and podcasts. The service is like a jukebox but presents content based on personal preferences and media consumption habits, and it was created to be "the best newsmagazine for you at the moment you want to listen," said Zach Bard, NPR's vice president of digital media.[29]

The app also accounts for listeners' interest in local news. "It's not just us saying local is important—we follow our audience, their behaviors, and our audience is *telling* us that local is important: When people don't hear local stuff, they say, 'Where's my local station?!'" said Sara Sarasohn, editorial lead for NPR One.[30]

NPR was also an early adopter in creating apps and social media solutions that improved the user experience of engaging with its content. Wilson formed distribution deals with Apple and car companies and created verticals to complement radio broadcasts on themed topics, such as race and identity, education, and global health.[31] The network established a Facebook group where listeners can easily post feedback and make requests.

In 2014 NPR hired former MTV and E! entertainment executive Jarl Mohn to spark additional innovation and growth. "I don't like incremental growth," Mohn announced to staffers shortly after taking the helm as CEO. "I want to take advantage of what I see as transformative opportunities. . . My job is to make sure you have the tools and the resources and the money for you to do the best work of your careers." Mohn has focused on growing the listenership of its flagship programs, *Morning Edition* and *All Things Considered,* and also capitalizing on the renewed popularity of podcasts. Sponsorship revenue for podcasts rose 200 percent between 2013 and 2015.[32]

NPR's ability to maintain brand loyalty can be partially attributed to the conversational style and palatable tone of its on-air talent. Over time, its news presenters become familiar names and voices to listeners. *Morning Edition's* Steve Inskeep, Rachel Martin, and previously Bob Edwards and Renee Montagne have successfully struck a welcoming chord with audiences seeking any given day's top stories.

Print journalism is also getting a facelift in terms of tone. Winston Ross is among the writers who are refreshingly bringing a breezier style of writing to legacy publications such as *Newsweek* without compromising journalistic integrity. Consider the difference between how Ross wrote about marijuana in 2015 and how Donna Foote wrote about it 14 years earlier. In *"In California, Smoke and Fire Over Pot,"* her 2001 *Newsweek* story on medical marijuana, Foote's lead paragraph read:

> They smoke lots of marijuana. They're gravely ill and dying. And they've got a lot on their minds besides politics. But California proponents of medical marijuana also have plenty of fight in them, particularly when authorities threaten to take away their painkiller of choice. Last week the U.S. Supreme Court unanimously rejected the "medical necessity" defense in federal marijuana cases, which may open the way for the Feds to close down cooperatives distributing cannabis to people suffering from diseases like AIDS and cancer. "We have no way of knowing what actions the Feds will take," said Scott Imler, president of the Los Angeles Cannabis Resource Center.[33]

In comparison, Ross's *Newsweek* cover story on "Cannabis Crusader" Travis Maurer is a nonfiction page turner—rich with description, texture, and a central character. Its lead paragraph reads:

> About 30 minutes before our plane is scheduled to take off, Travis Maurer strolls up to the gate at Portland International Airport in shorts and flip-flops, flashing a square-jawed smile. Broad-shouldered and affable,

Maurer looks like the perfect spokesman for any cause, and he deftly charms his way into a window seat. He's just eaten some ice cream, he tells me as we board, and he's in a surprisingly good mood for someone about to spend the next few hours in coach. A short while later, the plane lifts into the sky and Maurer falls asleep. The ice cream, it turns out, was laced with THC.[34]

In fairness, today's journalists are allowed more liberties than their predecessors when writing about marijuana use. Acceptance has shifted significantly. Ross and *Newsweek* might easily be accused of pandering to fulfill public curiosity. However, he is no lightweight. He has covered mass shootings, foreign dignitaries, and hardball politics. In an autobiographical blog post Ross wrote: "After 15 years mostly in newspapers, I landed my dream gig at *Newsweek* and *The Daily Beast,* then freelanced around Europe for a year, then back to *Newsweek,* serving for half of 2015 as the magazine's Europe Correspondent, then as a senior writer."[35]

Greg Barber, the director of digital news projects at the *Washington Post*, acknowledges the change in how legacy media now reports the news. "I've definitely seen just in my time at the *Post* the style of writing change in a way that I think is good," Barber told us. "I think that we need to tell stories in a way that is accessible to readers. Also, I think that giving ourselves more ability to tell our stories creatively and also to be able to utilize tech as we do it, means that we can have a greater impact."[36]

Publications that target ethnic audiences are also evolving. Nieman Lab reports that in New York City, "there's a vibrant ecosystem of ethnic media to serve a population that speaks more than 170 languages.[37] But a version of New York's mishmash exists in suburbs and small towns across America. Multicultural media are everywhere." Although much attention is focused on New York's three major daily newspapers, when you widen the scope of view, the city actually supports approximately 18 dailies with 9 published in languages other than English.

Ethnic television is also strong, particularly programs that target Latinos—the fastest-growing consumer market in the United States. In 2013 Univision finished first among U.S. broadcast networks in the coveted 18- to 49-year-old age demographic—beating NBC, CBS, ABC, and Fox.[38] Previously, on several occasions, it topped daily primetime ratings for a broader range of viewers. However, the Latino community continues to be underrepresented in newsrooms and underserved in terms of news coverage.

Rather than wait for legacy media companies to diversify, many entrepreneurial content creators are establishing their own. *Latin Heat* is an online site that covers Hollywood entertainment news, and LatinoRebels .com targets millennials.[39]

Rapid growth of ethnic publications, television, and online services is redefining the meaning of "mainstream media." These trends compel legacy news organizations to consider the merits of publishing in multiple languages. Journalist Sarah Maslin Nir advocated publishing "Unvarnished," her *New York Times* investigative series on unjust labor practices within the nail salon industry, in four languages.[40] Immigrant workers she met were enduring psychological and physical abuse and earning as little as $1.50 an hour. However, fearing retribution from their employers, most were reluctant to speak. To get their stories, Nir became a customer, which allowed her to collect 125 candid interviews. Publishing in English, Spanish, Korean, and Chinese enhanced the story's impact. The experiment was part of the *New York Times*' greater initiative to use automatic translation software to reach a broader audience.

Will Artificial Intelligence Empower Journalists or Replace Them?

"A machine will win a Pulitzer one day. We can tell the stories hidden in data."[41]

That was Kris Hammond's bold prediction in April 2016, only weeks before the Pulitzer Prize competition's 100th anniversary. Hammond is the co-founder and chief scientist at Narrative Science, a company that uses artificial intelligence to convert data into narrative prose, and he's no stranger to lofty promises. In 2011 he predicted it would take only *five years* for computers to reach the Pulitzer milestone (a timeline he later pushed back), and in 2012 he forecast that computers would soon be "more than 90 percent" of all news by 2027.[42] "Humans are unbelievably rich and complex, but they are machines," Hammond told *The Guardian*. "In 20 years, there will be no area in which Narrative Science doesn't write stories.[43]

Hammond's claims have garnered widespread media coverage (surely the intended effect), and they've sent a shiver down the spines of more than a few news veterans, including *Pasadena Star-News* columnist Robert Rector, who warned of a future where newspaper execs "build robots to replace reporters," reaping profits from a business model "with little or no overhead."[44] However, such doomsday predictions are far from the norm. More common is the relative indifference expressed by media economist Ken Doctor, who described robots as "just another tool of new journalism," and by Fredrick Kunkle, a *Washington Post* reporter and co-chair of the Washington-Baltimore News Guild, who shared similar optimism after the *Post* developed Heliograf, a tool to mine data sets (such as live election results) and automatically generate news stories.[45] "We're naturally wary about any technology that could replace human beings," Kunkle explained. "But this technology seems to have taken over only some of the grunt work."[46]

Magazine writer Kevin Roose is even more effusive in his praise of artificial intelligence, describing robo-reporters as "the best thing to happen to journalists in a long time," thanks to their ability to write "the kinds of stories that humans hate writing anyway."[47] Roose recalled his time as a business reporter for the *New York Times*, where his job included preparing "excruciatingly dull" corporate earnings stories—the type of formulaic content that Narrative Science's algorithms can now produce in a matter of seconds. Roose says journalists shouldn't hesitate to outsource this tedium to robots, nor should they worry that they're setting off down a slippery slope. He explains:

> Robots, as sophisticated as they are, can't approach the full creativity of a human writer. They can't contextualize Emmy snubs like Matt Zoller Seitz, assail opponents of Obamacare like Jonathan Chait, or collect summer-camp sex stories like Maureen O'Connor. My colleagues' jobs (and mine, knock wood) are too complex for today's artificial intelligence to handle; they require human skills like picking up the phone, piecing together data points from multiple sources, and drawing original, evidence-based conclusions.[48]

Roose is right that his work can't be replicated by today's artificial intelligence—not when Facebook's algorithms can't even get news curation right.[49] However, if current trends hold, *tomorrow's* artificial intelligence could be a different story. After years of overhyped expectations and underwhelming results, AI technology has taken dramatic steps forward over the last decade, sparking talk in Silicon Valley of an imminent "inflection point," beyond which computers will quickly gain the capacity to emulate human cognitive processes and displace human workers in both blue- and white-collar industries. "The combination of advanced sensors, voice recognition, artificial intelligence, big data, text-mining, and pattern recognition algorithms, is generating smart robots capable of quickly learning human actions, and even learning from one another," former U.S. Labor Secretary Robert Reich explains. "If you think being a 'professional' make your job safe, think again."[50]

Similarly, political economists and prolific authors Robert McChesney and John Nichols argue that creative destruction—the principle that technological innovation eventually replaces the jobs it destroys—may no longer apply in a world with intelligent machines. In this world, robots will become "far more sophisticated in their abilities and their applications than the clunky machines of old movies," McChesney and Nichols write. "They will be not only in factories, they will be everywhere."[51]

Can journalists expect to be immune from this trend? If the media business continues along its current path, doubling down on clickbait listicles, videos, and slideshows in pursuit of clicks and views, the answer is surely no. News organizations are already partnering with AI companies such as Wochit and Wibbitz to produce thousands of automated videos every month, and Tronc chairman Michael W. Ferro Jr. has set his sights on producing 20,000 videos *every day.*[52] Meanwhile, intelligent machines are quickly becoming sophisticated enough to perform the kind of aggregation, curation, and distribution work currently assigned to social media editors and entry-level reporters. Humans fill these positions for now, but corporate owners won't remain content with this arrangement forever. No CEO wants to be the *first* to replace their employees with robots, but if shareholders get antsy or the economy sinks into another recession, *someone* will say they've been left with no choice. And the rest of the dominos won't be far behind.

That's the bad news, but here's the bright side: at its best, journalism has always consisted of much more than stringing words and images together in a formulaic news package. In fact, now more than ever, the craft of journalism is about building relationships, facilitating conversations, and forging trust through the very best antidote to automation: the human touch. No matter how far technology advances, robots will never be able to draft handwritten thank-you notes for subscribers quite like Skip Foster at the *Tallahassee Democrat*, team up with community members to chase down a story quite like the Curious City team at WBEZ, or engage a community advisory board quite like jesikah maria ross at Capital Public Radio. If journalists put efforts like these at the heart of their work, robots will indeed continue to be tools in the newsroom, or at least junior colleagues, tasked with the mundane work that falls below the pay grade of professional human journalists.

Media scholar Seth Lewis perhaps says it best: "The essence of human journalism is that human connection," he explained. "In an idealized sense, journalists are representing communities—both by reflecting communities back to themselves and by helping communities find their best selves through knowledge, information and public deliberation. It's really hard to see how that becomes completely machine-oriented."[53]

Will Universities Help Point the Way toward Journalism's Digital Future?

Journalism schools have traditionally worked to prepare students for internships and entry-level positions at legacy media companies, often with the implied promise of career advancement. The premise was that students would expand upon classroom knowledge with on-the-job training in fundamental skills. Yet today, there is a reversal in expectations. Industry recruiters tell journalism professors they seek new hires who can *teach them* how to maximize the potential of Snapchat and a plethora of other emerging platforms that are unfamiliar to their established professionals.

"The world can now tweet, blog, take pictures, and more. Every workplace in America needs clear digital communicators. . . . To lead in any field—law, business, nonprofits, government—you need to be able to communicate," said Eric Newton, Innovation Chief at Arizona State University's Cronkite School of Journalism and Communication.[54]

Before joining ASU, Newton was a vice president and senior advisor at the John S. and James L. Knight Foundation, where he facilitated more than $250 million in grants to advance journalism with a specific emphasis on education.[55] However, he became critical of journalism schools, asserting they could be greater contributors to innovation.

"Universities must be willing to destroy and recreate themselves to be part of the future of news. They should not leave that future to technologists alone," Newton wrote.[56]

He took exception to an academic institutional culture within many journalism schools that resist change. At research-focused universities, teaching can become a secondary priority, and those who work within professional schools can feel undervalued.

In 2012 Newton and five other foundation executives wrote an open letter to the nation's university presidents calling them to task.[57] "Deans must find ways for their schools to evolve, rather than maintain the status quo. Simply put, universities must become forceful partners in revitalizing an industry at the very core of democracy," the letter stated.

We agree with Newton that universities can play a greater role as collaborators with industry to foster innovation. They must become incubators for experimentation and laboratories for change. "Universities must propel the profession forward and become the connective tissue between what's come before and what's still to come," said futurist Amy Webb.[58]

The notion of public universities partnering with consumer-driven corporations remains controversial. The two have fundamentally different missions. Universities exist to produce knowledge and serve students; corporations exist to produce profits and serve shareholders. Many academics fear that corporate money corrupts, and so it should have a limited role in research. Their concern is that consumer-driven companies will seek to control research agendas, thereby limiting the range of inquiry studied in social science. However, several top-tier universities have successfully forged relationships with industry that have fortified both academic and corporate aims, providing a model for journalism schools to follow.

Designing the Future: MIT

Harvard set the standard by which elite universities were measured until geologist William Barton Rogers conceived a bolder vision.[59] Founding the Massachusetts Institute of Technology in 1861, Rogers originated the concept of a science-based research university that would emphasize regional economic development by creating and spinning off high-technology companies.[60]

During the 1920s MIT Professor Vannevar Bush spent his own money and engaged his students in a failed attempt to patent and sell a new device. Burned by the experience and desiring to recover his losses, Bush began consulting high-tech firms in the Boston area. While earning social capital through networking, he also developed an eye for commercial opportunities and became a key figure in the formation of the Raytheon Corporation, which quickly emerged as a highly profitable venture.

Karl Compton, MIT's president during the 1930s and 1940s, further fulfilled Roger's vision by pioneering the practice of venture capital funding, which fueled academic and industry partnerships with startup dollars. Legions of MIT professors soon began supplementing their meager academic salaries by moonlighting as advisors for tech firms. The Arthur D. Little Company set up shop next door to MIT and paid professors retainers to consult exclusively for them.

Bush's students were integral to research and development (R&D) of innovations, testing their commercial worthiness. "I was an early professor and also a consultant to industry," Bush said. "It was a salutary combination; it drew me out of the ivory tower and put life into my teaching, and it greatly helped my family budget." [61]

The book *MIT and the Rise of Entrepreneurial Science* chronicles how Bush and his roommate Lawrence K. Marshall cultivated consulting relationships within the Boston investment community. Their efforts for the Spencer Thermostat Company led to a merger with Texas Instruments. Soon a "research row" emerged on Cambridge's Memorial Drive between MIT and Harvard.

Frederick Terman, one of Bush's former doctoral students, soon emulated MIT's model at Stanford. Terman was an electrical engineering professor who rose through the ranks to become Stanford's provost. Ingenuity led him to fund the institution's ambitions by leveraging its considerable real estate holdings to hire faculty and create robust research centers. What emerged was the concept of industrial research parks, which birthed numerous enterprises, including Hewlett-Packard. [62]

To appreciate fully how partnerships between universities and industries can be beneficial, one need only to look closer at the relationship between Stanford and Google. Founders Sergey Brin and Larry Page developed the company's PageRank algorithm while earning their PhDs at Stanford, which availed its significant infrastructure and gravitas to the venture. Stanford held 1.8 million shares of stock equating to a 10 percent interest in Google.[63] A year after the company went public in 2004, Stanford sold its stake for $336 million, an average of $187 per share. A rivalry between MIT and Stanford escalated, and in 1980, MIT elevated the competition to a higher level—this time with a direct play at media.

MIT Media Lab

Formal training as an architect led MIT Professor Nicholas Negroponte to conceive and design an interdisciplinary research lab aimed at "inventing the future" by establishing an unprecedented level of alliances between academic and industry collaborators. In 1985 Negroponte and MIT President Jerome Wiesner launched the MIT Media Lab to explore the convergence of multimedia, technology, science, and design.

With backing from a long list of corporate partners, the MIT Media Lab predicted, prototyped, and promoted ideas that were considered revolutionary at the time, including personal computing, wireless connectivity, and the home delivery of movies. Today they are common conveniences. "Demo or die" was the mantra among researchers who focused more on envisioning the future than creating marketable consumer products.[64]

Media Lab prototypes personalized news services decades before media curation and micro-blogging became mainstream. "Imagine turning on a computer, punching in a few commands, and accessing a newspaper filled with articles on the topics you're most interested in—say the space shuttle, MIT people in the news, and regional stories from the state where Grandma lives. How about an advice column that you can submit questions to with answers appearing in the next day's issue?" wrote Elizabeth Thompson in a 1994 Media Lab press release.[65]

In a freshmen seminar, students were challenged to invent the newspaper of the future. "We didn't tell them what's impossible, or what the state of our software is—we just asked them what they would like to see in such a paper," said MIT Professor Pascal Chesnais. The result was the *Freshman Fishwrap*, a speculative news service that relied on user profiles to customize its content. *The Boston Globe* and Knight-Ridder, Inc., were partners in the experiment, which also tested two-way communication between advertisers and customers and personalized coupons.

A subsequent iteration was dubbed *The Daily Me*, which would electronically deliver audio, video, or print stories. A 1994 *Advertising Age* article on the experiment marveled that a technical bookstore had made its whole inventory available for online purchase. And it also mentioned the development of a digital dining guide that would give the user restaurant reviews and maps based on his or her proximity to a given option.[66]

During the 1980s, university research and industry partnerships grew nearly 250 percent, and the number of patents received by U.S. universities tripled between 1984 and 1994. Today, MIT's Media Lab lists more than 100 corporate partners and manages a $45 million annual budget.[67] Members include Cisco Systems, Comcast, Estée Lauder, ExxonMobil, General Electric, Google, IBM, IKEA, Intel, Mercedes-Benz, PepsiCo, Sony Corporation, Target, Toyota, Univision, and Viacom.

Media Lab's explorations are as eclectic as its list of partners. Symphony Painter is under development by the Lab's Opera of the Future research group in partnership with Fisher-Price.[68] The intent is to create an "add-on" musical cartridge for Pixter Color, the company's popular digital drawing toy device. The Music, Mind, and Machine Group is developing Karaoke-on-Demand to make the social pastime more flexible and scalable.[69]

Media Lab has always worked to envision the unimaginable, yet one project ventures even further. Programmable Synthetic Hallucinations aims to create home appliances that display fantastical mirages.[70] Although whimsical in nature, the project seeks to delve beyond the boundaries of narrative storytelling. In that vein, another project explores Smell Narratives to "create more immersive and evocative experiences," the Media Lab's website states.

With a legacy that extends more than 30 years, Media Lab has earned an unquestionable track record as a hub for innovation. Karaoke, mirages, and smell narratives aside, it is fair to ask how Media Lab is addressing the stench that surrounds present-day journalism. What is it offering as a way forward during this ailing and defining moment in the trajectory of news media?

"When you're sinking, you have two ways to go," said Joi Ito, current director of the MIT Media Lab. "You can bet the house on something, go all in, or you can try to become smaller and smaller until you disappear." Ito was speaking about the lessons news organizations can learn from Silicon Valley technology firms. He asserted that in the digital world, rewards require risks. Ito believes that journalism is a risk-averse trade. "The problem with journalists, I find, and lawyers, is they understand risk very well. But they've never taken it," Ito said at a Media Lab event in 2013. He was pointing to the fact that journalism's credibility is rooted in precision and accuracy, not speculation. "Journalists, while skilled and trained in writing and editing, may be less prepared to build a new product or devise a new business model as a designer or developer," Ito stated further.[71]

Ito can speak with authority on the matter. He was an early investor in Twitter and Kickstarter and holds board seats at the *New York Times*, the Knight Foundation, and Creative Commons. He was joined by Ethan Zuckerman, director of the Center for Civic Media at MIT, about what it will take for journalism to reinvent itself.

Through an alliance with Media Lab, Zuckerman's center pursues such themes as "News in the Age of Participatory Media," where the future of journalism is considered an "engineering challenge."[72] Through its Media Cloud project, the center is inventing tools for better assessing the role of online media in civic discourse by tracking millions of online stories.[73] It adds 40,000 news stories a day to an archive of 550 million stories, all available to the public.[74] At a granular level, the Media Cloud analyzes 5 billion sentences for trends and common threads.

The Center's Dashboard tool mines the massive database to reveal how any given topic was spoken about through digital media within a specified time period. Media Mapper is a second tool that allows users to drill down to examine a topic in more depth to determine which aspects are gaining the most traction. Additionally, there is a cross-collaboration on projects with Harvard's Berkman Center for Internet and Society.

The Oregon Way

MIT enjoys a $13.2 billion endowment pool, and Stanford University's endowment fund is $22.4 billion.[75] At the University of Oregon School of Journalism and Communication, we take a scrappier approach to innovation and research, informed by the same pioneering spirit associated with the Pacific Northwest. It requires that we be resourceful and bold in ways that do not rely on access to an open checkbook. That sense of scrappiness is also one of our strong suits.

Within weeks of tech industry observers forecasting the debut of Apple's iPad tablet in 2009, we developed a mobile media content creation course. The class was already in session as iPads were hitting retail shelves. No textbooks or curriculum existed to guide our experimentations. We paired student groups with several publishing companies to create prototypes for mobile apps.

When Steve Jobs unveiled the device in January 2010, he was joined by Jennifer Brook, who developed the *New York Times'* first iPad app.[76] We called her the next day, and within a week she was engaging with our students via Skype. Our next move was to bring Brook to Portland to collaborate with our students.

A year later when Adobe announced its plans to release a digital publishing suite, we gained beta test–stage access. The result was *OR Magazine*, the first student-produced digital publication for the iPad using those tools.

The level of interactivity was revolutionary, allowing magazine readers to swipe, scroll, and spin through story elements in immersive and dynamic new ways. However, the student teams faced many of the unpredictable learning curves and technical setbacks inherent in working with pre-market software. UO students engaged in ongoing Skype sessions with innovators tackling similar design and technical challenges at Time-Warner, Conde Nast, and a wide range of startups. Now in its seventh year, *OR Magazine* is a multi-award–winning publication that continues to reimagine the possibilities of magazine experiences. Fast forward to 2017, now several recent *OR Magazine* alums are creating cutting-edge work for major companies, including Conde Nast, Nike, and AOL. Others are establishing their own groundbreaking media ventures, including The Locals Project and Combined Culture.

This flock of former Ducks returns to our campuses in Eugene and Portland regularly to interface with current students and share innovations they are bringing forth in the world. One recent alum now develops apps and user experiences for the *New York Times* and another is the chief technology officer for the forward-thinking online publication *The Outline*.[77] Both were previously with The Marshall Project, which is engaged in cutting-edge journalism centered on criminal justice issues.[78]

Inspired by MIT and Stanford, we are now drawing upon the expertise of these millennials as we work more closely with industry and philanthropic partners to solve pressing societal problems that relate to media, technology, and education. At UO, we're particularly focused on working with legacy and new media firms to explore more meaningful ways to engage and empower communities. For example, when the *New Yorker* revealed in a 2015 story that the Pacific Northwest was overdue for a major cataclysmic earthquake, the SOJC partnered with Oregon Public Broadcasting to produce "Don't Wait for the Quake," an interactive television special that allowed at-home and in-studio audiences to use a mobile app to give real-time responses to video stories.

Universities like ours are also facilitating more convenings that bring journalists and the public together to improve understanding. Our professors and students work together to connect with communities and invent new styles of storytelling that will resonate with younger audiences. However, approaches do not have to be new to be effective. Sometimes a vintage sensibility or archived image can evoke a sincere emotional response in ways that a shiny or new method does not. As an example, our colleagues and their students who examined climate change across four summers in Alaska through the Hearst award-winning Science + Memory project used handcrafted watercolor and recycled materials to depict the migration of salmon. In another instance, a group of students and faculty traveled to Sri Lanka to report on the resilience of people affected by civil war and a natural disaster. Upon their return, students created an interactive exhibit focused on simplicity, virtue, and character through imagery and music.

We challenge our partners and ourselves to step outside of storytelling conventions. Recently, we have been working with an American veteran who suffers from a spinal injury incurred while serving in Afghanistan. His story parallels those of many former service members who have struggled to transition back into civilian life. Rather than portray him as the "subject" of a story we might choose to craft, we're collaborating—to explore together how his story may unfold.

To be clear, we're not arguing for dispensing with all conventions or suggesting that journalists' roles be diminished. More so, we seek to break predictable patterns and to honor authentic voices as we encounter them. A cookie-cutter approach to journalism no longer works. Readers and audiences have higher expectations.

This kind of thinking is antithetical to what is often referred to by news organizations as the "daily grind" or "feeding the beast." When one is expected to schedule, write, shoot, edit, post, and engage with readers and audiences, there is little time for nuanced storytelling. Our colleague Peter Laufer and others in the "slow news" movement are calling for a more deliberate approach to news gathering and reporting. Journalism is stronger and more accurate when journalists have the time to thoughtfully gather news.

Real stories about real people, rather than "talking heads," have the power to move audiences to action and to show the world how events affect the disenfranchised, the forgotten, those too small to be heard. Journalism has always been about serving the public, giving "a voice to the voiceless."

As previously discussed, DSLR cameras now allow video journalists to bring cinematic qualities to stories that can immerse audiences in ways traditionally shot and edited news story packages do not. This technology is why VICE and RYOT are gaining a millennial following that eludes many legacy news organizations.

We've also hired innovators such as Andrew DeVigal, former multimedia director for the *New York Times*, to head UO's Portland-based Agora Journalism Center. While at the *Times*, DeVigal oversaw the development of the groundbreaking Snow Fall project.[79] The Agora Center focuses on civic engagement, working with Knight Foundation funding to develop a new online platform, Gather, to facilitate greater collaboration between journalists and enhance their ability to serve communities. It allows reporters to brainstorm project ideas, share and access resources, and support the progress of one another's work.

Education Is Journalism's Next Calling

Money and fame are rarely motivators for why someone becomes a journalist. Many speak of their choice as a "calling" they could not resist. Somewhere, inside, there was this sense that they were meant to serve, inform, and affect social injustice. Teachers often share the same sentiments.

It bears noting that journalists and teachers face similar challenges in our present times. Both professions face crises regarding credibility and societal support. Much finger pointing persists. The public questions their motives and their value. Ultimately, both journalists and teachers must take responsibility for shifting a narrative that too easily vilifies their roles and colors how they are perceived.

Fundamentally, journalists and teachers have similar roles within a society. They exist to educate us so we can collectively move our communities forward. Yet crises within K–12 education haunt our society's future prospects: if we're not raising generations of young people who are thoughtful and informed participants in our democratic process, then the future of journalism—and democracy—is very dark indeed.

These real concerns led to the establishment of the *Journalistic Learning Initiative* (JLI), which uses journalistic strategies to empower student voice and academic success through a collaboration between UO's School of Journalism and Communication and College of Education. It is a coalition of researchers, educators, community members, philanthropists, nonprofit organizations, corporate partners, government agencies, and allied stakeholders working together.

JLI facilitates *reverse mentorships* for teachers, a term coined to describe a strategy that Jack Welch implemented when he ran General Electric in the 1980s. Realizing that his seasoned executives were novices when it came to maximizing the potential of the Internet, Welch brought computer-savvy young people into the company. Similarly, JLI recruits talented millennials who are recent journalism and media college graduates, trains them in JLI methods, and offers them a gap year (or more) working alongside a middle or high school teacher to infuse journalism into the English and social studies curriculum. As newly designated *JLI Educators*, these millennials bring fresh ideas, technology skills, and media experience into classrooms where they are gravely needed.

The objective is not to spawn future journalists; the intent is to support students in becoming what we refer to as *informed thinkers*. Educators often speak about cultivating critical thinking, yet the term remains an elusive concept that does not fully encompass the levels of student engagement that young people need to navigate effectively in this increasingly complex and nuanced world.

An informed thinker is someone who thoroughly and thoughtfully researches a topic to make sure that what he or she is presenting is credible and valid. Informed thinking articulates a clearer method and result than does critical thinking. Students learn to distinguish fact from fiction and to detect biases and agendas.

We believe this approach makes students more than savvy consumers: informed thinkers become effective problem solvers, emerge as content creators, and learn to advocate for public good. The Maine Department of Education formulated this perspective 20 years ago and has since adopted it as a guiding principle.[80]

Our need to improve education is not optional; it is an obligation we must embrace.

A Parting Thought

When we set out to write this book about two years ago, Donald Trump's presidential campaign seemed like a benign publicity stunt, *Breitbart* was a fringe media player, and "fake news" referred primarily to late-night comedy, not Russian propaganda.

Boy, how quickly things change.

Even by the cyclonic standards of the digital age, the media landscape's evolution over the last 18 months has been remarkable in its reach and pace, and it has made writing this book both endlessly exciting and immeasurably challenging. Our hope is that we've helped untangle the challenges and opportunities facing media in this "post-truth" world, even if we haven't always reached clear and satisfying answers.

We also hope that this book will serve a catalyst for further conversation and debate about the trajectory of journalism's future. We welcome your feedback and pushback, and we invite you to illuminate our blind spots.

And, of course, we thank you for reading.

Notes

Introduction

1. Donald Trump, Twitter post, February 17, 2017, 1:48 p.m., https://twitter.com/realDonaldTrump.

2. Ted Cruz, Republican presidential debate moderated by John Harwood, Becky Quick, and Carl Quintanilla, October 28, 2015.

3. Frank Luntz, Twitter post, October 28, 2015, 5:48 p.m., https://twitter.com/FrankLuntz.

4. Eric Wemple, "Media-Bashing Ted Cruz Is Right," *Washington Post*, October 28, 2015, accessed July 10, 2017, https://www.washingtonpost.com/blogs/erik-wemple/wp/2015/10/28/media-bashing-ted-cruz-is-right/?utm_term=.3f2e1faf01f9; Rush Limbaugh, "CNBC's Shameless Kill Show Debate," transcript, October 29, 2015, accessed July, 10, 2017, https://www.rushlimbaugh.com/daily/2015/10/29/cnbc_s_shameless_kill_show_debate/; Bill Maher, Twitter post, October 28, 2015, accessed July 10, 2017, https://twitter.com/billmaher/status/659531873547190272.

5. Richard Norton Smith, "The Surprising George Washington: Part 1," *Prologue* 26.1 (1994).

6. @BamaStephen, Twitter post, October 28, 2015, 7:32 p.m., https://twitter.com/BamaStephen.

7. Anthony Boerio, Twitter post, October 28, 2015, 6:59 p.m., https://twitter.com/coachanthony79.

8. Sandra Lannis, Twitter post, October 28, 2015, 10:17 p.m., https://twitter.com/SandyLannis.

9. Art Swift, "Americans' Trust in Mass Media Sinks to New Low," Gallup, September 14, 2016, accessed July 10, 2017, http://www.gallup.com/poll/195542/americans-trust-mass-media-sinks-new-low.aspx.

10. Jim Norman, "Americans' Confidence in Institutions Stays Low," Gallup, June 13, 2016, accessed July 10, 2017, http://www.gallup.com/poll/192581/americans-confidence-institutions-stays-low.aspx.

11. "Today's Journalists Less Prominent," Pew Research Center, March 8, 2007, accessed July 5, 2017, http://www.people-press.org/2007/03/08/todays-journalists-less-prominent/.

12. *Fox News Sunday*, "Defense Secretary Robert Gates' Exit Interview; Jon Stewart Talks Politics; Media Bias," Fox News, June 19, 2011.

13. Paul Farhi, "Dear Readers: Please Stop Calling Us 'The Media.' There Is No Such Thing," *Washington Post*, September 23, 2016, accessed July 10, 2017, https://www.washingtonpost.com/lifestyle/style/dear-readers-please-stop-calling-us-the-media-there-is-no-such-thing/2016/09/23/37972a32-7932-11e6-ac8e-cf8e0dd91dc7_story.html?utm_term=.f636b7fcd43a.

14. *The O'Reilly Factor*, "Super Tuesday Analysis," Fox News, March 2, 2016.

15. Kristen Hare and Alexios Mantzarlis, "How the 2016 Political Campaign Changed Political Journalism," *Poynter*, November 8, 2016, accessed July 10, 2017, http://www.poynter.org/2016/how-the-2016-election-changed-political-journalism/437701/.

16. Kyle Pope, "An Open Letter to Trump from the US Press Corps," *Columbia Journalism Review*, January 17, 2017, accessed July 10, 2017, https://www.cjr.org/covering_trump/trump_white_house_press_corps.php.

17. Ibid.

18. John Motavalli, *Bamboozled at the Revolution: How Big Media Lost Billions in the Battle for the Internet* (New York City: Viking, 2002), 170.

19. As part of a wrongful termination lawsuit settlement in 2017, Tomi Lahren agreed to remove videos she'd created for TheBlaze from her Facebook page, according to the *Washington Post*. However, as of July 10, 2017, Lahren's monologue about Colin Kaepernick was still accessible on Facebook. See Tomi Lahren, Facebook post, August 29, 2016, https://www.facebook.com/TomiLahren/videos/1063123907114129/.

20. Jason Wilson, "The Rise of Tomi Lahren, the Media Star Lampooned as 'White Power Barbie," *The Guardian*, September 23, 2017, *The Guardian,* accessed July 10, 2017, https://www.theguardian.com/us-news/2016/sep/23/tomi-lahren-conservative-white-power-barbie.

21. danah boyd, "Reality Check: I Blame the Media," *Points*, November 9, 2016, accessed July 10, 2017, https://points.datasociety.net/reality-check-de447f2131a3.

22. David Morris, "American Voice 2004: Can Radio and TV Devote More Airtime to One National Convention than the Other?" Institute for Local Self-Reliance, June 1, 2004, accessed July 10, 2017, https://ilsr.org/can-radio-and-tv-devote-more-airtime-to-one-national-convention-than-another/.

23. Philosopher Thomas Nagel developed the idea of "the view from nowhere" in the 1980s, before media scholar Jay Rosen famously applied it to journalism in 2003. See Thomas Nagel, *The View From Nowhere* (Oxford: Oxford University Press, 1986); Jay Rosen, "The View From Nowhere," *PressThink*, September 18, 2003, accessed July 10, 2017, http://archive.pressthink.org/2003/09/18/jennings.html.

24. Amy Mitchell et al., "Political Polarization & Media Habits," Pew Research Center, October 21, 2014, accessed July 5, 2017, http://www.journalism.org /2014/10/21/political-polarization-media-habits/.

25. Scott Shane, "From Headline to Photograph, a Fake News Masterpiece," *New York Times*, January 18, 2017, accessed July 10, 2017, https://www.nytimes .com/2017/01/18/us/fake-news-hillary-clinton-cameron-harris.html?_r=0.

26. Craig Silverman and Lawrence Alexander, "How Teens in the Balkans Are Duping Trump Supporters with Fake News," *BuzzFeed*, November 3, 2016, accessed July 12, 2017, https://www.buzzfeed.com/craigsilverman/how-macedonia -became-a-global-hub-for-pro-trump-misinfo?utm_term=.blOQod26qb# .dcNb8KAZEQ.

27. Bill Kovach and Tom Rosenstiel, *The Elements of Journalism: What Newspeople Should Know and the Public Should Expect* (New York: Crown Publishers, 2001), 13.

28. *The Daily Show with Trevor Noah*, "Matt Taibbi," Comedy Central, January 23, 2017.

29. Barack Obama, interview by Bill Maher, *Real Time with Bill Maher*, HBO, November 4, 2017; Barack Obama, "Remarks by President Obama and Chancellor Merkel of Germany in a Joint Press Conference" (speech, November 17, 2016), The White House Office of the Press Secretary, https://obamawhitehouse.archives.gov /the-press-office/2016/11/17/remarks-president-obama-and-chancellor-merkel -germany-joint-press.

30. Barack Obama, "Farewell Address to the Nation from Chicago, Illinois" (speech, January 10, 2017), The American Presidency Project, http://www .presidency.ucsb.edu/ws/?pid=119928.

31. Jeffrey Gottfried and Elisa Shearer, "News Use Across Social Media Platforms 2016," Pew Research Center, May 26, 2016, accessed July 12, 2017, http:// www.journalism.org/2016/05/26/news-use-across-social-media-platforms-2016/.

32. Craig Silverman, "This Analysis Shows How Viral Fake Election News Stories Outperformed Real News on Facebook," *BuzzFeed*, November 16, 2016, accessed July 12, 2017, https://www.buzzfeed.com/craigsilverman/viral-fake -election-news-outperformed-real-news-on-facebook?utm_term=.vkBjqn kymZ#.levKb9GRZn.

33. Zeynep Tufekci, "Mark Zuckerberg Is in Denial," *New York Times*, November 15, 2016, accessed July 12, 2017, https://www.nytimes.com/2016/11/15 /opinion/mark-zuckerberg-is-in-denial.html?_r=0.

34. Sheera Frenkel, "Renegade Facebook Employees Form Task Force to Battle Fake News," *BuzzFeed*, November 14, 2016, accessed July 12, 2017, https:// www.buzzfeed.com/sheerafrenkel/renegade-facebook-employees-form-task -force-to-battle-fake-n?utm_term=.opnVpakAZO#.qaZy8wd1ql.

35. Michael Nunez, "Former Facebook Workers: We Routinely Suppressed Conservative News," *Gizmodo*, May 9, 2016, accessed July 12, 2017, http:// gizmodo.com/former-facebook-workers-we-routinely-suppressed-conser -1775461006.

36. Mark Zuckerberg, Facebook post, May 12, 2016, https://www.facebook.com/zuck/posts/10102830259184701.

37. Giulia Segreti, "Facebook CEO Says Group Will Not Become a Media Company," *Reuters*, August 29, 2016, accessed July 12, 2017, http://www.reuters.com/article/us-facebook-zuckerberg-idUSKCN1141WN.

38. Alan Yuhas, "Facebook Announces New Push Against Fake News After Obama Comments," *The Guardian*, November 19, 2016, accessed July 12, 2017, https://www.theguardian.com/technology/2016/nov/19/facebook-fake-news-mark-zuckerberg; Fidji Simo, "Introducing: The Facebook Journalism Project," January 11, 2017, accessed July 12, 2017, https://media.fb.com/2017/01/11/facebook-journalism-project/; Mark Zuckerberg, "Building Global Community," Facebook, February 16, 2017, https://www.facebook.com/notes/mark-zuckerberg/building-global-community/10154544292806634/.

39. Mark Zuckerberg, Facebook post, May 12, 2016, https://www.facebook.com/zuck/posts/10102830259184701; Mark Zuckerberg, "Note from Mark Zuckerberg," Facebook, April 27, 2016, https://newsroom.fb.com/news/2016/04/marknote/.

40. "Facebook Reports Fourth Quarter and Full Year 2016 Results," Facebook, February 1, 2017, https://investor.fb.com/investor-news/press-release-details/2017/facebook-Reports-Fourth-Quarter-and-Full-Year-2016-Results/default.aspx.

41. John Herrman, "Inside Facebook's (Totally Insane, Unintentionally Gigantic, Hyperpartisan) Political-Media Machine," *New York Times Magazine*, August 24, 2016, accessed July 12, 2017, https://www.nytimes.com/2016/08/28/magazine/inside-facebooks-totally-insane-unintentionally-gigantic-hyperpartisan-political-media-machine.html.

42. George Bush, "State of the Union Address," (speech, January 29, 2002), The White House Office of the Press Secretary, https://georgewbush-whitehouse.archives.gov/news/releases/2002/01/20020129-11.html.

43. "In Their Own Words: Who Said What When," PBS, accessed July 12, 2017, http://www.pbs.org/wgbh/pages/frontline/shows/truth/why/said.html.

44. Paul Krugman, "Errors and Lies," *New York Times*, May 18, 2015, accessed July 12, 2017, https://www.nytimes.com/2015/05/18/opinion/paul-krugman-errors-and-lies.html?_r=1.

45. *The Daily Show with Jon Stewart*, "Judith Miller," Comedy Central, April 29, 2015.

46. Lee Becker, Allan L. McCutcheon, and Tudor Vlad, "Who Really Thinks Saddam Was Personally Involved? Examining Changes in Misperceptions About the Iraq War" (paper presented to Midwest Association for Public Opinion Research, Chicago, Illinois, November 17–18, 2006).

47. Brett Cunningham, "Re-thinking Objectivity," *Columbia Journalism Review*, July/August 2003, accessed July 12, 2017, http://archives.cjr.org/feature/rethinking_objectivity.php.

48. Jeremy W. Peters, "Latest Word on the Trail? I Take it Back," *New York Times*, July 15, 2012, accessed July 12, 2017, http://www.nytimes.com/2012/07/16/us/politics/latest-word-on-the-campaign-trail-i-take-it-back.html.

49. Glenn Greenwald, "Inept Stenographers," *Salon*, July 17, 2012, accessed July 12, 2017, http://www.salon.com/2012/07/17/inept_stenographers/.

50. Carl Bialik, "Clinton Has Nearly Caught Up to Trump in Media Coverage," *FiveThirtyEight*, August 9, 2016, accessed July 12, 2017, https://fivethirtyeight.com/features/clinton-has-nearly-caught-up-to-trump-in-media-coverage/.

51. Lindsey Ellefson, "CBS CEO on Trump Campaign: It 'May Not be Good for America, But It's Damn Good for CBS,'" *Mediaite*, February 29, 2016, accessed July 12, 2017, http://www.mediaite.com/online/cbs-ceo-on-trump-campaign-it-may-not-be-good-for-america-but-its-damn-good-for-cbs/.

52. Brett Edkins, "Donald Trump's Election Delivers Massive Ratings for Cable News," *Forbes*, December 1, 2016, accessed July 12, 2017, https://www.forbes.com/sites/brettedkins/2016/12/01/donald-trumps-election-delivers-massive-ratings-for-cable-news/#d241596119e9.

53. Benjamin Mullin, "TV News Let the Public Down in Off-the-Record Meeting with Trump," *Poynter*, November 22, 2016, accessed July 12, 2017, https://www.poynter.org/2016/tv-news-let-the-public-down-in-off-the-record-meeting-with-trump/440044/.

54. Dana Milbank, "The Lap Dogs of Democracy Who Didn't Bark at Trump," *Washington Post*, October 24, 2016, accessed July 12, 2017, https://www.washingtonpost.com/opinions/the-lap-dogs-of-democracy-who-didnt-bark-at-trump/2016/10/24/26ba3418-9a28-11e6-9980-50913d68eacb_story.html?utm_term=.eea17ee2cb66.

55. Irvin Molotsky, "Dole Accuses Press and TV of Failing to Focus on Campaign Issue," *New York Times*, April 27, 1988, accessed July 12, 2017, http://www.nytimes.com/1988/04/27/us/dole-accuses-press-and-tv-of-failing-to-focus-on-campaign-issues.html.

56. Andrew Rosenthal, "More Questions About More Polls," *New York Times*, March 31, 1988, accessed July 12, 2017, http://www.nytimes.com/1988/03/31/us/more-questions-about-more-polls.html.

57. Thomas E. Patterson, *Out of Order* (New York: A. Knopf, 1993), 73–74.

58. David K. Perry, *The Roots of Civic Journalism: Darwin, Dewey, and Mead* (Landham, MD: University Press of America, 2003), 5–6.

59. Jeffrey A. Dvorkin, "Can Public Radio Journalism Be Re-Invented," NPR, n.d., accessed July 12, 2017, http://www.npr.org/yourturn/ombudsman/2001/010705.html.

60. Bob Steele, "The Ethics of Civic Journalism: Independence as a Guide," *Poynter*, August 25, 2017, accessed July 12, 2017, http://www.poynter.org/2002/the-ethics-of-civic-journalism-independence-as-the-guide/2128; Jay Rosen, *What Are Journalists For?* (New Haven, CT: Yale University Press, 1999), 75.

61. Rosen, *What Are Journalists*, 262.

62. William Glaberson, "A New Press Role: Solving Problems," *New York Times*, October 3, 1994, accessed July 12, 2017, http://www.nytimes.com/1994/10/03/business/the-media-business-a-new-press-role-solving-problems.html; Tony Case, "Public Journalism Denounced," *Editor & Publisher*, November 12,

1994, accessed July 12, 2017, http://www.editorandpublisher.com/news/public -journalism-denounced-p-14/.

63. Case, "Public Journalism."

64. Geneva Overholser, "Civic Journalism, Engaged Journalism: Tracing the Connections," Democracy Fund, August 3, 2016, accessed July 12, 2017, http:// www.democracyfund.org/blog/entry/civic-journalism-engaged-journalism -tracing-the-connections.

65. Ibid.

66. "State of the News Media 2006," Pew Research Center, n.d. accessed July 12, 2017, http://www.stateofthemedia.org/2006/network-tv-intro/audience/.

67. Stephen Earl Bennett, "Young Americans' Indifference to Media Coverage of Public Affairs," *PS: Political Science & Politics* 31, no. 3 (1998): 535.

68. "State of the News Media 2016," Pew Research Center, June 2016.

69. Paula M. Poindexter, *Millennials, News and Social Media: Is News Engagement a Thing of The Past?* (New York: Peter Lang, 2012).

70. Amy Mitchell et al., "The Modern News Consumer," Pew Research Center, July 2016.

71. Andy Kohut, "Pew Surveys of Audience Habits Suggest Perilous Future for News," *Poynter*, October 4, 2013, accessed July 12, 2017, https://www.poynter .org/2013/pew-surveys-of-audience-habits-suggest-perilous-future-for-news /225139/.

72. David M. Gross and Sophfronia Scott, "Living: Proceed with Caution," *Time*, July 16, 1990, accessed July 12, 2017, http://content.time.com/time/magazine /article/0,9171,970634,00.html.

73. Robert G. Kaiser, "The Bad News for News," *The Brookings Essay*, October 16, 2014, accessed July 13, 2017, http://csweb.brookings.edu/content/research /essays/2014/bad-news.html.

74. Mitchell, "Modern News Consumer"; Amy Mitchell, Jeffrey Gottfried, and Katerina Eva Matsa, "Millennials No Less Trusting (or Distrusting) of News Sources," Pew Research Center, June 1, 2015, accessed July 13, 2017, http://www .journalism.org/2015/06/01/millennials-no-less-trusting-or-distrusting-of-news -sources/.

75. "How Millennials Get News: Inside the Habits of America's First Digital Generation," American Press Institute," March 16, 2015, accessed July 13, 2017, https://www.americanpressinstitute.org/publications/reports/survey-research /millennials-news/.

76. Christopher K. Sopher, "The Kids Are Alright: How News Organizations Can Tap the Vast Potential of Younger Consumers," *NiemanLab*, August 18, 2010, accessed July 13, 2017, http://www.niemanlab.org/2010/08 /the-kids-are-alright-how-news-organizations-can-tap-the-vast-potential-of -younger-consumers/.

77. Ken Doctor, "The News Media and Trump," *Politico*, November 10, 2016, accessed July 13, 2017, http://www.politico.com/media/story/2016/11/the-news -media-and-trump-004850.

78. Ken Doctor, "Newsonomics: The Halving of America's Daily Newsrooms," *NiemanLab*, July 28, 2015, accessed July 13, 2017, http://www.niemanlab.org/2015 /07/newsonomics-the-halving-of-americas-daily-newsrooms; Penelope Muse Abernathy, *The Rise of a New Media Baron and the Emerging Threat of News Deserts* (Chapel Hill, NC: University of North Carolina Press, 2016), 12.

79. Ken Doctor, "Newsonomics: After John Oliver, The You-Get-What-You-Pay-For Imperative Has Never Been Clearer," *NiemanLab*, August 10, 2016, accessed July 13, 2017, http://www.niemanlab.org/2016/08/newsonomics-after -john-oliver-the-you-get-what-you-pay-for-imperative-has-never-been-clearer/.

80. Paul Starr, "Goodbye to the Age of Newspapers (Hello to a New Era of Corruption), *New Republic*, March 9, 2009, accessed July 13, 2017, https://newrepublic .com/article/64252/goodbye-the-age-newspapers-hello-new-era-corruption; Joshua Benton, "The Forces that Drove this Election's Media Failure are Likely to Get Worse," *NiemanLab*, November 9, 2016, accessed July 13, 2017, http://www .niemanlab.org/2016/11/the-forces-that-drove-this-elections-media-failure-are -likely-to-get-worse/; Steven Waldman, *The Information Needs of Communities: The Changing Media Landscape in a Broadband Age* (Washington, D.C.: Federal Communication Commission, 2011), 12.

81. David Griner, "U.S. Newspapers Make $40 Billion Less From Ads Today Than in 2000," *Adweek*, October 24, 2014, accessed July 13, 2017, http://www .adweek.com/digital/us-newspapers-make-40-billion-less-ads-today-2000 -160966/; "State of the News Media 2015," Pew Research Center, April 2015.

82. "State of the News Media 2016," Pew Research Center, June 2016.

83. "Revised Fourth-Quarter and Full-Year 2000 Earnings," Tegna, February 8, 2001, accessed July 13, 2017, http://www.tegna.com/revised-fourth -quarter-and-full-year-2000-earnings/.

84. "Dot-Com Layoffs and Shutdowns," *Wall Street Journal*, last modified November 28, 2001, accessed July 13, 2017, http://interactive.wsj.com/public /resources/documents/dotcomlayoffs.htm; Tim Jones, "Gannett Agrees to Buy Central Newspapers," *Chicago Tribune*, June 29, 2000, accessed July 13, 2017, http://articles.chicagotribune.com/2000-06-29/business/0006290125_1 _central-newspapers-gannett-dailies; "Gannett's Fourth-Quarter Earnings Up 5.6 Percent," *Washington Post*, January 27, 2005, accessed July 13, 2017, https:// www.washingtonpost.com/archive/business/2005/01/27/gannetts-fourth -quarter-earnings-up-56-percent/c94296bd-820c-4775-b926-e42c71ce10cc/ ?utm_term=.8c9e8d1b16be.

85. Michael Wolff, *The Man Who Owns the News: Inside the Secret World of Rupert Murdoch* (New York: Broadway Books, 2008), 87; Waldman, *Information Needs*, 37.

86. Donna Lampkin Stephens, *If It Ain't Broke, Break It: How Corporate Journalism Killed the* Arkansas Gazette (Fayetteville, AR: University of Arkansas Press, 2015), 25.

87. Eli M. Noam, *Media Ownership and Concentration in America* (Oxford, UK: Oxford University Press, 2009), 139–141; Abernathy, *New Media Baron*, 15.

88. Abernathy, *New Media Baron, 28.*

89. Ibid., 7.

90. Ibid., 40.

91. Felix Gillette, "The Sinclair Revolution Will Be Televised. It'll Just Have Low Production Values," *Bloomberg Businessweek*, July 20, 2017, accessed July 28, 2017, https://www.bloomberg.com/news/features/2017-07-20/the-sinclair-revolution-will-be-televised-it-ll-just-have-low-production-values.

92. Emily Bell, "How Mark Zuckerberg Could Really Fix Journalism," *Columbia Journalism Review*, February 21, 2017, accessed July 13, 2017, https://www.cjr.org/tow_center/mark-zuckerberg-facebook-fix-journalism.php.

93. Thomas Jefferson to Walter Jones, 2 January 1814, in *The Papers of Thomas Jefferson, Retirement Series, Vol. 7: 28 November 1813 to 30 September 1814*, ed. J. Jefferson Looney (Princeton, NJ: Princeton University Press, 2010), 100–104.

94. Thomas Jefferson to John Norvell, 14 June 1807, in *The Works of Thomas Jefferson*, Vol. 10, ed. Paul Leicester Ford (New York: G.P. Putnam's Sons, 1905), 417.

95. Thomas Jefferson to Adamantios Coray, 31 October 1823, *Founders Online*, National Archives, http://founders.archives.gov/documents/Jefferson/98-01-02-3837.

96. Michael M. Grynbaum, Sydney Ember, and Charlie Savage, "Trump's Urging That Comey Jail Reporters Denounced as an 'Act of Intimidation,'" *New York Times*, May 17, 2017, accessed July 13, 2017, https://www.nytimes.com/2017/05/17/business/media/trumps-urging-that-comey-jail-reporters-denounced-as-an-act-of-intimidation.html?_r=1.

97. Donald Trump, Twitter post, September 30, 2016, 12:20 a.m., https://twitter.com/realDonaldTrump.

98. Alex Jones, *The Alex Jones Show*, Genesis Communications Network, August 11, 2016.

99. Kyle Cheney et al., "Donald Trump's Week of Misrepresentations, Exaggerations and Half-Truths," *Politico*, September 25, 2016, accessed July 13, 2017, http://www.politico.com/magazine/story/2016/09/2016-donald-trump-fact-check-week-214287.

100. Ibid.

101. Swift, "Trust in Mass Media."

102. Joe Concha, "Trump Administration Seen As More Truthful Than News Media: Poll," *The Hill*, February 8, 2017, accessed July 13, 2017, http://thehill.com/homenews/media/318514-trump-admin-seen-as-more-truthful-than-news-media-poll.

103. Stephanie Kirchgaessner, "If Berlusconi Is Like Trump, What Can America Learn From Italy?" *The Guardian*, November 21, 2016, accessed July 13, 2017, https://www.theguardian.com/world/2016/nov/21/if-berlusconi-is-like-trump-what-can-italy-teach-america.

104. Roger Cohen, "Trump and the End of Truth," *New York Times*, July 25, 2016, accessed July 13, 2017, https://www.nytimes.com/2016/07/26/opinion/trump-and-the-end-of-truth.html.

105. Ken Pope, "Here's to the Return of the Journalist as Malcontent," *Columbia Journalism Review*, November 9, 2016, accessed July 13, 2017, https://www.cjr.org/criticism/journalist_election_trump_failure.php.

Chapter 1

1. Timothy Snyder, "20 Lessons From the 20th Century on How to Survive in Trump's America, *In These Times*, November 21, 2016, accessed July 5, 2016, http://inthesetimes.com/article/19658/20-lessons-from-the-20th-century-on-how-to-survive-in-trumps-america.

2. *Crossfire,* "Jon Stewart's America," CNN, October 15, 2004.

3. Jon Stewart et al., *America (The Book): A Citizen's Guide to Democracy* (New York: Warner Books, 2004), 133.

4. American Perspectives, "Presidential Election Politics," *CSPAN*, October 14, 2004.

5. *The Daily Show with Jon Stewart*, "Christina Hendricks," Comedy Central, April 22, 2013.

6. Benjamin Mullin, "Journalists on the Media Beat Critique Jon Stewart on His Last Day," *Poynter*, August 6, 2015, accessed July 5, 2017, http://www.poynter.org/2015/journalists-on-the-media-beat-critique-jon-stewart-on-his-last-day/363157/.

7. Jennifer Keishin Armstrong, "Meet the Woman Who Invented 'The Daily Show,'" *DAME*, January 27, 2015, accessed July 5, 2017, https://www.damemagazine.com/2015/01/27/daily-show-creator-i-cant-believe-cbs-put-another-white-man-late-night.

8. Lizz Winstead, *Lizz Free or Die: Essays* (New York: Riverhead Books, 2013), 221.

9. Armstrong, "Meet the Woman."

10. John Colapinto, "Jon Stewart: The Most Trusted Name in News," *Rolling Stone*, October 14, 2004, accessed July 5, 2017, http://www.rollingstone.com/tv/features/the-most-trusted-name-in-news-20041028.

11. Amanda Holpuch, "Jon Stewart Calls *Daily Show* Guest Hugh Grant 'A Big Pain in the Ass,'" *The Guardian*, December 14, 2012, accessed July 5, 2017, https://www.theguardian.com/media/tvandradioblog/2012/dec/14/jon-stewart-daily-show-hugh-grant.

12. *The Daily Show with Jon Stewart*, "Dennis Miller," Comedy Central, April 10, 2003.

13. Bill Carter, "CNN Will Cancel 'Crossfire' and Cut Ties to Commentator," *The New York Times*, January 6, 2017, accessed July 5, 2017, http://www.nytimes.com/2005/01/06/business/media/cnn-will-cancel-crossfire-and-cut-ties-to-commentator.html?_r=1.

14. Amy Mitchell et al., "Political Polarization & Media Habits," Pew Research Center, October 21, 2014, accessed July 5, 2017, http://www.journalism.org/2014/10/21/political-polarization-media-habits/.

15. "Today's Journalists Less Prominent," Pew Research Center, March 8, 2007, accessed July 5, 2017, http://www.people-press.org/2007/03/08/todays-journalists-less-prominent/.

16. Matt Taibbi, "'Objective Journalism' Is an Illusion," *The New York Times*, August 6, 2015, accessed July 5, 2017, https://www.nytimes.com/roomfordebate/2015/08/06/did-jon-stewart-have-a-serious-lesson-for-journalists/objective-journalism-is-an-illusion.

17. Matt Carlson and Jason T. Peifer, "The Impudence of Being Earnest: Jon Stewart and the Boundaries of Discursive Responsibility," *Journal of Communication* 63 (2013): 340.

18. Mullin, "Journalists on the Media Beat."

19. "Journalism, Satire, or Just Laughs? 'The Daily Show with Jon Stewart,' Examined," Pew Research Center, May 8, 2008, accessed July 5, 2017, http://www.journalism.org/2008/05/08/journalism-satire-or-just-laughs-the-daily-show-with-jon-stewart-examined/.

20. Thomas F. Gieryn, *Cultural Boundaries of Science: Credibility on the Line* (Chicago: University of Chicago Press, 1999), 1.

21. Matt Carlson and Seth C. Lewis, "What Are the Boundaries of Today's Journalism, and How Is the Rise of Digital Changing Who Defines Them?" *Nieman Lab*, April 27, 2015, accessed July 5, 2017, http://www.niemanlab.org/2015/04/what-are-the-boundaries-of-todays-journalism-and-how-is-the-rise-of-digital-changing-who-defines-them/; Matt Carlson, "Introduction: The Many Boundaries of Journalism," in *Boundaries of Journalism*: *Professionalism, Practices and Participation*, ed. Matt Carlson and Seth C. Lewis (New York: Routledge, 2015), 2.

22. Jane B. Singer, "Out of Bounds: Professional Norms as Boundary Markers," in *Boundaries of Journalism*: *Professionalism, Practices and Participation*, ed. Matt Carlson and Seth C. Lewis (New York: Routledge, 2015), 23.

23. Michael Schudson, *Discovering the News: A Social History of American Newspapers* (New York: Basic Books, 1978), 6.

24. "The Daily Show Cast on 'Personal Beliefs' @ Paley Center," The Paley Center for Media, July 29, 2008, accessed July 5, 2017, https://www.youtube.com/watch?v=FpSw0j8-4_o.

25. *The Daily Show with Jon Stewart*, "John Goodman," Comedy Central, November 27, 2011.

26. Chris Smith, *The Daily Show (The Book): An Oral History as Told by Jon Stewart, the Correspondents, Staff and Guests* (New York: Grand Central Publishing, 2016), 51.

27. Allison Adato, "Anchor Astray," *George*, May 2000.

28. Jon Stewart, Interview with Bill Moyers, *NOW with Bill Moyers*, PBS, July 11, 2003.

29. Katrina vanden Heuvel, "Jon Stewart's Progressive Legacy, *The Washington Post,* July 28, 2015, accessed July 5, 2017, https://www.washingtonpost.com/opinions/jon-stewarts-progressive-legacy/2015/07/28/f6587a2a-34a5-11e5-adf6-7227f3b7b338_story.html?utm_term=.09e628616536.

30. Amanda Holpuch and Tom McCarthy, "Jon Stewart Made Fake News Meaningful Without Sacrificing Comedic Bite," *The Guardian*, February 11, 2015, accessed July 5, 2017, https://www.theguardian.com/media/2015/feb/11/jon-stewart-daily-show-legacy-iraq-war-bush-cnn.

31. Michiko Kakutani, "Is Jon Stewart the Most Trusted Man In America," *The New York Times*, August 15, 2008, accessed July 5, 2017, http://www.nytimes.com/2008/08/17/arts/television/17kaku.html; Nate Scott, "How Jon Stewart Became the Voice of a Generation," *USA Today*, August 6, 2015, accessed July 5, 2017, http://ftw.usatoday.com/2015/08/jon-stewart-somehow-became-the-voice-of-a-generation; Colapinto, "Most Trusted Name in News"; Matthew Gilbert, "Jon Stewart's Game-Changing Legacy, *The Boston Globe*, August 4, 2015, accessed July 5, 2017, https://www.bostonglobe.com/arts/2015/08/03/jon-stewart-game-changing-legacy/3J6m3DuwVab28YBzUTw14L/story.html.

32. Stewart, Interview with Bill Moyers.

33. David T. Z. Mindich, *Just the Facts: How 'Objectivity' Came to Define American Journalism* (New York: New York University Press, 1998), 1.

34. Bill Keller, "Is Glenn Greenwald the Future of News?" *The New York Times*, October 27, 2013, accessed July 5, 2017, http://www.nytimes.com/2013/10/28/opinion/a-conversation-in-lieu-of-a-column.html.

35. Keller, "Future of News."

36. "The Marshall Project Mission Statement," *The Marshall Project*, accessed July 5, 2017, https://www.themarshallproject.org/about#.qSJ653C84.

37. Danny Funt, "Marshall Project Stakes Out High Ground on Journalism's Slippery Slope," *Columbia Journalism Review,* September/October 2015, accessed July 5, 2017, https://www.cjr.org/analysis/marshall_project_bill_keller.php.

38. Jaya Vengadesan, "Former *New York Times* Editor Bill Keller Discusses the Practice of Journalism in the Age of Trump," *The Highlander*, March 13, 2017, accessed July 5, 2017, https://highlandernews.org/28365/former-new-york-times-editor-bill-keller-discusses-practice-journalism-age-trump/.

39. Jay Rosen, Twitter post, September 17, 2016, 9:34 a.m., https://twitter.com/jayrosen_nyu; Peter Beinart, "The Death of 'He Said, She Said' Journalism," *The Atlantic*, September 19, 2016, accessed July 5, 2017, https://www.theatlantic.com/politics/archive/2016/09/the-death-of-he-said-she-said-journalism/500519/.

40. David Uberti, "Martha Raddatz and the Case for a More Assertive Debate Moderator," *Columbia Journalism Review*, October 10, 2016, accessed July 5, 2017, https://www.cjr.org/covering_the_election/martha_raddatz_anderson_cooper_debate_moderator_trump.php.

41. *Reliable Sources*, "Charles Osgood Retirement, J.D. Vance Joins Panels on Trump Coverage, Kathleen Carroll Addresses AP Tweets," CNN, August 28, 2016.

42. Sarah Posner, "How Donald Trump's New Campaign Chief Created an Online Haven for White Nationalists," *Mother Jones,* August 22, 2016, accessed October 15, 2017, http://www.motherjones.com/politics/2016/08/stephen-bannon-donald-trump-alt-right-breitbart-news/.

43. "What Is Crooked Media," *Crooked Media*, January 9, 2017, accessed July 5, 2017, https://getcrookedmedia.com/here-have-a-mission-statement-e365a663d004.

44. Alexander Nazaryan, "Crooked Media Fights Trump with 'Pod Save America,'" *Newsweek*, March 26, 2017, accessed July 5, 2017, http://www.newsweek.com/crooked-media-fights-trump-pod-save-america-jon-favreau-jon-lovett-tommy-570695.

45. Comedy Central launched *The Nightly Show with Larry Wilmore* in January 2015 as a successor to *The Colbert Report*. Despite receiving critical acclaim, the show was discontinued in August 2016 due to poor ratings.

46. *The Nightly Show with Larry Wilmore*, "Walter Scott Shooting & Rand Paul 2016," Comedy Central, April 8, 2015.

47. Ryan Grim and Nick Wing, "Here's a News Report We'd Be Reading if Walter Scott's Killing Wasn't on Video," *Huffington Post*, April 8, 2015, accessed July 6, 2017, http://www.huffingtonpost.com/2015/04/08/walter-scott-shooting-without-video_n_7024404.html.

48. Stuart Hall et al., *Policing the Crisis: Mugging, The State, and Law and Order* (London: Macmillan Press, 1978), 53–54.

49. Reagan Jackson, "White Bias in Media Is Ruining Your Life, Whether You Realize It or Not," *The Seattle Globalist*, July 11, 2016, accessed July 6, 2017, http://www.seattleglobalist.com/2016/07/11/white-bias-media-ruining-your-life/53546/.

50. "ASNE Releases 2016 Diversity Survey Results," *ASNE*, September 9, 2016, accessed July 6, 2017, http://asne.org/content.asp?contentid=447.

51. Jose Antonio Vargas, Twitter post, January 22, 2016, 12:57 p.m., https://twitter.com/joseiswriting.

52. David Itzkoff, "Trevor Noah on 'The Daily Show' and His 'Jewish Yoda,' Jon Stewart," *The New York Times*, September 23, 2015, accessed July 6, 2017, https://www.nytimes.com/2015/09/27/arts/television/trevor-noah-daily-show-jon-stewart.html?_r=0.

53. Lauren Williams, "The Daily Show's Jessica Williams on Race, Comedy, and Her Role in 'Girls,'" *Mother Jones*, January/February 2014, accessed July 6, 2017, http://www.motherjones.com/media/2014/01/interview-jessica-williams-daily-show-race-comedy-girls/.

54. Chava Gourarie, "Why Samantha Bee Is the Political Commentator We've Been Waiting For," *Columbia Journalism Review*, June 6, 2016, accessed July 6, 2017, https://www.cjr.org/criticism/samantha_bee_politics_trump.php.

55. Kenneth Olmstead, Paul Hitlin, and Nancy Vogt, "Net Neutrality: A Made-for-Web Debate," Pew Research Center, May 15, 2014, accessed July 6, 2017, http://www.pewresearch.org/fact-tank/2014/05/15/net-neutrality-a-made-for-web-debate/.

56. Marvin Ammori, "John Oliver's Hilarious Net Neutrality Piece Speaks the Truth," *Slate*, June 6, 2014, accessed July 6, 2017, http://www.slate.com/articles/technology/future_tense/2014/06/john_oliver_s_net_neutrality_segment_speaks_the_truth.html; Tim Wu, Twitter post, June 4, 2014, 4:07 p.m., https://twitter.com/superwuster.

57. Brian Steinberg, "How John Oliver and HBO Shattered TV's Comedy-News Format," *Variety*, July 2, 2014, accessed July 6, 2017, http://variety.com/2014/tv/news/how-john-oliver-and-hbo-shattered-tvs-comedy-news-format-1201257084/.

58. Walter Lippmann, *Public Opinion* (New York: Harcourt, Brace and Company, 1922), 358.

59. Thomas E. Patterson, *Out of Order: An Incisive and Boldly Original Critique of the News Media's Domination of America's Political Process*, (New York: Knopf Doubleday Publishing Group, 2011), 180.

60. Lippmann, *Public Opinion*, 358.

61. Ezra Klein, "Vox Is Our Next," *The Verge*, January 26, 2014, accessed July 6, 2017, https://www.theverge.com/2014/1/26/5348212/ezra-klein-vox-is-our-next.

62. Tom Rosenstiel, "The Future of News: Sense-Making and Other Strategies for Survival," *Poynter*, June 9, 2006, accessed July 6, 2017, http://www.poynter.org/2006/the-future-of-news-sense-making-and-other-strategies-for-survival/75655/.

63. Sarah Kliff, "Everything You Need to Know about Obamacare," *Vox.com*, January 5, 2017, accessed July 6, 2017, https://www.vox.com/cards/obamacare.

64. Carolyn Y. Johnson, "This Is How Obamacare Might Actually Explode," *The Washington Post,* April 11, 2017, accessed July 6, 2017, https://www.washingtonpost.com/news/wonk/wp/2017/04/11/this-is-how-obamacare-might-actually-explode/?utm_term=.22ba6c5c6226.

65. We borrow parts of this argument from Monika Bauerlein and Clara Jeffery, who discussed the importance of time and money for investigations like Shane Bauer's private prison reporting. See Monika Bauerlein and Clara Jeffery, "This Is What's Missing From Journalism Right Now," *Mother Jones,* August 17, 2016, accessed July 6, 2017, http://www.motherjones.com/media/2016/08/whats-missing-from-journalism/.

66. *The Colbert Report*, "Douglas Kmiec," Comedy Central, April 16, 2000.

67. Ibid.

68. Andy Towle, "National Organization for Marriage Thanks Colbert, Slams Schmidt," *Towleroad,* April 20, 2009, accessed July 6, 2017, http://www.towleroad.com/2009/04/national-organization-for-marriage-thanks-colbert-slams-schmidt/.

69. Heather LaMarre, Kristen D. Landreville, and Michael A. Beam, "The Irony of Satire: Political Ideology and the Motivation to See What You Want to See in The Colbert Report," *The International Journalism of Press/Politics* 14.2 (2009): 212.

70. Maureen Dowd, "Jon Stewart and Stephen Colbert: America's Anchors," *Rolling Stone*, November 16, 2006, accessed July 6, 2017, http://www.rollingstone.com/tv/news/americas-anchors-20061116.

71. Harry Enfield, interview with Malcolm Gladwell, "The Satire Paradox," *Revisionist History*, podcast audio, http://revisionisthistory.com/episodes/10-the-satire-paradox.

72. Matthew Dessem, "Here's Everything Samantha Bee Has Called Donald Trump on Full Frontal," *Slate*, November 5, 2016, accessed July 6, 2017, http://www

.slate.com/blogs/browbeat/2016/11/05/here_s_everything_samantha_bee_has
_called_donald_trump.html.

73. Last Week Tonight, "Voting," *HBO*, Feb. 14, 2016.

74. Adam Felder, "The Limits of the Late-Night Comedy Takedown," *The Atlantic*, April 17, 2016, accessed July 6, 2017, https://www.theatlantic.com/entertainment
/archive/2016/04/late-night-comedy/475485/.

75. *The Daily Show with Jon Stewart*, "Louis C.K.," Comedy Central, August 5, 2015.

76. Bill Brioux, "Don't Tell John Oliver He's Making a Difference," *The Toronto Star*, February 12, 2016, accessed July 6, 2017, https://www.thestar
.com/entertainment/television/2016/02/12/dont-tell-john-oliver-hes-making
-a-difference.html.

77. Barack Obama, "Farewell Address to the Nation from Chicago, Illinois" (speech, January 10, 2017), The American Presidency Project, http://
www.presidency.ucsb.edu/ws/?pid=119928.

Chapter 2

1. Gloria Steinem attributes this advice to a group of Gandhian reformers whom she met in India. See Gloria Steinem, *My Life on the Road* (London: Oneworld Publications, 2015), 37.

2. Liz Spayd, "Want to Attract More Readers? Try Listening to Them," *New York Times*, July 9, 2016, accessed July 6, 2017, https://www.nytimes.com/2016
/07/10/public-editor/liz-spayd-new-york-times-public-editor.html?_r=1.

3. Kristen Hare, "The Washington Post's Marty Baron Will Spend Election Day Waiting," *Poynter,* November 7, 2017, accessed July 6, 2017, http://www
.poynter.org/2016/the-washington-posts-marty-baron-will-spend-election-day
-waiting/437983/.

4. Marty Baron, "Commencement Address at the CUNY Graduate School of Journalism," (speech, December 16, 2016), *WashPost PR Blog*, https://www
.washingtonpost.com/pr/wp/2016/12/16/washington-post-executive-editor
-martin-baron-delivers-commencement-address-at-the-cuny-graduate-school-of
-journalism/?utm_term=.1dee774f8766.

5. Chuck Todd, "Analysis: As Election Day Arrives, Plenty of Blame to Go Around," *NBC News*, November 8, 2016, accessed July 6, 2017, http://www
.nbcnews.com/storyline/2016-election-day/analysis-election-day-arrives-plenty
-blame-go-around-n679356.

6. Margaret Sullivan, "The Media Didn't Want to Believe Trump Could Win. So They Looked the Other Way," *Washington Post*, November 9, 2017, accessed July 6, 2017, https://www.washingtonpost.com/lifestyle/style/the
-media-didnt-want-to-believe-trump-could-win-so-they-looked-the-other
-way/2016/11/09/d2ea1436-a623-11e6-8042-f4d111c862d1_story.html?utm
_term=.9f2f9806c659.

7. Nicholas Kristof, "Lies in the Guise of News in the Trump Era," *New York Times*, November 12, 2016, accessed July 6, 2017, https://www.nytimes.com/2016/11/13/opinion/sunday/lies-in-the-guise-of-news-in-the-trump-era.html.

8. Matt Taibbi, "President Trump: How America Got It Wrong," *Rolling Stone*, November 10, 2016, accessed July 6, 2017, http://www.rollingstone.com/politics/features/president-trump-how-america-got-it-so-wrong-w449783.

9. Matt Abbott, "Listening to Communities Is How We Shape the Journalism of the Future #GdnCMS," Centre for Community Journalism blog, March 15, 2017, accessed July 6, 2017, https://www.communityjournalism.co.uk/blog/2017/03/15/listening-to-communities-is-how-we-shape-the-journalism-of-the-future-gdncms-2/.

10. "Message from Diane McFarlin," University of Florida College of Journalism and Communications, accessed July 6, 2017, https://www.jou.ufl.edu/home/message-from-diane-mcfarlin/.

11. Melanie Sill, Twitter post, November 9, 2016, 6:42 a.m., https://twitter.com/melaniesill?lang=en.

12. Andrew Losowsky, "After the Election, News Organizations Need to Listen More than Ever," *Poynter,* November 17, 2016, accessed July 6, 2017, http://www.poynter.org/2016/after-the-election-news-organizations-need-to-listen-more-than-ever/439644/.

13. Kelly McBride, "Journalists, It's Time to Get Back to Work," *Poynter*, November 9, 2016, accessed July 6, 2017, http://www.poynter.org/2016/journalists-its-time-to-get-back-to-work/438452/.

14. Josh Stearns, "Creating a Trust Toolkit for Journalism," *First Draft*, December 19, 2016, accessed July 6, 2017, https://firstdraftnews.com/creating-a-trust-toolkit-for-journalism/.

15. danah boyd, "Reality Check: I Blame the Media," *Points*, November 9, 2016, accessed July 6, 2017, https://points.datasociety.net/reality-check-de447f2131a3.

16. Angelica Das, *Pathways to Engagement: Understanding How Newsrooms are Working with Communities*, ed. Jessica Clark (Washington, DC: Democracy Fund, 2017), 11.

17. Andrew Haeg, "Beyond Broadcast: Why We Need to Listen," *Medium*, July 15, 2016, accessed July 6, 2017, https://medium.com/@andrewhaeg/beyond-broadcast-why-we-need-to-listen-6c3d7b05aebc.

18. Alicia C. Shepard, "The Gospel of Public Journalism," *American Journalism Review* (September 1994): 28.

19. Jay Rosen, "The People Formerly Known as the Audience," *PressThink*, June 27, 2006, accessed July 6, 2017, http://archive.pressthink.org/2006/06/27/ppl_frmr.html.

20. Ibid.

21. Jeff Jarvis, *Geeks Bearing Gifts: Imagining New Futures for News* (New York: CUNY Journalism Press, 2014), 11-12.

22. Tracie Powell, "Building Reader Relationships," *NiemanLab,* accessed July 7, 2016, http://www.niemanlab.org/2016/12/building-reader-relationships/.

23. Joy Mayer, "How Building Trust with News Consumers Is Like Dating," *Reynolds Journalism Institute,* February 23, 2017, accessed July 7, 2017, https://www.rjionline.org/stories/how-building-trust-with-news-consumers-is-like-dating.

24. Andrew Haeg, "The Year of Listening," *NiemanLab,* accessed July 7, 2017, http://www.niemanlab.org/2016/12/the-year-of-listening/.

25. Isaac Chotiner, "The NYT's New Public Editor Has Some Terrible Advice for the Paper," *Slate,* July 10, 2016, accessed July 7, 2016, http://www.slate.com/blogs/the_slatest/2016/07/10/liz_spayd_s_first_nyt_public_editor_column_is_real_bad.html.

26. Jennifer Brandel, "A Serious Problem the News Industry Does Not Talk About," *Medium,* April 19, 2016, accessed July 7, 2017, https://medium.com/we-are-hearken/a-serious-problem-the-news-industry-does-not-talk-about-346caaa6d1cd.

27. Laurie Penny, "Laurie Penny: A Woman's Opinion Is the Mini-Skirt of the Internet," *The Independent,* November 4, 2011, accessed July 7, 2017, http://www.independent.co.uk/voices/commentators/laurie-penny-a-womans-opinion-is-the-mini-skirt-of-the-internet-6256946.html/.

28. Jessica Valenti, "Not All Comments Are Created Equal: The Case for Ending Online Comments," *The Guardian,* September 10, 2015, accessed July 7, 2017, https://www.theguardian.com/commentisfree/2015/sep/10/end-online-comments.

29. Chotiner, "New Public Editor."

30. Rebecca Bowring, "Listen Up! Hearken's Got Something to Say," *A Matter-Driven Narrative,* July 19, 2016, accessed July 7, 2017, https://medium.com/matter-driven-narrative/listen-up-hearkens-got-something-to-say-7560d098cdc5.

31. "ProPublica Is Hiring an Engagement Editor," *ProPublica,* accessed July 7, 2017, https://www.propublica.org/atpropublica/item/propublica-is-hiring-an-engagement-reporter.

32. Jeff Jarvis, "Social Journalism: Proposing a New Degree at CUNY," *Medium,* April 24, 2014, accessed July 7, 2017, https://medium.com/whither-news/social-journalism-39c0edce8a9.

33. Ben DeJarnette, "Toward an Inclusive Journalism: Reflecting the Communities We Represent," *MediaShift,* January 19, 2016, accessed July 7, 2017, http://mediashift.org/2016/01/toward-an-inclusive-journalism-reflecting-the-communities-we-represent/.

34. Mathew Ingram, "What the Missouri Protests Say About Where the Media Is Now," *Fortune,* November 10, 2015, accessed July 7, 2017, http://fortune.com/2015/11/10/missouri-media/.

35. Jake Batsell, *Engaged Journalism: Connecting with Digitally Empowered News Audiences* (New York: Columbia University Press, 2015), 7.

36. Ibid., xv.

37. Ibid.

38. Ben DeJarnette, "Before Interviewing, Journalists Must Listen Deeply," *MediaShift*, January 14, 2016, accessed July 8, 2017, http://mediashift.org/2016/01/before-interviewing-journalists-must-listen-deeply/.

39. Lizzy Acker, "Black-Owned Portland Cupcake Shop Accused of Racism," *OregonLive*, October 10, 2016, accessed July 8, 2017, http://www.oregonlive.com/foodday/index.ssf/2016/10/black-owned_portland_cupcake_s.html#comments.

40. Andrew Haeg, "The Engagement Manifesto: Part I," *Medium*, February 25, 2016, accessed July 8, 2017, https://medium.com/groundsource-notes/the-engagement-manifesto-part-i-9c348b34200f.

41. Robin Amber, "Six Tunnels Hidden Under Chicago's Loop," WBEZ, June 20, 2013, accessed July 8, 2017, https://www.wbez.org/shows/curious-city/six-tunnels-hidden-under-chicagos-loop/a4a5fc40-fbd6-415e-96b1-29d767363e57; Lewis Wallace, "Being a Breadwinner on $8.25 an Hour," WBEZ, May 21, 2013, accessed July 8, 2017, https://www.wbez.org/shows/wbez-news/being-a-breadwinner-on-825-an-hour/d25ca7f6-8b01-426e-baf4-79825fe276d2; Chris Bentley, "How Much Road Salt Ends Up In Lake Michigan, WBEZ, March 5, 2015, accessed July 8, 2017, https://www.wbez.org/shows/curious-city/how-much-road-salt-ends-up-in-lake-michigan/6d75b490-1bee-42e0-9679-1b1bedb5e1bb.

42. Mark Brush, "What's the Status of the Old Oil Pipeline Under Lake Michigan? We Need More Information to Know," Michigan Radio, October 9, 2014, accessed July 8, 2017, http://michiganradio.org/post/whats-status-old-oil-pipeline-under-lake-michigan-we-need-more-information-know; Latoya Dennis, "South Side of Milwaukee, Your Bar Dice Rules Aren't Wrong—Just Different," WUWM, November 4, 2016, accessed July 8, 2017, http://wuwm.com/post/south-side-milwaukee-your-bar-dice-rules-arent-wrong-just-different#stream/0.

43. Ben DeJarnette, "One Year In, Hearken's Audience Engagement Platform is Catching Fire, *MediaShift*, March 1, 2016, accessed July 8, 2017, http://mediashift.org/2016/03/one-year-in-hearkens-audience-engagement-platform-is-catching-fire/; Ben DeJarnette, "How Michigan Radio Created its Own 'Curious' Project," Gather, n.d., accessed July 8, 2017, https://interact.fmyi.com/sites/20801?e=4167341; Vignesh Ramachandran, "'Curious City' Inspires Scalable Model for Engagement Journalism That Answers People's Questions," Knight Foundation, July 27, 2015, accessed July 8, 2017, https://www.knightfoundation.org/articles/curious-city-inspires-scalable-model-engagement-journalism-answers-peoples-questions; Kate Lesniak, "Bitch Media: Turning Readers Into Funders," Institute for Nonprofit News, May 16, 2017, accessed July 8, 2017, https://innovation.inn.org/2017/05/16/turning-readers-into-funders/.

44. Brandel, "Serious Problem."

45. David A. Fahrenthold, "David Fahrenthold Tells the Behind-the-Scenes Story of His Year Covering Trump," *Washington Post*, December 29, 2016, accessed July 8, 2017, https://www.washingtonpost.com/lifestyle/magazine/david-fahrenthold-tells-the-behind-the-scenes-story-of-his-year-covering-trump/2016/12/27/299047c4-b510-11e6-b8df-600bd9d38a02_story.html?utm_term=.5f15edefd76c.

46. David A. Fahrenthold and Jose A. DelReal, "Media Scrutiny Over Charitable Donations to Veterans Riles Up Trump," *Washington Post,* May 31, 2016, accessed July 8, 2017, https://www.washingtonpost.com/politics/media-scrutiny-over -charitable-donations-to-veterans-riles-up-trump/2016/05/31/cbb1fecc-272f -11e6-b989-4e5479715b54_story.html?tid=a_inl&utm_term=.d9259b519665.

47. Fahrenthold, "Behind-the-Scenes Story."

48. Dan Gillmor, "How One Reporter Turned to His Readers to Investigate Donald Trump," *The Atlantic*, December 21, 2016, accessed July 8, 2017, https:// www.theatlantic.com/politics/archive/2016/12/what-journalists-can-learn-from -david-fahrentholds-trump-coverage/511277/.

49. Jelmer Mommers, "Dear Shell Employees: Let's Talk," *De Correspondent*, n.d., accessed July 8, 2017, https://thecorrespondent.com/4049/dear-shell -employees-lets-talk/446236241-89c4a65a.

50. Ernst-Jan Pfauth, "How Reader Engagement Helped Unearth the Shell Tape," *Medium*, March 6, 2017, accessed July 8, 2017, https://medium.com/de -correspondent/reader-engagement-shell-4bb6d0b8fb84.

51. Ibid.

52. Mimi Onuoha, Jeanne Pinder, and Jan Schaffer, *Guide to Crowdsourcing* (New York: Tow Center for Digital Journalism, 2015), 4.

53. Terry Parris Jr. (engagement editor, *ProPublica*), in discussion with the author, October 2016.

54. Charles Ornstein, "Are You a Vietnam Veteran? Help Us Investigate the Impact of Agent Orange," *ProPublica*, June 23, 2015, accessed July 8, 2017, https:// www.propublica.org/getinvolved/item/vietnam-veterans-agent-orange -propublica-investigate.

55. Parris Jr., discussion.

56. "The Counted," *The Guardian*, accessed July 8, 2017, https://www .theguardian.com/us-news/ng-interactive/2015/jun/01/the-counted-police -killings-us-database.

57. Jamiles Lartey and Jon Swaine, "Philando Castile Shooting: Officer Said He Felt in Danger After Smelling Pot in Car, *The Guardian*, June 20, 2017, accessed July 8, 2017, https://www.theguardian.com/us-news/2017/jun/20/philando-castile -shooting-marijuana-car-dashcam-footage.

58. *AC360*, "Obama Cutting Overseas Trip Short, Will Visit Dallas Next Week; Protesters Gather After Deadly Dallas Ambush . . . ," CNN, July 8, 2016.

59. Todd Gitlin, "Media Ignore What It Means to Have a Read Conversation About Race," *BillMoyers.com*, July 12, 2016, accessed July 8, 2017, http://billmoyers .com/story/mean-conversation-race/.

60. "Under Our Skin," *Seattle Times*, n.d., accessed July 8, 2017, http:// projects.seattletimes.com/2016/under-our-skin/#.

61. Ibid.

62. Some of the comments, including this one, were removed from the "Under Our Skin" project page during the production of this book. However, this comment still appeared in a Google search as of July 8, 2017.

63. Adam Jude, "UW Coach Chris Petersen, Inspired by 'Under Our Skin' Series, Encourages Dialogue on Race," *Seattle Times*, September 1, 2016, accessed July 8, 2017, http://www.seattletimes.com/sports/uw-husky-football/uw-coach -chris-petersen-inspired-by-under-our-skin-series-encourages-dialogue-on -race/.

64. Mónica Guzmán, "Seattleites Took a 10-Hour Road Trip to Cross a Political Divide," *The Evergrey,* March 7, 2017, accessed July 8, 2017, https://theevergrey .com/took-10-hour-road-trip-cross-political-divide-heres-happened/.

65. Yu Vongkiatkajorn, "How Discourse Media's Brielle Morgan Got Canadians Talking About Child Welfare," Gather, n.d., accessed October 1, 2017, https:// gather.fmyi.com/sites/20801?e=4181350.

66. Erin Millar, "Why Discourse Pressed Pause and What Comes Next," Discourse Media newsletter, May 2017, accessed July 8, 2017, http://mailchi.mp /discoursemedia/why-discourse-pressed-pauseand-what-comes-next.

Chapter 3

1. Daniel Robson, "Punk Icon Lydon Shows Fondness for Japan in Book," *The Japan Times*, March 4, 2011, accessed July 29, 2017. http://www.japantimes .co.jp/culture/2011/03/04/music/punk-icon-lydon-shows-fondness-for-japan-in -book/#.WXxpzMeGNPY.

2. Lacy Rose, "Warning! This Shane Smith Interview Has 52 F-Bombs: "If I Can Come Up With the New Algorithm, Then I Win"," *Hollywood Reporter*, February 03, 2016, accessed June 2017, http://www.hollywoodreporter.com/features /warning-shane-smith-interview-has-861227.

3. Ben Quinn, "Murdoch Firm Dips into Hipsters' Bible with $70m Stake in Vice," *The Guardian*, August 16, 2013, accessed June 2017, https://www.theguardian .com/media/2013/aug/17/rupert-murdoch-vice-magazine-stake; Mathew Ingram, "Vice Media sells a 10-Percent Stake to Disney and Hearst, Valuing the Company at $2.5B," *gigaom.com*, August 29, 2014, accessed June 2017, https://gigaom.com /2014/08/29/vice-media-sells-a-10-percent-stake-to-disney-and-hearst-valuing -the-company-at-2-5b/.

4. 2017 Doug Herzog interview by Dr. Ed Madison.

5. Ibid.

6. BBC Radio 4, "Shane Smith," BBC Radio presented by Mark Coles, produced by Ben Crighton, British Broadcasting Corporation, http://www.bbc .co.uk/programmes/b04hmdks.

7. Jason Tanz, "The Snarky Vice Squad Is Ready to Be Taken Seriously. Seriously." *Wired*, October 18, 2007, accessed June 2017, https://www.wired.com/2007 /10/ff-vice/?currentPage=2.

8. Graham Winfrey, "How Vice Grew to a $4 Billion Media Powerhouse This Year," *Inc.*, November 18, 2015, accessed June 2017, https://www.inc.com /graham-winfrey/vice-media-2015-company-of-the-year-nominee.html.

9. Ibid.

10. "Shane Smith, the Hard-Partying Mogul Who Has Won Over the Millennials," *Ft.com*, https://www.ft.com/content/ad90e5d2-f227-11e3-9015-00144 feabdc0#axzz3MgFLB98x.

11. "HBO and VICE Enter Major News Content Deal," *Timewarner.com*, March 26, 2015, accessed June 2017, http://www.timewarner.com/newsroom /press-releases/2015/03/26/hbo-and-vice-enter-major-news-content-deal.

12. Ibid.

13. Jack Shafer, "The timeless appeal of Vice Media," *Reuters*, June 25, 2014, accessed June 2017, http://blogs.reuters.com/jackshafer/2014/06/25/the-timeless -appeal-of-vice-media/.

14. Isobel Yeung, "Activists Couldn't Stop 10,000 Dogs from Being Eaten Last Weekend in China," *Vice*, June 24, 2014, accessed June 2017, https://www .vice.com/en_us/article/locals-bite-back-at-yulin-dog-meat-festival; Jak Phillips, "I Ate a Dog in Hanoi," *Vice*, January 31, 2013, accessed June 2017, https://www .vice.com/en_us/article/i-ate-dog-in-hanoi.

15. Timesvideo: " 'Page One': David Carr Confronts Vice," *The New York Times*, February 13, 2015, accessed June 2017, https://www.nytimes.com/video /business/100000003509105/page-one-david-carr-confronts-vice.html; James Rainey, "*New York Times*' David Carr Holds 'Page One' A Final Time (Appreciation)," *Variety*, February 13, 2015, accessed June 2017, http://variety.com/2015 /biz/news/new-york-times-david-carr-holds-page-one-a-final-time-appreciation -1201433495/.

16. Brendan James, "Watch NYT's David Carr Completely Own The Top Executives At VICE," *Talking Points Memo*, February 13, 2015, http://talkingpoints memo.com/livewire/david-carr-vice-interview-page-one.

17. Ibid.

18. Gabriel Snyder, "*The New York Times* Claws Its Way into the Future," *Wired*, February 12, 2017, accessed June 2017, https://www.wired.com/2017/02 /new-york-times-digital-journalism.

19. Corinne Grinapol, "How *The New York Times* Went From Avoiding to Embracing Innovation in a Few Short Years," *Adweek*, February 13, 2017, accessed June 2017, http://www.adweek.com/digital/how-the-new-york-times-went-from -avoiding-to-embracing-innovation-in-a-few-short-years/.

20. Ibid.

21. NYT Press Release, *The New York Times* Company Reports 2016 Fourth Quarter and Full-Year Results, February 2, 2017, http://investors.nytco.com/press /press-releases/press-release-details/2017/The-New-York-Times-Company -Reports-2016-Fourth-Quarter-and-Full-Year-Results/default.aspx, accessed October 17, 2017.

22. Ken Doctor, "Trump Bump Grows Into Subscription Surge—and Not Just for *the New York Times*," *Thestreet*, March 3, 2017, accessed June 2017, https:// www.thestreet.com/story/14024114/1/trump-bump-grows-into-subscription -surge.html.

23. Vicky Huang, "New York Times and Spotify Look to Create Beautiful Music Together," *Thestreet*, February 11, 2017, accessed June 2017, https://www

.thestreet.com/story/13998230/1/new-york-times-and-spotify-look-to-create
-beautiful-music-together.html.

24. Lucia Moses, "The Favorite Publisher Trick that Makes Their Digital Audiences Look Bigger and Younger," *digiday.com,* February 18, 2016, accessed June 2017, https://digiday.com/media/favorite-publisher-trick-makes-digital-audiences-look
-bigger-younger/; Andrew Wallenstein, "Vice Media Traffic Plummets, Underscoring Risky Web Strategy," *Variety*, March 21, 2016, accessed June 2017, http://variety
.com/2016/digital/news/vice-media-traffic-plummets-underscoring-risky-web
-strategy-1201733673/.

25. Merissa Marr, "Pittman Envisions New Life for Radio," *The Wall Street Journal*, October 14, 2012, accessed June 2017, https://www.wsj.com/articles/SB1
00008723963904446578045780486234562 95566; T.L. Stanley, "MTV Founder Bob Pittman Is Our First Media Visionary," *Adweek*, December 15, 2013, accessed June 2017, http://www.adweek.com/brand-marketing/mtv-founder
-bob-pittman-our-first-media-visionary-154510/.

26. 2017 Doug Herzog interview by Dr. Ed Madison.

27. Paul Kaplan, "CNN/Sports Illustrated Channel to Go Off Air in May," *highbeam.com*, April 6, 2002, accessed June 2017, https://www.highbeam.com
/doc/1G1-122954265.html.

28. Paul Taylor and George Gao, "Generation X: America's Neglected 'Middle Child'," *Pew Research Center*, June 5, 2014, accessed June 2017, http://
www.pewresearch.org/fact-tank/2014/06/05/generation-x-americas-neglected
-middle-child/.

29. Jered Leto interview, Cannes Lions International Festival of Creativity, YouTube: https://youtu.be/9SWtKnevQmM, accessed October 17, 2017.

30. Rance Crain, "Bob Pittman's Winning Formula: Making the World More Convenient for Consumers," *adage.com*, June 15, 2015, accessed June 2017, http://
adage.com/article/rance-crain/bob-pittman-making-world-convenient
-consumers/299029/; Rick Andrews, "5 Facts You May Not Know About MTV," *mix941kmxj.com*, July 22, 2013, accessed June 2017, http://mix941kmxj.com/5
-facts-you-may-not-know-about-mtv/.

31. Steve Guttenberg, "MTV and the 'Day' the Music Died," *Cnet*, December 21, 2011, accessed June 2017, https://www.cnet.com/news/mtv-and-the-day-the
-music-died/; MTV Music Television Profile, Cable Network Information, *Parentstv.org*, accessed June 2017, http://www.parentstv.org/PTC/campaigns/Skins
/MTV%20Music%20Television%20Profile.htm.

32. 2017 Doug Herzog interview by Dr. Ed Madison.

33. Linda Holmes, "Did 'The Real World' Really Kill MTV?" *NPR*, November 7, 2011, accessed June 2017, http://www.npr.org/sections/monkeysee/2011/11/07
/142101549/did-the-real-world-really-kill-mtv.

34. "MTV: How Internet Killed the Video Star," *Independent*, June 5, 2008, accessed June 2017, http://www.independent.co.uk/news/media/mtv-how-internet
-killed-the-video-star-841393.html.

35. Karen De Witt, "The 1992 Campaign: Media; MTV Puts the Campaign on Fast Forward," *The New York Times*, February 8, 1992, accessed June 2017,

http://www.nytimes.com/1992/02/08/us/the-1992-campaign-media-mtv-puts-the
-campaign-on-fast-forward.html, Dan Fastenberg, "Ready For My Close Up: Boxers
or Briefs? Clinton Answers," *Time*, Thursday, July 29, 2010, accessed June 2017,
http://content.time.com/time/specials/packages/article/0,28804,2007228
_2007230_2007258,00.html.

36. Interview, Learner.org, accessed June 22, 2017, http://www.learner.org
/catalog/extras/interviews/kloder/kl03.html.

37. Lloyd Grove, "Will Viacom Be Here in a Decade? Big Media's Digital
Dilemma," The Daily Beast, August 21, 2015, accessed June 2017, http://www
.thedailybeast.com/will-viacom-be-here-in-a-decade-big-medias-digital
-dilemma.

38. Felix Gillette and Lucas Shaw, "Viacom Is Having a Midlife Crisis: Why
Nobody Wants Their MTV," *Bloomberg*, July 1, 2015, accessed June 2017, https://
www.bloomberg.com/graphics/2015-viacom-mtv-sumner-redstone/.

39. Christine Lagorio, "Viacom Demands YouTube Nix 100,000 Clips," *CBS
News*, February 2, 2007, accessed June 2017, http://www.cbsnews.com/news
/viacom-demands-youtube-nix-100000-clips/; Sean Alfano, "Viacom Sues You-
Tube, Google For $1B," *CBS News*, March 13, 2007, accessed June 2017, http://
www.cbsnews.com/news/viacom-sues-youtube-google-for-1b/; Peter Kafka, "It's
Over! Viacom and Google Settle YouTube Lawsuit," *recode.net*, March 18, 2014,
accessed June 2017, https://www.recode.net/2014/3/18/11624656/its-over-viacom
-and-google-settle-youtube-lawsuit; Greg Sandoval, "Viacom Moves On Without
YouTube," *Cnet*, February 9, 2007, accessed June 2017, https://www.cnet.com
/news/viacom-moves-on-without-youtube/.

40. Caitlin Fitzsimmons, "Monty Python DVD Sales Soar Thanks to You-
Tube Clips," *The Guardian*, February 26, 2009, accessed June 2017, https://
www.theguardian.com/media/pda/2009/feb/26/monty-python-dvd-sales-soar.

41. Shalini Ramachandran and Lukas I. Alpert, "Comcast Raises Its Bet on
New Media," *The Wall Street Journal*, august 18, 2015, accessed June 2017, https://
www.wsj.com/articles/comcasts-nbcuniversal-agrees-to-invest-in-buzzfeed
-1439927427; Mathew Ingram, "New Media and Old Media Are Getting Together
Because They Need Each Other," *Fortune*, august 13, 2015, accessed June 2017,
http://fortune.com/2015/08/13/comcast-invests-in-vox/;   Benjamin   Mullin,
"BuzzFeed News Gets Its First Pulitzer Citation," *poynter.com*, April 10, 2017,
accessed June 2017, https://www.poynter.org/2017/buzzfeed-news-gets-its-first
-pulitzer-citation/455406/; Benjamin Mullin, "Digital Digging: How BuzzFeed
Built an Investigative Team Inside a Viral Hit Factory," *poynter.com*, February 15, 2016, accessed June 2017, https://www.poynter.org/2016/how-buzzfeed
-built-an-investigative-team-from-the-ground-up/396656/; Vox   Media   Network. https://www.quantcast.com/p-d9vfr8QTWnvlE.

42. Oriana Schwindt, "Viceland Ratings: Here's How Many People Are Watching Vice Media's New Cable TV Network," *International Business Times*, March 25,
2016, accessed June 2017, http://www.ibtimes.com/viceland-ratings-heres-how
-many-people-are-watching-vice-medias-new-cable-tv-network-2343335.

43. Bloomberg News, "Vice's New Cable Network Is More Popular on YouTube Than TV," *Bloomberg*, March 23, 2016, accessed June 2017, https://www.bloomberg.com/news/articles/2016-03-23/vice-s-new-cable-network-is-more-popular-on-youtube-than-on-tv.

44. Ibid., 47.

45. Andrew Wallenstein, Vice Media Traffic Plummets, Underscoring Risky Web Strategy, *Variety*, accessed October 17, 2017, http://variety.com/2016/digital/news/vice-media-traffic-plummets-underscoring-risky-web-strategy-1201733673/.

46. Jordan Valinsky, "Vice's Shane Smith: 'Expect a Bloodbath' in Media Within the Next Year," *digiday.com*, May 20, 2016, accessed June 2017, https://digiday.com/media/shane-smith-vice-media-interview/.

47. Laura Jamison, "Forests Can Resist Climate Change, So Humans Should Too," *Vice Impact*, April 25, 2017, accessed June 2017, https://impact.vice.com/en_us/article/forests-can-resist-climate-change-so-humans-should-too; Larry Towell, "Bangladeshi Sweatshops Continue to Imperil Workers' Lives," *Vice*, September 20, 2015, accessed June 2017, https://www.vice.com/en_us/article/lost-lessons-from-rana-plaza-0000741-v22n9.

48. Anonymous Employee, "Hipster Sweatshop that Would Make Aldous Huxley Roll in His Grave," *glassdoor.com*, March 24, 2015, accessed June 2017, https://www.glassdoor.com/Reviews/Employee-Review-Vice-Media-RVW6187877.htm.

49. Ibid.

50. Hamilton Nolan, "Working at Vice Media Is Not As Cool As It Seems," *gawker*.com, May 30, 2014, accessed June 2017, http://gawker.com/working-at-vice-media-is-not-as-cool-as-it-seems-1579711577.

51. Jeremy Barr, "Facebook Is Taking Over the Media Business, Vice CEO Shane Smith Says," *adage.com*, May 20, 2016, accessed June 2017, http://adage.com/article/media/candid-shane-smith-sizes-vice-media-industry/304112/.

52. Jeff Bercovici, "Vice News Launches, Promising 'Changing of the Guard in Media'," *Forbes*, March 4, 2014, accessed July 27, 2017, https://www.forbes.com/sites/jeffbercovici/2014/03/04/vice-news-launches-promising-changing-of-the-guard-in-media/#c80bf2c2271f.

53. Bootie Cosgrove-Mather, "Al Gore Buying Int'l News Channel," *CBS News*, May 4, 2004, accessed June 2017, http://www.cbsnews.com/news/al-gore-buying-intl-news-channel/.

54. Maisie McCabe, "Al Gore's Current Media Abandons Plans for NYSE Listing," April 14, 2009, accessed June 2017, http://www.campaignlive.co.uk/article/al-gores-current-media-abandons-plans-nyse-listing/898262?src_site=mediaweek; Lisa Derrick, "Al Gore's Current TV Lays Off 80 Staff, Changes Direction," *Huffington Post*, March 18, 2010, accessed June 2017, http://www.huffingtonpost.com/lisa-derrick/al-gores-current-tv-lays_b_355248.html.

55. Brian Steinberg, "Al Jazeera America Already Has a Suitor: Herring Broadcasting," *Variety*, January 13, 2016, accessed June 2017, http://variety.com/2016/tv/news/al-jazeera-america-herring-broadcasting-suitor-1201679331/; Alicia P.Q.

Wittmeyer, "Is Al Jazeera America Simply CNN, Minus Wolf Blitzer?" *foreignpol-icy.com*, September 16, 2013, accessed June 2017, http://foreignpolicy.com/2013
/09/16/is-al-jazeera-america-simply-cnn-minus-wolf-blitzer/; Paul Farhi, "Al
Jazeera America: Was the TV News Network Cursed from the Start?" *The Wash-ington Post*, January 13, 2016, accessed June 2017, https://www.washingtonpost
.com/lifestyle/style/al-jazeera-america-news-channel-to-close-up-shop/2016/01
/13/aa3ab180-ba1f-11e5-99f3-184bc379b12d_story.html?hpid=hp_hp-top-table
-main_aljazeera-250pm%3Ahomepage%2Fstory&utm_term=.863016779d68.

56. Forbes Profile, "Jeffrey Skoll Real Time Net Worth," *Forbes*, June 22, 2017, accessed June 2017, https://www.forbes.com/profile/jeffrey-skoll/.61. Press Release, "Participant Media Announces Plan to Wind Down Pivot TV Cable Network," *participantmedia.com*, August 17, 2016, accessed June 2017, http://www.participantmedia.com/2016/08/participant-media-announces-plan -wind-down-pivot-tv-cable-network.

57. Ibid.

58. Liam Corcoran, "The Biggest Facebook Video Publishers in June," *news-whip.com*, June 30, 2015, accessed June 2017, https://www.newswhip.com/2015 /06/biggest-facebook-video-publishers-june/#abcpfPTXyfLgYHuq.97.

59. Ryot's Manifesto, accessed June 2017, https://www.ryot.org/about.

60. Jack Marshall, "Verizon's AOL Buys Virtual Reality Video Specialist RYOT," *The Wall Street Journal*, April 20, 2016, accessed June 2017, https://www.wsj.com /articles/verizons-aol-buys-virtual-reality-video-specialist-ryot-1461153651.

61. Arianna Huffington and Bryn Mooser, HuffPost RYOT, "Lights, Camera, Impact" HuffPost Blog, April 20, 2016, accessed October 17, 2017, https://www .huffingtonpost.com/arianna-huffington/huffpost-ryot-lights-came_b_9727240 .html.

62. Jason Tanz, "The Snarky Vice Squad Is Ready to Be Taken Seriously. Seriously." *Wired*, October 18, 2007, accessed June 2017, https://www.wired.com /2007/10/ff-vice/?currentPage=2.

63. Class discussion at the University of Oregon, May 24, 2017

64. Jack Marshall and Lukas I. Alpert, "Publishers Take On Ad-Agency Roles With Branded Content," *The Wall Street Journal*, December 11, 2016, accessed June 2017, https://www.wsj.com/articles/publishers-take-on-ad-agency-roles-with -branded-content-1481457605.

65. Fred Jacobs, "Reinventing Radio," *jacobsmedia.com*, February 18, 2016, accessed June 2017, http://jacobsmedia.com/reinventing-radio/.

66. About Us, accessed June 2017, https://www.thisamericanlife.org/about; John Wenzel, "Ira Glass Is a Clear Window into the Future of Radio," *The Denver Post*, February 11, 2016, accessed June 2017, http://www.denverpost.com/2016 /02/11/ira-glass-is-a-clear-window-into-the-future-of-radio/.

67. Jamie Doerschuck, "5 Things You Can Learn About Storytelling from Ira Glass," *medium.com*, August 5, 2016, accessed June 2017, https://medium.com/@the _doerco/what-you-can-learn-about-storytelling-from-ira-glass-335014cb7cdd.

68. Stuart Dredge, "Serial Podcast Breaks iTunes Records as It Passes 5m Downloads and Streams," *The Guardian*, November 18, 2014, accessed June 2017,

https://www.theguardian.com/technology/2014/nov/18/serial-podcast-itunes
-apple-downloads-streams; Dan Frommer, "What S-Town's Success Says about
the State of Podcasting," May 9, 2017, accessed June 2017, https://www.recode.net
/2017/5/9/15592044/s-town-podcast-ira-glass-nicholas-quah-million-listeners.

69. Ibid.

70. Chris Giliberti, "3 Reasons Why Millennials Want Long Form Storytelling Over 'Snackable' Content," *Forbes*, Mar 8, 2016, accessed June 2017, https://
www.forbes.com/sites/under30network/2016/03/08/3-reasons-why-millennials
-want-long-form-storytelling-over-snackable-content/#74109016380e.

71. Ibid.

72. Ibid

73. Sherry Turkle, *Reclaiming Conversation: The Power of Talk in a Digital Age*
(New York: Penguin Press, 2015).

74. Class discussion at the University of Oregon, May 24, 2017.

75. About Us—TV Show, accessed June 2017, https://www.thisamericanlife
.org/about/about-our-television-show.

76. Ibid.

77. Ibid.

78. Kimberly Meltzer, *TV News Anchors and Journalistic Tradition: How Journalists Adapt to Technology* (New York: Peter Lang Publishing, Inc.), 55–56.

79. Mary Elizabeth Williams, "Goodbye to Katie Couric, 'Perky' News Anchor?"
Salon, April 4, 2011, accessed June 2017, http://www.salon.com/2011/04/04/katie
_couric_leaving_cbs_news_report/.

80. Makers, "Katie Couric: Perky," *Makers*, July 20, 2012, YouTube Video,
00:55, July 20, 2012, https://www.youtube.com/watch?v=rL7El-b-XhY.

81. Margaret Sullivan, "If You Think Fox News is Changing, Rupert Murdoch's Internal Memo Shows It Isn't. At All." Washington Post. May 2, 2017,
https://www.washingtonpost.com/lifestyle/style/if-you-think-fox-news-is
-changing-rupert-murdochs-internal-memo-shows-it-isnt-at-all/2017/05/02
/99764a72-2f39-11e7-8674-437ddb6e813e_story.html?utm_term=
.d9ae69b3cf5e Accessed October 17, 2017.

82. Makers, 84.

83. J. K. Trotter, "Fox News Uses a 'Leg Cam' to Ogle Female Panelists" *Gawker*,
November 22, 2013, accessed October 17, 2017, http://gawker.com/fox-news-uses
-a-leg-cam-to-ogle-female-panelists-legs-1469841162; posted by Face Company,
"Report: The Female Exec Just Promoted at Fox News Used to Enforce a 'Mini-
Skirt Dress Code'," May 1, 2017, accessed June 2017, https://news.fastcompany
.com/report-the-female-exec-just-promoted-at-fox-news-used-to-enforce-a-mini
-skirt-dress-code-4036293.

84. Lindsey Ellefson, "Fox News Women Are Wearing Pants—Here's Why
That Matters," *mediaite.com*, May 2, 2017, accessed June 2017, http://www.mediaite
.com/online/fox-news-women-are-wearing-pants-heres-why-that-matters/.

85. Michael Parrish and Donald W. Nauss, "NBC Admits It Rigged Crash,
Settles GM Suit," *Los Angeles Times*, February 10, 1993, accessed June 2017, http://
articles.latimes.com/1993-02-10/news/mn-1335_1_gm-pickup.

86. Stone Phillips, "Why It's Not Entrapment," *NBC News*, February 1, 2006, accessed June 2017, http://www.nbcnews.com/id/11131562/.

87. Tiara M. Ellis, "Charges Dropped in Internet Sex-Sting Cases," *The Dallas Morning News*, June 7, 2007, accessed June 2017, http://archive.li/k60v9#selection -9283.3-9283.43.

88. Clarissa Cruz, "*Ocean's Eleven*'s Clooney Leads A New Rat Pack," *Entertainment Weekly*, December 10, 2001, accessed June 2017, http://ew.com/article /2001/12/10/oceans-elevens-clooney-leads-new-rat-pack/.

89. Sophia A. McClennen, "Bill O'Reilly Ruined the News: 10 Ways He and Fox News Harassed Us All," *Salon*, April 22, 2017, accessed June 2017, http://www .salon.com/2017/04/22/bill-oreilly-ruined-the-news-10-ways-he-and-fox-news -harassed-us-all/.

90. Punditfact, "Bill O'Reilly's File," http://www.politifact.com/personalities /bill-oreilly/.

91. Indiana University—Media Relations. "Content Analysis of O'Reilly's Rhetoric Finds Spin to Be a 'Factor'," May 2, 2007, accessed June 2017, https://web .archive.org/web/20070504040310/http://newsinfo.iu.edu/news/page/normal /5535.html; Mike Conway, Maria Elizabeth Grabe, and Kevin Grieves, "Villains, Victims, and the Virtuous in Bill O'Reilly's 'No Spin Zone'," *Journalism Studies* 8, no. 2 (2007), 214–218, accessed June 2017, DOI:10.1080/14616700601148820, https://web.archive.org/web/20070613215838/http://journalism.indiana.edu /papers/oreillyjourstud07.pdf.

92. Ibid., 95.

93. Pew Research, "Millennials, Media and Information," *Pew Research Center*, Washington, D.C. March 11, 2010, accessed June 2017, http://www .pewresearch.org/2010/03/11/millennials-media-and-information/.

94. Jennifer Maerz, "The Best Practices for Reaching a Millennial Audience," *American Press Institute*, October 16, 2015, accessed June 2017, https://www .americanpressinstitute.org/publications/reports/strategy-studies/millennials -best-practices/.

95. Don Irvine, "24 Hour News Cycle Takes a Toll," *Accuracy In Media*, July 21, 2010, accessed June 2017, http://www.aim.org/don-irvine-blog/24 -hour-news-cycle-takes-a-toll/.

96. Bob Papper, "RTDNA Research: Local News by the Numbers," *Newsroom Research Project*, May 31, 2016, accessed June 2017, https://www.rtdna.org /article/rtdna_research_local_news_by_the_numbers; Bob Papper, "RTDNA Research: Newsroom Staffing," *Newsroom Research Project*, July 25, 2016, accessed June 2017, https://www.rtdna.org/article/rtdna_research_newsroom _staffing.

97. David Dunkley Gyimah, "What Is Cinema Journalism?" posted 2016, Vimeo video, 04:46, accessed June 2017, https://vimeo.com/157988974.

98. Thom Powers, "The Kennedy Films of Robert Drew & Associates: Capturing the Kennedys," *The Criterion Collection*, April 26, 2016, accessed June 2017, https://www.criterion.com/current/posts/4030-the-kennedy-films-of-robert -drew-associates-capturing-the-kennedys.

99. Deborah D. McAdams, "Survey: 17 Percent of U.S. Households Are OTA-Only," *tvtechnology.com,* July 13, 2016, accessed June 2017, http://www.tvtechnology.com/news/0002/17-percent-of-us-households-are-otaonly/278987; TV Technology Staff, "CEA Study Says Seven Percent of TV Households Use Antennas," *tvtechnology.com,* July 30, 2013, accessed June 2017, http://www.tvtechnology.com/news/0002/cea-study-says-seven-percent-of-tv-households-use-antennas/220585; Jennifer Van Grove, "Digital Life Why TV antennas Are Making a Comeback," *The San Diego Union-Tribune,* January 20, 2017, accessed June 2017, http://www.sandiegouniontribune.com/business/technology/sd-fi-digitallife-antennas-20170120-story.html.

100. John Hockenberry guest speaking at the University of Oregon, May 24, 2017. As this book went to press, Hockenberry was one of several prominent media figures accused of inappropriate behavior in the workplace.

101. Ibid.

102. Ibid.

103. Nico Lang, "Why Teens Are Leaving Facebook: It's 'Meaningless'," *The Washington Post,* February 21, 2015, accessed June 2017, https://www.washingtonpost.com/news/the-intersect/wp/2015/02/21/why-teens-are-leaving-facebook-its-meaningless/?utm_term=.91e8533634be.

104. Thomas Shambler, "Snap to the Future: The Rise of Evan Spiegel," *Arabian Business,* June 22, 2017, accessed June 2017, http://www.arabianbusiness.com/snap-the-future—rise-of-evan-spiegel-677957.html; Celeb, "Bobby Murphy—Family, Family Tree," *celebfamily.com,* accessed June 2017, https://www.celebfamily.com/internet/bobby-murphy-family.html.

105. J.J. Colao, "Snapchat: The Biggest No-Revenue Mobile App Since Instagram," *Forbes,* November 27, 2012, accessed June 2017, https://www.forbes.com/sites/jjcolao/2012/11/27/snapchat-the-biggest-no-revenue-mobile-app-since-instagram/#312b7e357200.

106. Dan Moseley, "Snapchat: Impermanence Is Here to Stay," *wearesocial.com,* 18 November 2015, accessed June 2017, https://wearesocial.com/us/thought-leadership/snapchat-impermanence-stay.

107. John Koetsier, "Snapchat Installs PayPal: Planning Mobile Commerce Feature?" *Forbes,* Jun 5, 2017, accessed June 2017, https://www.forbes.com/sites/johnkoetsier/2017/06/05/snapchat-installs-paypal-planning-mobile-commerce-feature/#40efd94f1e16.

108. Jordan Novet, "Snapchat by the Numbers: 161 Million Daily Users in Q4 2016, Users Visit 18 Times a Day," *venturebeat.com,* February 2, 2017, accessed June 2017, https://venturebeat.com/2017/02/02/snapchat-by-the-numbers-161-million-daily-users-in-q4-2016-users-visit-18-times-a-day/.

109. Salman Aslam, "Snapchat by the Numbers: Stats, Demographics & Fun Facts," January 22, 2017, accessed June 2017, https://www.omnicoreagency.com/snapchat-statistics/.

110. Sarah Frier and Cynthia Hoffman, "Facebook's Clones Attack Snapchat," *Bloomberg,* February 22, 2017, accessed June 2017, https://www.bloomberg.com/graphics/2017-snapchats-copycats/.

111. Kerry Flynn, "Twitter Will Soon Have Ads Like Snapchat, Within Moments," *mashable.com*, May 4, 2017, accessed June 2017, http://mashable.com /2017/05/04/twitter-moments-ads-snapchat/#P5MB4EzXNaqw.

112. Kaya Yurieff, "Snapchat Unveils Custom Stories, Amid Battle with Facebook," *money.com*, May 23, 2017, accessed June 2017, http://money.cnn.com/2017 /05/23/technology/snapchat-custom-story/.

113. Company Profile: Snap, https://www.fastcompany.com/company/snapchat.

114. Lisa de Moraes, " 'Saturday Night Live' Launches Its First Snapchat Show, 'Boycott'," *deadline.com*, February 10, 2017, accessed June 2017, http://deadline .com/2017/02/saturday-night-live-snapchat-show-boycott-1201908073/.

115. Andrew Wallenstein, "Snapchat Shows: Inside the Plan to Reimagine TV for the Mobile Era," *Variety*, May 23, 2017, accessed June 2017, http://variety.com /2017/digital/news/snapchat-shows-inside-the-plan-to-reimagine-tv-for-the -mobile-era-1202440096.

116. Andrew Wallenstein, "Snapchat Launches 'Tonight Show Starring Jimmy Fallon' Offshoot," *Variety*, November 3, 2016, accessed June 2017, http://variety .com/2016/digital/news/snapchat-launches-tonight-show-starring-jimmy-fallon -offshoot-1201907463/.

117. A.J. Katz, "NBC News Will Produce the First Daily News Show for Snapchat," *Adweek*, May 23, 2017, accessed June 2017, http://www.adweek.com/tvnewser /nbc-news-will-produce-the-first-daily-news-show-for-snapchat/329981.

118. Ibid., 122.

119. Ibid.

120. Farhad Manjoo, "While We Weren't Looking, Snapchat Revolutionized Social Networks," *The New York Times*, November 30, 2016, accessed June 2017, https://www.nytimes.com/2016/11/30/technology/while-we-werent-looking -snapchat-revolutionized-social-networks.html.

121. Todd Spangler, "Snapchat Parent Loses $6 Billion in Market Value Overnight," *Variety*, May 11, 2017, accessed June 2017, http://variety.com/2017/digital /news/snapchat-market-cap-loss-6-billion-q1-earnings-1202423304/.

122. Tim Baysinger, "Snapchat 2017 Ad Revenue Forecast Trimmed to $770 Million: eMarketer," *Reuters*, March 14, 2017, accessed June 2017, http://www .reuters.com/article/us-snap-advertising-idUSKBN16L1JC.

123. Janko Roettgers, "Snapchat Earnings Disappoint With Slow User Growth, Lower-Than-Expected Revenue," *Variety*, May 10, 2017, accessed June 2017, http:// variety.com/2017/digital/news/snapchat-q1-2017-earnings-1202422693.

124. Christina Warren, "Holy Crap Snapchat Is Losing a Ton of Money," *gizmodo.com*, February 2, 2017, accessed June 2017, http://gizmodo.com/holy-crap -snapchat-is-losing-a-ton-of-money-1791938528.

Chapter 4

1. Rick Edmonds et al., "Newspapers: By the Numbers," *2013 State of the News Media*, Pew Research Center, May 7, 2013, accessed July 21, 2017, http:// www.stateofthemedia.org/2013/newspapers-stabilizing-but-still-threatened

/newspapers-by-the-numbers/; Ken Doctor, "Newsonomics: The Halving of America's Daily Newsrooms," *NiemanLab*, July 28, 2015, accessed July 21, 2017, https://www.americanpressinstitute.org/publications/reports/strategy-studies /events-revenue/.

2. Sarah Ellison and Jennifer S. Forsyth, "Zell Wins Tribune in Bid to Revive a Media Empire," *Wall Street Journal*, April 3, 2007, accessed July 26, 2017, https://www.wsj.com/articles/SB117551431653956734.

3. Gustavo Arellano, "Is Aaron Kushner the Pied Piper of Print," *OC Weekly*, December 13, 2012, accessed July 26, 2017, http://www.ocweekly.com/news/is -aaron-kushner-the-pied-piper-of-print-6424909.

4. Mary Ann Milbourn, "Register Owners Reflect on Their First Year," *Orange County Register*, July 27, 2013, accessed July 26, 2017, http://www.ocregister.com /2013/07/27/register-owners-reflect-on-their-first-year/; Arellano, "Pied Piper."

5. Arellano, "Pied Piper."

6. Ryan Chittum, "An Ink-Stained Stretch," *Columbia Journalism Review*, May/June 2013, accessed July 26, 2017, http://archives.cjr.org/feature/an_ink -stained_stretch.php.

7. Mark Katches, Twitter post, September 7, 2012, 5:16 p.m., https://twitter .com/markkatches.

8. Ravi Somaiya, "Aaron Kushner, Entrepreneur with Plans to Lead a California Newspaper Renaissance, Steps Aside," *New York Times*, March 11, 2015, accessed July 26, 2017, https://www.nytimes.com/2015/03/12/business/media /aaron-kushner-entrepreneur-with-plans-to-lead-a-california-newspaper -renaissance-steps-aside.html?_r=0.

9. Robert Kuttner, "The Race," *Columbia Journalism Review*, March/April 2007, accessed July 26, 2017, http://archives.cjr.org/cover_story/the_race.php.

10. Dean Starkman, "Confidence Game," *Columbia Journalism Review*, November/December 2011, accessed July 26, 2017, http://archives.cjr.org/essay/confidence _game.php.

11. Clay Shirky, "Newspaper and Thinking the Unthinkable," Skirky.com, March 13, 2009, accessed July 26, 2017, http://www.shirky.com/weblog/2009/03 /newspapers-and-thinking-the-unthinkable/.

12. Jeff Jarvis, *What Would Google Do?: Reverse Engineering the Fastest-Growing Company in the History of the World* (New York: Harper Business, 2009), 78.

13. Vivian Schiller, "A Letter to Readers About TimesSelect," *New York Times*, n.d., accessed July 26, 2017, http://www.nytimes.com/ref/membercenter /lettertoreaders.html.

14. Starkman, "Confidence Game."

15. Justin Ellis, "A Twin Cities Turnaround? The Star Tribune Carves a Path Back Through Growing Audience," *NiemanLab*, May 1, 2012, accessed July 26, 2017, http://www.niemanlab.org/2012/05/a-twin-cities-turnaround-the-star -tribune-carves-a-path-back-through-growing-audience/.

16. Alan D. Mutter, "Why Paywalls Are Scary," *Reflections of a Newsosaur*, April 10, 2013, accessed July 26, 2017, http://newsosaur.blogspot.com/2013/04 /why-paywalls-are-scary.html.

17. Joe Coscarelli, "*The New York Times* Is Now Supported by Readers, Not Advertisers," *New York*, July 26, 2012, accessed July 26, 2017, http://nymag.com /daily/intelligencer/2012/07/new-york-times-supported-by-readers-not -advertisers.html.

18. "Digital First CEO John Paton Discusses Future," *The Times Herald*, April 6, 2013, accessed July 26, 2017, http://www.timesherald.com/article/JR /20130406/FINANCE01/130409613.

19. Ken Doctor, "As Digital First Media Announces Its Paywalls, 41 Percent of US Dailies Will Soon Have Them," *Newsonomics*, November 18, 2013, accessed July 26, 2017, http://newsonomics.com/as-digital-first-media-announces-its -paywalls-41-of-us-dailies-will-soon-have-them/.

20. "State of the News Media 2015," Pew Research Center, April 2015.

21. "The State of the Blocked Web: 2017 Global AdBlock Report," PageFair, February 2017.

22. Mark Scott, "Rise of Ad-Blocking Software Threatens Online Revenue," *New York Times*, May 30, 2016, accessed July 26, 2017, https://www.nytimes.com /2016/05/31/business/international/smartphone-ad-blocking-software-mobile .html.

23. "2016 Publisher Outlook: Monetizing in the Age of Mobile & Video," AOL Publishers, n.d., accessed July 26, 2017, https://tankanyc.com/dev/aol /publisher-outlook/r2/us/#state-of-the-industry.

24. "State of the News Media 2016," Pew Research Center, June 2016.

25. In 2014 the Pew Research Center estimated that $5 billion in digital ad revenue was collected by news properties; in 2017 analyst Gordon Borrell put that number closer to $12 billion. See Jesse Holcomb and Amy Mitchell, "A Deeper Look at the Digital Advertising Landscape," Pew Research Center, March 26, 2014, accessed July 26, 2017, http://www.journalism.org/2014/03/26/a-deeper-look-at -the-digital-advertising-landscape/; Rick Edmonds, "After Google and Facebook Scarf Down Most of the Local Ad Pie, There's Still $12 Billion Left," *Poynter*, May 24, 2017, accessed July 26, 2017, http://www.poynter.org/2017/after-google -and-facebook-scarf-down-most-of-the-local-ad-pie-theres-still-12-billion-left /460759/.

26. Jake Kanter, "Former Guardian Editor: Facebook Sucked Up $20 Million of Our Online Ad Revenue Last Year," *Business Insider*, September 5, 2016, accessed July 26, 2017, http://uk.businessinsider.com/alan-rusbridger-blames-facebook -guardian-digital-revenue-2016-9?international=true&r=UK&IR=T.

27. "IAB Podcast Ad Revenue Study: An Analysis of the Largest Players in the Podcasting Industry," Interactive Advertising Bureau, June 2017.

28. "IAB Internet Advertising Revenue Report: 2016 Full Year Results," Interactive Advertising Bureau, April 2017.

29. Noah Kulwin, "Tribune Publishing Chairman: We Want to Start Publishing 2,000 Videos a Day with Artificial Intelligence," *Recode*, June 6, 2016, accessed July 26, 2017, https://www.recode.net/2016/6/6/11871908/tribune -publishing-artificial-intelligence-videos.

30. Antonis Kalogeropoulos, Federica Cherubini, and Nic Newman, *The Future of Online News Video* (Oxford, UK: Reuters Institute for the Study of Journalism, 2016), 8.

31. Sahil Patel, "Reality Check: Video Won't Save the Day for Digital Publishers Desperate for Growth," *Digiday*, April 11, 2016, accessed July 26, 2016, https://digiday.com/media/reality-check-video-wont-save-day-digital-publishers-desperate-growth/.

32. Dean Starkman, "A New Consensus on the Future of News," *Columbia Journalism Review*, February 28, 2014, accessed July 26, 2017, http://archives.cjr.org/the_audit/a_new_consensus_on_the_future.php.

33. Ryan Chittum, "Anti-Paywall Dead-Enders," *Columbia Journalism Review*, December 3, 2012, accessed July 26, 2017, http://archives.cjr.org/the_audit/zombie_lies_of_the_anti-paywal.php.

34. David Streitfeld, "'The Internet Is Broken': @ev is Trying to Salvage It," *New York Times*, May 20, 2017, accessed July 26, 2017, https://www.nytimes.com/2017/05/20/technology/evan-williams-medium-twitter-internet.html?_r=0.

35. Mike Ananny and Leila Bighash, "Why Drop a Paywall? Mapping Industry Accounts of Online of News Decommodification," *International Journal of Communication* 10 (2016): 3362.

36. Sydney Ember, "*New York Times* Co. Reports Rising Digital Profit as Print Advertising Falls," *New York Times*, May 3, 2017, accessed July 26, 2017, https://www.nytimes.com/2017/05/03/business/new-york-times-co-q1-earnings.html.

37. Gabriel Snyder, "The *New York Times* Claws Its Way into the Future," *Wired*, February 12, 2017, accessed July 26, 2017, https://www.wired.com/2017/02/new-york-times-digital-journalism/.

38. Joshua Benton, "A *New York Times* TimesSelect Flashback: Early Numbers are Nice, But Growth Over Time Is Nicer," *NiemanLab*, April 21, 2001, accessed July 26, 2017, http://www.niemanlab.org/2011/04/a-new-york-times-timesselect-flashback-early-numbers-are-nice-but-growth-over-time-is-nicer/.

39. Ken Doctor, "Newsonomics: The *New York Times* Is Setting Its Sights on 10 Million Digital Subscribers," *NiemanLab*, December 5, 2016, accessed July 26, 2017, http://www.niemanlab.org/2016/12/newsonomics-the-new-york-times-is-setting-its-sights-on-10-million-digital-subscribers/.

40. "Journalism That Stands Apart: The Report of the 2020 Group," *New York Times*, January 2017.

41. Ricardo Bilton, "The Boston Globe Is Getting Smarter About Digital Subscriptions—And Tightening Up Its Paywall," *NiemanLab*, May 31, 2017, accessed July 26, 2017, http://www.niemanlab.org/2017/05/the-boston-globe-is-getting-smarter-about-digital-subscriptions-and-tightening-up-its-paywall/.

42. Ben DeJarnette, "MECLABS Study Points to Major Opportunity for Online News Subscriptions," *MediaShift*, April 6, 2016, accessed July 26, 2017, http://mediashift.org/2016/04/meclabs-study-points-to-major-opportunity-for-online-news-subscriptions/.

43. Lucia Moses, "How the Washington Post Grew Digital Subscriptions 145 Percent," *Digiday*, July 12, 2016, accessed July 26, 2017, https://digiday.com /media/washington-post-grew-digital-subscriptions-145-percent/.

44. Daniel Funke, "'You Can't Shrink Your Way to Profitability': Jeff Bezos Talks About the Future of Newspapers," *Poynter*, June 21, 2017, accessed July 26, 2017, http://www.poynter.org/2017/you-cant-shrink-your-way-to-profitability-jeff -bezos-talks-about-the-future-of-newspapers/464243/.

45. Kathleen Kingsbury (former managing editor for digital, *Boston Globe*), in discussion with the author, September 2016.

46. Ken Doctor, "Newsonomics: 10 Numbers on *The New York Times'* 1 Million Digital-Subscriber Milestone," *NiemanLab*, August 6, 2015, accessed July 26, 2017, http://www.niemanlab.org/2015/08/newsonomics-10-numbers-on-the-new -york-times-1-million-digital-subscriber-milestone/.

47. Ibid.

48. Ariel Stulberg, "Testing News Paywalls: Which Are Leaky, and Which Are Airtight?" *Columbia Journalism Review*, May 23, 2017, accessed July 26, 2017, https://www.cjr.org/business_of_news/news-paywalls-new-york-times-wall -street-journal.php.

49. "Republican Platform 2016," Republican National Convention, July 2016.

50. "Guardian US Launches This Land Is Your Land, a New Editorial Series and Reader Contribution Campaign on the Growing Threat to America's Public Lands," *The Guardian*, June 5, 2017, accessed July 26, 2017, https://www .theguardian.com/guardian-us-press-office/2017/jun/05/guardian-us-launches -this-land-is-your-land-a-new-editorial-series-and-reader-contribution -campaign-on-the-growing-threat-to-americas-public-lands.

51. Joe Amditis, "We're Launching Another Collaborative Reporting Project. Join Us," Center for Cooperative Media, March 29, 2016, accessed July 26, 2017, https://medium.com/centerforcooperativemedia/we-re-launching-another -collaborative-reporting-project-d289b7cd73f7.

52. Monika Bauerlein and Clara Jeffery, "Now It's About Much More than Trump and Russia," *Mother Jones*, May 12, 2017, accessed July 26, 2017, http:// www.motherjones.com/media/2017/05/facts-trump-russia/.

53. Jason Alcorn, "We Asked the Public to Crowdfund Reporting on the Washington State Legislature," *Medium*, March 8, 2016, accessed July 26, 2017, https://medium.com/@jasonalcorn/we-asked-the-public-to-crowdfund -reporting-on-the-washington-state-legislature-1a2a165bf142.

54. Gabe Bullard, "Crowdfunding the News," *NiemanReports*, September 26, 2016, accessed July 26, 2017, http://niemanreports.org/articles/crowdfunding-the -news/.

55. "Investigating the Intern Economy," Kickstarter, accessed July 26, 2017, https://www.kickstarter.com/projects/propublica/investigating-the-intern -economy.

56. "New Boston Review Web Site," Kickstarter, accessed July 26, 2017, https://www.kickstarter.com/projects/1617105743/new-boston-review-web-site /description.

57. Nancy Vogt and Amy Mitchell, "Crowdfunded Journalism: A Small But Growing Addition to Publicly Driven Journalism," Pew Research Center, January 20, 2016, accessed July 26, 2017, http://www.journalism.org/2016/01/20/crowdfunded-journalism/.

58. Ernst-Jan Pfauth, "How We Turned a World Record in Journalism Crowd-Funding into an Actual Publication," *Medium*, November 27, 2013, accessed July 26, 2017, https://medium.com/de-correspondent/how-we-turned-a-world-record-in-journalism-crowd-funding-into-an-actual-publication-2a06e298afe1.

59. Ibid.

60. Loes Witschge, "A Dutch Crowdfunded News Site Has Raised $1.3 Million and Hopes for a Digital-Native Journalism," *NiemanLab*, April 5, 2013, accessed July 26, 2017, http://www.niemanlab.org/2013/04/a-dutch-crowdfunded-news-site-has-raised-1-3-million-and-hopes-for-a-digital-native-journalism/.

61. Ernst-Jan Pfauth, "A Short Guide to Crowdfunding Journalism," *Medium*, April 16, 2015, accessed July 26, 2017, https://medium.com/de-correspondent/a-short-guide-to-crowdfunding-journalism-b495ecba710.

62. Bullard, "Crowdfunding the News."

63. Josh Stearns, "Journalism Live: How News Events Foster Engagement and Expand Revenue," Democracy Fund, n.d., accessed July 26, 2017, https://localnewslab.org/guide/events/.

64. Kristen Hare, "Gannett Takes the Idea Behind Arizona Storytellers Project Nationwide," *Poynter*, September 15, 2015, accessed July 26, 2017, https://www.poynter.org/2015/gannett-takes-the-idea-behind-arizona-storytellers-project-nationwide/371421/.

65. Stearns, "Journalism Live."

66. Leslie Kaufman, "Media Outlets Embrace Conferences as Profits Rise," *New York Times*, October 27, 2013, accessed July 26, 2017, http://www.nytimes.com/2013/10/28/business/media/media-outlets-embrace-conferences-as-profits-rise.html; Ken Doctor, "The Newsonomics of the New Chattanooga (Events) Choo-Choo," *NiemanLab*, September 18, 2013, accessed July 26, 2017, http://www.niemanlab.org/2013/09/the-newsonomics-of-the-new-chattanooga-events-choo-choo/; Jake Batsell, "How MinnPost Raised $160,000 While Having Fun With Its Audience," *MediaShift*, May 6, 2017, accessed July 26, 2017, http://mediashift.org/2014/05/how-minnpost-raised-160000-while-having-fun-with-its-audience/; Anna Clark, "Amid Big Changes in Philly Media, Startup Billy Penn Sticks to Its Vision," *Columbia Journalism Review*, February 4, 2016, accessed July 26, 2017, https://www.cjr.org/united_states_project/billy_penn.php.

67. Kevin Loker, "The Best Strategies for Generating Revenue Through Events," American Press Institute, August 7, 2014, accessed July 26, 2017, https://www.americanpressinstitute.org/publications/reports/strategy-studies/events-revenue/.

68. "Code of Ethics," *Texas Tribune*, accessed July 26, 2017, https://www.texastribune.org/about/ethics/.

69. Celeste LeCompte, "Find Your Trampoline" (presentation, ONA16, Denver, CO, October 15, 2016).

70. Celeste LeCompte (director of business development, ProPublica), in discussion with the author, September 2016.

71. Ricardo Bilton, "ProPublica's Data Store, Which Has Pulled in $200k, Is Now Selling Datasets for Other News Orgs," *NiemanLab*, October 7, 2016, accessed July 26, 2017, http://www.niemanlab.org/2016/10/propublicas-data-store-which -has-pulled-in-200k-is-now-selling-datasets-for-other-news-orgs/.

72. Ibid.

Chapter 5

1. Eric Hoffer, *Reflections on the Human Condition* (New York: Harper & Row, 1973), 22.

2. Robert W. McChesney and John Nichols outlined a detailed proposal for taxpayer-subsidized journalism in 2010. See Robert W. McChesney and John Nichols, *The Death and Life of American Journalism: The Media Revolution That Will Begin the World Again* (New York: Nation Books, 2010), 157–212.

3. AJ Vicens, "Two GOP Congressmen Suggest Trump May Have Committed Impeachable Offense," *Mother Jones*, May 17, 2017, accessed July 18, 2017, http://www.motherjones.com/politics/2017/05/amash-trump-impeachment/.

4. Alan Rappeport, "Donald Trump Threatens to Sue The Times Over Article on Unwanted Advances," *New York Times*, October 13, 2016, accessed July 18, 2017, https://www.nytimes.com/2016/10/14/us/politics/donald-trump -lawsuit-threat.html?_r=0.

5. "Joe Concha, "Trump Administration Seen as More Truthful than News Media: Poll," *TheHill,* February 8, 2017, accessed July 19, 2017, http:// thehill.com/homenews/media/318514-trump-admin-seen-as-more-truthful -than-news-media-poll.

6. Jennifer De Pinto et al., "Republicans Blame Bill, Not Trump, for Health Care Defeat," CBS News, "March 29, 2017," accessed July 19, 2017, http://www .cbsnews.com/news/republicans-health-care-trump-approval-russia-election -meddling-cbs-news-poll/.

7. Southern Poverty Law Center, "April 29, 2016," *Intelligence Report* 162, Spring 2017, 12.

8. Julia Ioffe, Twitter post, April 28, 2016, 9:10 a.m., https://twitter.com /juliaioffe.

9. Martin Baron, "Washington Post Editor Marty Baron Has a Message to Journalists in the Trump Era," *Vanity Fair*, November 30, 2016, accessed July 19, 2017, http://www.vanityfair.com/news/2016/11/washington-post-editor-marty -baron-message-to-journalists.

10. Jeff Jarvis, "Trump & The Press: A Murder-Suicide Pact," *Buzzmachine*, February 19, 2017, accessed July 19, 2017, http://buzzmachine.com/2017/02/19 /trump-press-murder-suicide-pact/.

11. Ibid.

12. "Poll Finds Huge Gab in How GOP, Dems View the Media's Watchdog Role," NBC News, May 10, 2017, accessed July 19, 2017, http://www.nbcnews.com /politics/first-read/poll-finds-huge-gap-how-gop-dems-view-media-s-n757346.

13. Pamela Shoemaker, Jaime Riccio, and Philip Johnson, "Gatekeeping," published October 29, 2013, accessed July 20, 2017. DOI: 10.1093/OBO/9780199756841 -0011 http://www.oxfordbibliographies.com/view/document/obo-9780199756841 /obo-9780199756841-0011.xml.

14. Jeff John Roberts, "Why Facebook Won't Admit It's a Media Company," *Fortune*, published November 14, 2016, accessed July 20, 2017, http://fortune .com/2016/11/14/facebook-zuckerberg-media/; Joshua Benton, "The Forces that Drove This Election's Media Failure Are Likely to Get Worse," *Nieman Lab*, published November 9, 2016, accessed July 20, 2017, http://www.niemanlab.org/2016 /11/the-forces-that-drove-this-elections-media-failure-are-likely-to-get-worse/.

15. Max Read, "Donald Trump Won Because of Facebook," *New York Magazine*, published November 9, 2016, accessed July 20, 2017, http://nymag.com /selectall/2016/11/donald-trump-won-because-of-facebook.html.

16. Jessica Guynn, "Facebook: Don't Call Us a Media Company," *USA Today*, published October 25, accessed July 20, 2017, https://www.usatoday.com/story /tech/news/2016/10/25/facebook-says-its-not-a-media-company/92744614/.

17. Ibid., 14

18. Sarah and Max Chafkin, "Zuckerberg's New Mission for Facebook: Bringing the World Closer" *Bloomberg*, published June 22, 2017, accessed October 23, 2017, https://www.bloomberg.com/news/articles/2017-06-22/zuckerberg-s-new -mission-for-facebook-bringing-the-world-closer.

19. Heather Kelly, Mark Zuckerberg Explains Why He Just Changed Facebook's Mission, *CNN Tech*, published June 22, 2017, accessed October 23, 2017, http://money.cnn.com/2017/06/22/technology/facebook-zuckerberg-interview /index.html.

20. Facebook, "Facebook Journalism Project," https://www.facebook.com /facebookmedia/get-started/facebook-journalism-project.

21. Sydney Schaedel, "Did the Pope Endorse Trump?" *factcheck.org*, published October 24, 2016, accessed July 20, 2017, http://www.factcheck.org/2016 /10/did-the-pope-endorse-trump/.

22. Tennessee Watson, "To Test Your Fake News Judgment Play This Game," NPR.org. published July 3, 2017, accessed October 23, 2017, http://www.npr.org /sections/ed/2017/07/03/533676536/test-your-fake-news-judgement-play-this -game.

23. Drudge Report, https://www.quantcast.com/drudgereport.com.

24. ABC News, "Drudge Report Sets Tone for National Political Coverage," ABC News, published October 1, 2006, accessed July 20, 2017, http://abcnews .go.com/WNT/story?id=2514276&page=1.

25. A.J. Katz, "February 2017 Ratings: MSNBC Beats CNN in Total Prime Time Viewers," *Adweek*, published February 28, 2017, accessed July 20, 2017,

http://www.adweek.com/tvnewser/february-2017-ratings-msnbc-is-the-no-2
-cable-news-network-in-prime-time/322241.

26. Dawn C. Chmielewski, "YouTube Gives Wacky Anchorman Philip DeFranco Greater Exposure," *Los Angeles Times*, published August 28, 2012, accessed July 21, 2017, http://articles.latimes.com/2012/aug/28/entertainment/la-et-ct-youtube -news-philip-defranco-elections-hub-20120828.

27. Lewis Wallace, Sexiest Geeks of 2008, as Voted by Wired.com Readers, *Wired.com*, published December 31, 2008, accessed October 23, 2017, https:// www.wired.com/2008/12/sexiest-geeks-o/.

28. Philip DeFranco, "Giving Back vs. Keeping Mine," YouTube Video, published January 21, 2015, accessed October 23, 2017.

29. Shan Wang, "Out of Many, NPR One: The App that Wants to Be the "Netflix of Listening" Gets More Local," *Nieman Lab*, published January 11, 2016, accessed July 20, 2017, http://www.niemanlab.org/2016/01/out-of-many -npr-one-the-app-that-wants-to-be-the-netflix-of-listening-gets-more-local.

30. Ibid.

31. David Folkenflik, "In Forcing Out Senior Executive, New CEO Mohn Puts Stamp On NPR," *NPR*, published October 17, 2014, accessed July 20, 2017, http:// www.npr.org/2014/10/17/356998435/in-forcing-out-senior-executive-new-ceo -mohn-puts-stamp-on-npr.

32. Brett Zongker, "NPR Chief Says Network Positioned for Growth After Struggles," AP News, published June 11, 2015, accessed July 20, 2017, https:// apnews.com/450dfef0f1384b409bf69aebb2415194/npr-chief-says-network -positioned-growth-after-struggles.

33. Donna Foote, "In California, Smoke and Fire Over Pot," *Newsweek,* published May 27, 2001, accessed October 23, 2017, http://www.newsweek.com /california-smoke-and-fire-over-pot-152685.

34. Winston Ross, "A Cannabis Crusader Brings the Fight for Legal Weed to America's Heartland," Newsweek, published November 25, 2017, accessed October 23, 2017, http://www.newsweek.com/2015/12/04/cannabis-crusader-brings -fight-legal-weed-americas-heartland-397956.html.

35. Winston Ross, "About Winston," Blog, accessed October 23, 2017 https:// winstonross.wordpress.com/about/.

36. 2016 interview by Dr. Madison.

37. Sarah Bartlett, "Ethnic Media Is More Than a Niche: It's Worth Your Attention," *Nieman Lab*, published July 25, 2013, accessed July 21, 2017, http:// www.niemanlab.org/2013/07/ethnic-media-is-more-than-a-niche-its-worth -your-attention/.

38. Mark Hugo Lopez, "What Univision's Milestone Says about U.S. Demographics," *Pew Research Lab*, published July 29, 2013, accessed July 21, 2017, http:// www.pewresearch.org/fact-tank/2013/07/29/what-univisions-milestone-says -about-u-s-demographics/.

39. Latin Heat, http://www.latinheat.com.

40. Lene Bech Sillesen, "Why a *New York Times* Nail Salon Exposé Is Published in Four Languages," *Colombia Journalism Review*, published May 8, 2015, accessed July 21, 2017, https://www.cjr.org/hit_or_miss/why_a_new_york_times _nail_salon_expose_is_published_in_four_languages.php.

41. Jonathan Holmes, "AI Is Already Making Inroads into Journalism But Could It Win a Pulitzer?" *The Guardian*, April 3, 2016, accessed July 19, 2017, https://www.theguardian.com/media/2016/apr/03/artificla-intelligence-robot -reporter-pulitzer-prize.

42. Steve Lohr, "In Case You Wondered, a Real Human Wrote This Column," *New York Times*, September 10, 2017, accessed July 19, 2017, http://www.nytimes .com/2011/09/11/business/computer-generated-articles-are-gaining-traction .html; Steven Levy, "Can an Algorithm Write a Better News Story Than a Human Reporter?" *Wired*, April 24, 2012, accessed July 19, 2017, https://www.wired.com /2012/04/can-an-algorithm-write-a-better-news-story-than-a-human-reporter/.

43. Levy, "Write a Better News Story."

44. Robert Rector, "In the Age of Algorithms, Will Robots Replace Real Reporters," *Pasadena Star-News*, August 2, 2016, accessed July 19, 2017, http:// www.pasadenastarnews.com/media/20160802/in-the-age-of-the-algorithim -will-robots-replace-real-reporters.

45. Joe Keohane, "What News-Writing Bots Mean for the Future of Journalism," *Wired*, February 16, 2017, accessed July 19, 2017, https://www.wired.com /2017/02/robots-wrote-this-story/.

46. Levy, "Write a Better News Story."

47. Kevin Roose, "Robots Are Invading the News Business, and It's Great for Journalists," *New York*, July 11, 2017, accessed July 11, 2014, http://nymag.com /daily/intelligencer/2014/07/why-robot-journalism-is-great-for-journalists.html.

48. Ibid.

49. Facebook's attempt to replace its human trending news curators with algorithms went poorly in 2016, when the software promoted several fake news stories, including a report that Fox News had fired anchor Megyn Kelly for treason. That story generated thousands of shares on social media and was seen by millions before being removed. See Caitlin Dewey, "Facebook Has Repeatedly Trended Fake News Since Firing Its Human Editors," *Washington Post*, October 12, 2016, accessed July 19, 2017, https://www.washingtonpost.com /news/the-intersect/wp/2016/10/12/facebook-has-repeatedly-trended-fake-news -since-firing-its-human-editors/?utm_term=.7e1f1c230781.

50. Robert W. McChesney and John Nichols, *People Get Ready: The Fight Against a Jobless Economy and a Citizenless Democracy* (New York: Nation Books, 2016), 97.

51. Ibid., 94.

52. Noah Kulwin, "Tribune Publishing Chairman: We Want to Start Publishing 2,000 Videos a Day with Artificial Intelligence," *Recode*, June 6, 2016, accessed July 19, 2017, https://www.recode.net/2016/6/6/11871908/tribune -publishing-artificial-intelligence-videos.

53. Ben DeJarnette, "Seth Lewis Joins SOJC as Shirley Papé Chair in Electronic Media," *AroundtheO*, May 16, 2016, accessed July 17, 2017, https://around .uoregon.edu/content/seth-lewis-joins-sojc-shirley-pape-chair-electronic-media.

54. Eric Newton, "Searchlights and Sunglasses," Knight Foundation, https:// archive.org/stream/SearchlightsAndSunglassesEricNewton/Searchlights-and -Sunglasses_djvu.txt.

55. Eric Newton, Profile, http://www.niemanlab.org/author/enewton/.

56. Eric Newton, "Eric Newton: Journalism Education Isn't Evolving Fast Enough, and You Should Help Change That," *Nieman Lab*, published October 17, 2013, accessed July 20, 2017, http://www.niemanlab.org/2013/10/eric-newton -journalism-education-isnt-evolving-fast-enough-and-you-should-help-change -that/.

57. Eric Newton, "An Open Letter to America's University Presidents," Knight Foundation, published August 3, 2012, accessed July 20, 2017, https:// knightfoundation.org/articles/open-letter-americas-university-presidents.

58. Amy Webb, *How to Make J-School Matter (Again)* (Cambridge, MA: Nieman Foundation for Journalism at Harvard, 2015).

59. "Harvard, MIT Lead Most Prestigious Universities, Study Reports," https://www.bloomberg.com/news/articles/2011-03-10/harvard-mit-ranked -most-prestigious-universities-study-reports.

60. Acts of 1861, Chapter 183, "Acts and Resolves of the General Court Relating to the Massachusetts Institute of Technology," published 1861, http:// libraries.mit.edu/archives/mithistory/pdf/1861%20Charter.pdf.

61. MIT Facts "Origins and Leadership" http://web.mit.edu/facts/origins.html;

62. Henry Etzkowitz, *MIT and the Rise of Entrepreneurial Science* (New York: Routledge, 2002); Vannevar Bush, "Pieces of the Action" (Morrow, New York, 1970).

63. Mohit Jain, "How Much Equity Did Stanford Hold in Google When the Company Was Formed?" *quora.com*, answered May 30, 2013, accessed July 20, 2017, https://www.quora.com/How-much-equity-did-Stanford-hold-in-Google -when-the-company-was-formed.

64. "Inventing the Future @ The Media Lab," MIT Media Lab, published April 2012, accessed July 20, 2017, https://www.media.mit.edu/files/inventing -future.pdf.

65. Elizabeth A. Thomson, "Freshman Publishing Experiment Offers Made-to-Order Newspapers," MIT News, published March 9, 1994, accessed July 20, 2017, http://news.mit.edu/1994/newspaper-0309.

66. Christy Fisher, "MIT Media Lab Developing a 'Daily Me' for Everyone," *AdvertisingAge*, published on April 25, 1994, accessed July 20, 2017, http://adage .com/article/news/mit-media-lab-developing-a-daily/87417/.

67. MIT Media Lab, "Media Lab Membership Member FAQs," https://www .media.mit.edu/members/member-faqs/.

68. Margaret K. Evans, "Member Collaboration: Symphony Painter," MIT Media Lab, published November 8, 2016, accessed July 20, 2017, https://www .media.mit.edu/posts/symphony-painter/.

69. Margaret K. Evans, "Member Collaboration: Karaoke-on-Demand," MIT Media Lab, published December 12, 2016, accessed July 20, 2017, https://www.media.mit.edu/posts/member-collaboration-karaoke-on-demand/.

70. MIT Media Lab, "Programmable Synthetic Hallucinations," https://www.media.mit.edu/projects/programmable-synthetic-hallucinations/overview/.

71. Justin Ellis, "Risk and Reward: Joi Ito on What News Orgs Could Learn from Tech Companies About Innovation," *Nieman Lab*, published October 9, 2013, accessed July 20, 2017, http://www.niemanlab.org/2013/10/risk-and-reward-joi-ito-on-what-news-orgs-could-learn-from-tech-companies-about-innovation/.

72. Ethan Zuckerman, "News and Participatory Media" Syllabus, Massachusetts Institute of Technology, 75 Amherst/20 Ames St., Cambridge, MA, http://web.media.mit.edu/~ethanz/news.html.

73. Media Cloud, "Our Tools," https://mediacloud.org/tools.

74. Rahul Bhargava, "Hiring a Media Cloud Contract Software Engineer," MIT, published June 22, 2017, accessed July 20, 2017, https://civic.mit.edu/blog/rahulb/hiring-a-media-cloud-contract-software-engineer.

75. MIT News Office, "MIT Releases Endowment Figures for 2016," MIT News, published September 9, 2016, accessed July 20, 2017, http://news.mit.edu/2016/mit-releases-endowment-figures-2016-0909.

76. Jennifer Brook, Profile, http://jenniferbrook.co/about.

77. The Outline, "It's Not for Everyone, It's for You," https://theoutline.com/about.

78. The Marshall Project, "Nonprofit Journalism about Criminal Justice," https://www.themarshallproject.org/#.g8hk0KMlL.

79. John Branch, "Snow Fall the Avalanche at Tunnel Creek," *The New York Times*, published on December 20, 2012, accessed July 20, 2017, http://www.nytimes.com/projects/2012/snow-fall/#/?part=tunnel-creek.

80. Maine Department of Education, *Understanding Maine's Guiding Principles* (Augusta, ME: Maine Department of Education).

Index

About the Authors

Ed Madison, PhD, is assistant professor at the University of Oregon School of Journalism and Communication in Eugene, Oregon. He began his media career at age 16, as an intern at the CBS affiliate television station in Washington, DC, during the Watergate scandal. Shortly after completing his undergraduate degree at Emerson College, he was recruited to join the team that launched CNN as executive producer. For 23 years, Madison produced programs for CBS, ABC, A&E, Paramount, Disney, and Discovery. He is the author of *Newsworthy: Cultivating Critical Thinkers, Readers, and Writers in Language Arts Classrooms.* His website is www.edmadison.com.

Ben DeJarnette is an engagement strategist and freelance journalist in Portland, Oregon. His writing has appeared in print and online with *Pacific Standard, Men's Journal,* InvestigateWest, *High Country News,* MediaShift, *Oregon Quarterly,* and others. In 2015 he earned his master's degree in media studies from the University of Oregon School of Journalism and Communication. His website is www.bendejarnette.com.